D1452828

CAMBRIDGE STUDIES IN LATIN AMERICAN
AND IBERIAN LITERATURE 1

The Cuban condition

The sense of the radical newness of Spanish America found in literary works from the chronicles of the conquest to the work of the *criollistas* has more recently given way to a stronger recognition of the transatlantic roots of much Spanish American literature. This indebtedness does not imply subservience; rather, the New World's cultural and literary autonomy lies in the distinctive ways in which it assimilated its cultural inheritance.

Professor Pérez Firmat explores this process of assimilation or transculturation in the case of Cuba, and proposes a new understanding of the issue of Cuban national identity through revisionary readings of both literary and non-literary works by Juan Marinello, Fernando Ortiz, Nicolás Guillén, Alejo Carpentier and others, dating from the early decades of the twentieth century, a time of intense self-reflection in the nation's history. Using a critical vocabulary derived from these works, he argues that Cuban identity is translational rather than foundational and that *cubanía* emerges from a nuanced, self-conscious recasting of foreign models.

CAMBRIDGE STUDIES IN LATIN AMERICAN AND IBERIAN LITERATURE

Latin American literature, steeped as it is in myth, history and prophecy, ranks among the most original and innovative in the Western world. In its early phases this literary tradition produced such major writers as Bernal Díaz, the Inca Garcilaso and Sor Juana Inés de la Cruz. More recently, authors of the stature of Darío, Neruda, Borges, Paz, García Márquez, Fuentes, Vargas Llosa and Severo Sarduy have shed light on the many-faceted nature of Latin America, commenting with both wit and insight on the aspirations and anxieties of the modern self. This extensive body of texts has also probed deeply into the paradoxical nature of power and into the dynamics of revolutionary movements.

The aim of this series is to promote the best scholarship on Latin American literature and to provide a major forum for diverse critical approaches. At the same time, recognizing the significant affinities which exist between Iberian literature and that of Latin America, the series will include studies on Spanish and Portuguese topics. It will provide an important opportunity for the productive convergence of scholars in all these fields, as well as those interested in Romance studies, comparative literature and literary theory.

The Cuban condition
Translation and identity in modern Cuban literature

GUSTAVO PÉREZ FIRMAT

Professor of Romance Languages, Duke University

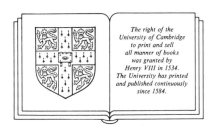

*The right of the
University of Cambridge
to print and sell
all manner of books
was granted by
Henry VIII in 1534.
The University has printed
and published continuously
since 1584.*

CAMBRIDGE UNIVERSITY PRESS

CAMBRIDGE

NEW YORK   NEW ROCHELLE

MELBOURNE   SYDNEY

Published by the Press Syndicate of the University of Cambridge
The Pitt Building, Trumpington Street, Cambridge CB2 1RP
32 East 57th Street, New York, NY 10022, USA
10 Stamford Road, Oakleigh, Melbourne 3166, Australia

© Cambridge University Press 1989

First published 1989

Printed in Great Britain at
the University Press, Cambridge

British Library cataloguing in publication data
Pérez Firmat, Gustavo, 1949– .
The Cuban condition: translation and identity
in modern Cuban literature. –
(Cambridge studies in Latin American and Iberian literature).
1. Spanish literature. Cuban writers, 1888–.
Special subjects. National identity. Critical studies.
1. Title
860.9′358

Library of Congress cataloguing in publication data
Pérez Firmat, Gustavo, 1949–
The Cuban condition: translation and identity in modern
Cuban literature / Gustavo Pérez Firmat.
p.   cm. – (Cambridge studies in Latin American and Iberian literature).
Bibliography.
Includes index.
ISBN 0 521 32747 4
1. Cuban literature – 20th century – History and criticism.
2. Assimilation (Sociology) in literature.   3. Literature and
society – Cuba.   1. Title.   11. Series.
PQ7378.P47   1989.
860′.9′97291 – dc19   88-23454   CIP

ISBN 0 521 32747 4

For us

Somos a través de un idioma que es nuestro siendo extranjero.

Juan Marinello

On n'écrit jamais ni dans sa propre langue ni dans une langue étrangère.

Jacques Derrida

Yo soy tú alucinado.

Virgilio Piñera

Contents

Acknowledgments

I would like to thank the John Simon Guggenheim Memorial Foundation, the National Endowment for the Humanities, and the Duke University Research Council for their generous support in the writing of this book.

Earlier versions of chapters 4 and 9 originally appeared in *Callaloo* and *MLN*; I am grateful to the editors for permission to reprint. Several colleagues and friends aided me with their encouragement and advice: Jorge Olivares, Enrique Pupo-Walker, María Salgado, Marcel Tetel, Lisa Ryan, and Pedro Gómez. I would also like to thank Ricardo Castells for preparing the index and proofreading. As always, Rosa Perelmuter Pérez remains my toughest critic and my biggest fan.

Introduction: In other words

Some years ago I was at a Cuban–Jewish wedding in Miami, Florida, where the entertainment was provided by Willie Chirino, a popular Cuban-born singer and composer. If you have been to a Jewish wedding, you know that at some point the band has to play Hava-Nagilah. No Jewish wedding is complete without Hava-Nagilah. On this particular night, Chirino played all sorts of music – Cuban, American, Cuban–American – but no Hava-Nagilah. Late into the evening, sensing what his audience expected, he said something like, "No se preocupen, que ayer nos pasamos la tarde ensayando Hava-Nagilah en guaguancó" ["Don't worry, we spent all of yesterday afternoon rehearsing Hava-Nagilah in a Latin beat"]. Thereupon followed a rendition of Hava-Nagilah, or perhaps I should say, "Havana-gilah," for Chirino did indeed play this traditional Jewish song but in a *guaguancó* rhythm, and this prompted a *horah* with *salsa* steps.

At the time I made a note to myself that Chirino's performance illustrated the "translation sensibility" that defines many Cuban cultural products. There was something peculiarly Cuban, I thought, in that irreverent, creole translation of this Hebrew song. Like Chirino's performance, Cuban culture results from the importation, and even the smuggling, of foreign goods. Of course, since similar phenomena can be observed in other parts of the New World, these transactions are not peculiar to Cuba, and I hope that my discussion may have instructive implications for those interested generally in the connections between Old World and New World culture. What may be peculiar, however, is the pervasiveness of the phenomenon in Cuba, and this for well-documented historical reasons. As is well known, Cuban culture lacks the indigenous substratum that is so strong a presence in other parts of Spanish America. Since Cuban culture is composed entirely from exogenous ingredients, in Cuba the indigenous, in the narrow sense of the word, is little more than a poetic commonplace popularized during the Romantic period. In a memorable but forgotten essay entitled "El estilo en Cuba y su sentido histórico" (1944), Jorge Mañach summed up the situation in this way:

Cuba tuvo que partir de una tabla rasa, o poco menos. El indígena cubano no rebasó, como es sabido, el nivel infracultural. Ningún fondo tradicional de imágenes autóctonas alimentó, pues, la sensibilidad criolla primeriza. Nuestra expresión se vió así consignada, *ab initio*, a la adopción de formas europeas, principalmente, por supuesto, españolas. No por obvio y sencillo es este hecho menos capital.

[Cuba had to start from little more than a *tabula rasa*. The Cuban indian, as is known, did not surpass the infracultural level. No traditional stock of autochthonous images nourished the initial creole sensibility. Our means of expression, from the beginning, had to adopt European forms, principally, of course, Spanish ones. This fact is no less important for being simple and obvious.][1]

As Mañach goes on to explain, the difficulties stemming from the absence – or, more exactly, the extermination – of native culture were exacerbated by Cuba's place in Spain's New World empire. Because the island lacked precious metals, it was not considered valuable for itself; rather, its value was strategic: positioned at the entrance to the New World, Cuba was the logical way-station for travelers going to or returning from the continental mainland. From the time of its discovery until the beginning of the nineteenth century, Cuba was for the most part a crossroads, a temporary haven for "migratory birds" on their way to some other destination.[2] This circumstance not only accentuated the foreignness of vernacular culture but gave it a provisional, makeshift character. Cuban culture was doubly lacking: if the extermination of aboriginal civilizations erased its past, the restlessness of its Spanish colonizers undermined its future. In Mañach's words: "Si no tuvimos pasado al nacer, tampoco casi tuvimos futuro. Desvanecidas las primeras ilusiones sobre la riqueza aurífera de la isla, ésta vino a ser pronto tierra accesoria y provisional. No se estaba en ella por ella, ni con ánimo de permanencia" ["If we were born without a past, we were also almost born without a future. When the early illusions about auriferous wealth faded, the island quickly became a subordinate and provisional land. One did not come to it for its own sake, nor with the intention of staying"] (p. 113).

Slowed by this conspiracy of circumstances, the development in Cuba of a sense of cultural wholeness – what Mañach terms a "style" – is a relatively recent event. Not until the last century, with the advent of such figures as José de la Luz y Caballero (1800–1862), Domingo del Monte (1804–1853), and José María Heredia (1803–1839), does an incipient sense of cultural autonomy begin to flower. The development of this autonomy, which coincided with the movement for political independence, can be usefully imaged as a process of isolation, of *aislamiento*, in both the geographical and psychological senses of the word. For Cuba to have a cultural identity, there had to be a recognition of the island's insularity, of its geographical and cultural separateness. But Mañach's thesis is that this spiritual isolation, which he terms a "conciencia de isla" ["insular consciousness"] (p. 136), never materialized. Writing in 1944 he maintains that Cuba has yet to develop a genuine sense of cultural integrity. In his view, even after its independence from Spain, Cuba remained a nation without nationhood, a "patria sin nación," in his striking formulation (p. 64).

Mañach's ideas on this score can be usefully contrasted to those of the Puerto Rican Antonio Pedreira who, writing at approximately the same time, attributes his island's ills precisely to its "tragic isolation" (*Insularismo*, p. 165). Unlike Cuba, Puerto Rico was not a commercial center during the centuries of Spanish domination; hence it was seldom frequented by ships and travelers coming from or returning to the Iberian peninsula (Pedreira records the melancholy testimony of Juan Pérez de Guzmán who, in 1662, noted that for eleven years not one Spanish ship had touched port in Puerto Rico). In Pedreira's view, this lack of communication has been the cause of what he sees as Puerto Rico's cultural enervation; the island's isolation, its *insularismo*, has produced a deficient sense of national purpose and identity. Mañach, on the contrary, traces some of the same ills to exactly the opposite cause. In his scheme of things, if Cuba has yet to develop a sense of national selfhood, it is because of excessive contact with the outside world. In Cuba the continuous influx and outflow of peoples and goods have made it difficult to hold the sustained intramural discussion required for national self-definition. For him Cuba suffers the consequences, not of neglect, but of contagion.

My initial hypothesis derives from Mañach's: I believe that one important result of Cuba's lack of *insularismo* is what I have called a "translation sensibility." Because of the island's peculiar history, the Cuban writer or artist is especially sensitive to opportunities for translation, in both the geographical and linguistic senses of the word. Not having a native store of cultural goods, and conditioned by history to the ways of the transient rather than the settler, the Cuban writer has the habit of looking outward, of being on the lookout for opportunities for displacement, graphic and topographic. In my opinion, this outward glance, this "outlook," underlies translational (and, in this case, transnational) performances like Chirino's Hava-Nagilah, a performance that I regard as typical of a crucial strain in many Cuban texts. Cuban culture subsists in and through translation.

Unlike Mañach, however, I do not believe that Cuban culture lacks "style." If Mañach could not locate a Cuban style, it was perhaps because he underrated the creative possibilities inherent in translation. Recognizing Cuba's dependence on foreign models, he regarded this dependence as symptomatic of timidity and derivativeness (p. 113). But the use of foreign models need not be timid or irreflective. As the Cuban Hava-Nagilah shows in a small way, translation can be a recreative endeavor, in both senses of the adjective; as such, it can be a powerful instrument in the creation of a national style, as I will be arguing in the succeeding chapters. In other words: Cuban style *is* translation style – this, in brief, is the thesis of the present book.

I use "translation" not only in the strict sense of a recasting, in a second language, of statements from a first. In fact, most of my examples will not cross the language barrier. My usage of the term generally corresponds to what Roman Jakobson has called "intralingual translation," that is, a restatement or paraphrase that occurs within the matrix of a single language ("On linguistic aspects of translation," p. 232). What draws me to the notion of intralingual translation is the following consideration. Unlike interlingual translation, intralingual translation is constantly threatened by the proximity of the original. In interlingual translation, the original text is an ever-receding theoretical horizon; as we all know, *traduttore, traditore*: the translator can only hope to approximate, not reproduce, his original text. But when translation occurs in a monolingual setting, the situation is far different. For the intralingual translation, the possibility of identical reproduction is always available: all you have to do is quote (but without quotation marks). This means that an intralingual translation, in order *not* to collapse into the original, in order to maintain its integrity *as* translation, needs to keep its distance. Normally this distance is built into the insurmountable barrier between languages, but here it has to be staked out through different means. An intralingual translation, even as it attempts to restate the original, must deviate from it in perceptible ways. That is to say, intralingual translation strives precisely after that "insular consciousness" propounded by Mañach. So as to maintain its separateness, the translation needs to insulate itself, to stake out a piece of earth in what Edward Said has called "the endless sea of linguicity." This variety of translation gives full force to the topographical meaning of the word: translation as displacement. The intralingual translator is someone who knows that in order to pick his words, he has to keep his distance.

The purpose of this book is then twofold: I want to examine the specific ways in which this distance is achieved in an important group of twentieth-century Cuban texts, and I want to explore how this insulation contributes to Cuba's cultural and literary self-definition. I am broadly interested, therefore, in how certain Cuban works emerge from the translation of exogenous models and forms. More specifically, I am interested in works written by writers who were roughly Mañach's contemporaries, that is, writers who belonged to the first and second generations of the Republican era, and whose best work was done during the first three or four decades of this century. My choice of this period is dictated by historical reasons. Coming in the wake of the island's independence from Spain, and punctuated by several episodes of United States interventionism, the first decades of this century were a time of intense national reflection. It is not an exaggeration to say that this was the time when the Cuban "ethos" was being formed, a period of several

decades when the dominant concern of Cuban writers and intellectuals was nothing less than the forging of a national identity. It is
enough to peruse the contents of such journals as *Cuba Contemporánea*, *Revista Bimestre Cubana*, *Revista de Avance*, *Social*, or *Archivos del
Folklore Cubano* to get a sense of the vigorous discussion that was
taking place during these years, a discussion that involved all strata
of Cuban culture, material as well as ideological, high-brow as well
as popular. This was the period that saw the publication of such
seminal works as Ramiro Guerra's *Azúcar y población en las Antillas*
(1925), Mañach's *Indagación del choteo* (1928), Juan Marinello's
Cubanismo y americanismo literarios (1932), and Fernando Ortiz's *Contrapunteo cubano del tabaco y el azúcar* (1940), to name only a few. The
authors of these works, like the other participants in this national
debate, repeatedly return to the same set of related issues: the
"Cuban character," the meaning of a national culture, the tension
between Cuba's Iberian and African heritage, and the effects of U.S.
imperialism.[3]

If for Cuban politicians and intellectuals generally the burning
question was the design and destiny of the Cuban polity, for the
Cuban writer the issue was narrower and more easily grasped.
Fundamentally it had to do with his search for what I will call a
literary vernacular, that is, a literary idiom that respects and reflects
the specificity of Cuban life, a language possessed also of "insular
consciousness." The common thrust of the work of writers as
dissimilar as Fernando Ortiz, Nicolás Guillén, and Carlos Loveira,
to name only three of the ones discussed in this book, was the
creation of a vernacular literary language from within the matrix of
the mother tongue. This was a project in translation. From Europe
and Spain the Cuban writer inherited a set of artistic and literary
resources, a grammar of literary and linguistic usage, as it were. His
task was now to produce a vernacular equivalent of this grammar by
combining elements from the European tradition with those from
other cultures. It is no accident, therefore, that several important
lexicographical works appeared during this period – works like
Constantino Suárez's *Diccionario de voces cubanas* (1921) or Ortiz's own
Catauro de cubanismos (1923) and *Glosario de afronegrismos* (1925);[4] like
other dictionaries, these compendia are essentially exercises in
intralingual translation. On the one hand, they register the local

names of universal phenomena; on the other, they explain idiosyn-
crasies of speech or behavior by translating them into "standard"
language.

What held true for common speech also held true for literary
language. The aim here was also to find or found a Cuban expression, and one of the crucial questions faced by a writer like Nicolás
Guillén was precisely how to marry common speech with literary
language, for only such a marriage could engender an authentic
literary vernacular. In a recent book, *History of the Voice*, Edward
Brathwaite discusses the development, in the anglophone Caribbean, of "nation language," a creole variant of "standard" English
that bears the imprint of conditions of life in the New World. The
subject of my book is the development, on the plane of literary
expression, of a Cuban "nation language." I am interested, therefore, in the history of the "Cuban voice" – its tone, its timbre, its
modulations; and the purpose of the chapters that follow is to study
one particularly important episode in the history of that voice. (The
paradox that this study is being undertaken in English is not lost on
me, and it shapes the modulations of my own critical voice, as will
soon become evident.)

In the broader context of Spanish-American literature, the
writers I will be discussing belong to the movement that usually
goes by the name of *criollismo* or *mundonovismo*.[5] In Cuba, the land-
marks of literary criollism are such works as José Antonio Ramos's
Tembladera (1916), *Coaybay* (1927), *Caniquí* (1936), and many others;
Jorge Mañach's *Estampas de San Cristóbal* (1925) and *Tiempo muerto*
(1928); Agustín Acosta's *La zafra* (1926); Carlos Loveira y Chirino's
Juan Criollo (1927); Marcelo Salinas's *Alma guajira* (1928) and *La
tierra...* (1928); Nicolás Guillén's *Motivos de son* (1930) and *Sóngoro
cosongo* (1931); Eugenio Florit's *Trópico* (1930), Alejo Carpentier's
Ecue-Yamba-O (1933); Lino Novás Calvo's *El negrero* (1933) and *La
luna nona* (1942); Emilio Ballagas's *Cuaderno de poesía negra* (1934);
Luis Felipe Rodríguez's *Relatos de Marcos Antilla* (1932) and *Ciénaga*
(1937); and a few others. With a couple of notable exceptions,
however, most of these works are all but forgotten. In part, their
oblivion stems from the prominence of the following generation of
writers – the *Orígenes* group – a generation that has all but mono-
polized, and understandably so, the attention of students of modern

Cuban literature. In part also, the neglect of criollist writers is due to a general lack of interest in the literature of criollism, which is usually not thought to raise the complicated theoretical issues that hold the attention of present-day critics of Spanish-American literature.

Although the temporal limits of *criollismo* are imprecise (criollism is still practiced today), there is fairly widespread agreement on the aesthetic program of this tendency. As the word suggests, works of this persuasion attempted, arguably for the first time, to capture the specificity of American nature and culture. Thus, criollist literature is characterized by its attention to native landscapes, regional dialects, rustic characters, and autochthonous themes. Mario Vargas Llosa has called criollist writers "primitives" – a somewhat misleading characterization but one that does reflect the current consensus on this body of work. For Vargas Llosa, these writers are "primitive" in two related senses: first, because of their anachronistic literary technique, and second, because of their concentration on "primitive" themes like the struggle between man and nature.[6] According to this view, which has been perpetuated in countless essays and manuals, criollism is a nativist reaction to the cosmopolitan excesses of *modernismo*. Unlike his *modernista* predecessor, the criollist writer was someone who had his gaze fixed on American reality. As Rufino Blanco Fombona once said, criollism is "tener dentro del pecho un corazón americano y no un libro extranjero" ["having in your breast an American heart and not a foreign book"] ("El criollismo," p. 263).

Against this opinion, I want to argue for the "cosmopolitanism" of criollist literature. Although many of these works are indeed "sample cases of folklore,"[7] other works in the criollist canon raise and explore issues that have little to do with folklorism. My own position is that, at least as regards Cuban criollism, foreign books are not incompatible with American feeling; indeed, American feeling is nothing other than a certain way of reading foreign books. Said differently: Cuban criollism is translational rather than foundational. For example, as we will see more fully in chapter 3, a work like Fernando Ortiz's *Contrapunteo cubano del tabaco y el azúcar*, for all of its local flavor, cannot be properly appreciated unless one sees it for what it is: a modern, creole version of the dispute between Carnival and Lent in the *Libro de Buen Amor*; Ortiz's criollism cannot be understood unless one examines the textual counterpoint between his essay and its model. I will claim, in fact, that the "Cubanness" of this work principally resides in the counterpoint itself, in Ortiz's translation of the medieval genre of the allegorical debate.

To be sure, many works of criollist intent are little more than registers of regional customs. But there is another side – an outside if you will – to criollism. The most powerful works of this persuasion compel precisely by their attention to foreign precedent, by their deliberate and nuanced cosmopolitanism. My term for this tendency is "critical criollism." I use the adjective to underscore the exegetical slant of these works, which do not limit themselves to a docile emulation of foreign usage; their stance is "critical" in that it entails a self-conscious, selective, and sometimes even willful manipulation of literary tradition. As intralingual translation, a work of critical criollism knows it must follow its precursors, but from a distance. These works have a double edge. On the one hand, and as one has come to expect, they record regionalisms of all kinds; but on the other hand, their regional bias is countered by or filtered through an awareness of the inherited or traditional forms that local usage has displaced. The result is an interesting tug-of-words between insular usage and peninsular precedent. Recognizing that the search for a literary vernacular can be furthered only by recasting, refashioning, adapting – in short, by translating – exogenous models, critical criollists shade local color with foreign hues.

Let me provide a small but clear-cut example of this shading. In Carlos Loveira y Chirino's *Juan Criollo*, a novel that I will discuss later in some detail, one finds the following sentence: "Dentro de tal estado de cosas llegó la gran comida, o no hablando en criollo, la gran cena" ["In this state of affairs the great meal arrived, or, not speaking in creole, the great repast"].[8] This remark displays the translation sensibility that I already attributed to that other Chirino of Cuban culture, Willie. By saying both *cena* and *comida*, Loveira makes a point of mixing the exotic and the demotic, of recording the "standard" word as well as its local equivalent. Even if his overall aim is to write *en criollo*, there is a certain pressure upon his text that manifests itself in the acknowledgment of peninsular usage, and this pressure complicates and enriches a novel that begins to broadcast its "criollism" on the title page. Loveira's double focus is typical of the "critical" strain within Cuban criollism, and I could say that the subject of my study is simply the counterpoint between *cena* and *comida*. Like this sentence from *Juan Criollo*, works of critical criollism willingly get caught up in a *contrapunteo* between the native and the foreign. The best among them – and Loveira's novel is an example – find interesting and innovative ways of resolving the counterpoint, of having their *comida* and eating it too. Fittingly enough, Fernando Ortiz imaged the results of process with a culinary metaphor: the *ajiaco*, a Cuban stew characterized by the heterogeneity of its ingredients. In the best of cases, the translational, contrapuntal performances of critical criollism produce a savory linguistic and literary *ajiaco*: food for thought, words of mouth.

We must realize, moreover, that exogenous pressure is inevitable in any event. As Juan Marinello points out in "Americanismo y cubanismo literarios," a crucial text for any discussion of criollism, the Spanish-American writer who writes in Spanish cannot help feel the pressure of linguistic and literary tradition. Initially a review of Luis Felipe Rodríguez's collection of stories, *Relatos de Marcos Antilla* (1932), this essay is actually an extensive and subtle meditation on the difference between the "primitive" and "critical" approaches to criollism. Like the other writers I will discuss, Marinello rejects the view that it is enough to describe ostensibly local phenomena in order to create a vernacular literature; instead, he insists that no amount of indigenous overlay can cover up the transatlantic roots of New World literature. For Marinello, the New World writer is caught in a bind: even when he speaks most personally or provincially, his voice continues to resonate with a foreign accent. Marinello expresses this situation with genealogical and prison imagery: the New World writer is a "prisoner" enfettered by the "learned chains of Europe," or he is the "grandchild" that fatally resembles parents and grandparents. It is not enough, therefore, to use local words, for these words, if they are Spanish, fatally betray their transatlantic relations. As he puts it in one of the many quotable passages in the essay,

Sudaremos de echar criollismos sobre la lengua matriz y cuando queramos innovar seriamente el habla derivaremos formas que tuvieron hace siglos vida lozana en Andalucía o Extremadura. O que pudieron tenerla. Es que la sangre claustral que es toda lengua recuerda fatalmente a sus padres y enniña sin quererlo nietos que se le parecen.

[We will strain to secrete criollisms onto the mother tongue and when we make a serious effort to innovate our speech we will come up with linguistic forms that lived a youthful existence centuries ago in Andalusia or Extremadura. Or forms that could have had such a life. The cloistral blood that is language fatally recalls its parents and engenders grandchildren that cannot help resembling them.] (p. 49)

And yet, the possibility for innovation is not entirely foreclosed. The command of the Spanish language, a possession that possesses in turn, is also a "key" with which we unlock the chains. The key is distance: the "great distance" that turns the Spanish-American writer into an "impassioned spectator."

Hasta tal punto es lo idiomático alimento maternal y llave específica, que si penetramos en lo literario español – en el subsuelo alimentador de lo literario español – es por la lengua. Franz Tamayo afirmaba en cierta ocasión que el hispanoamericano no podía sentir el *Quijote*. Creemos que el hispanoamericano, como haya crecido en la disciplina hispánica auténtica, puede sentir el *Quijote* mejor que el español porque está inmerso en la realidad espiritual que la lengua cristaliza en su intimidad y muy parado en la gran distancia que lo hace espectador apasionado.

[To such an extent is language maternal nourishment and specific key that if we penetrate into Spanish literature – into the subsoil that feeds Spanish literature – it is through language. Franz Tamayo once said that someone from Spanish America could not feel the *Quijote*. We believe that a Spanish American, if he has been reared within an authentically Hispanic discipline, can feel the *Quijote* better than the Spaniard, since he is immersed in the spiritual reality of language and standing in the great distance that makes him an impassioned spectator.] (p. 49)

If, on the one hand, the derivativeness of New World culture locks the writer into certain molds of expression, the distance from the source implicit in the very notion of derivativeness gives him a privileged hermeneutic position with respect to the cultural products of the Old World. As an "impassioned spectator," the Spanish-American writer occupies a middle distance between involvement and detachment. This phrase, which echoes the title of another of Marinello's essays, "Margen apasionado," is something of an oxymoron. An impassioned spectator is someone who is both involved in and removed from the objects of his attention. Even if he is physically distant, his passion constitutes an effective link to the reality he contemplates. To some degree, such a spectator is himself part of the spectacle. This ambivalence captures the essential relation between New World and Old World culture, a relation to be savored rather than severed.

Criollism's potential for original achievement resides in this combination of involvement and detachment. As Marinello makes clear, this achievement will be a hermeneutic feat. Implicit in his argument is the notion that New World culture in general and criollist literature in particular are decidedly hermeneutic, that they emerge from a reading, a repossession – call it also a "translation" – of the master texts of the European tradition. This achievement will be no easy task, and in texts that attempt it one will always find a certain stress that bears witness to the tension between the New World and the old words. This tension, though, is not only inevitable but productive, and the only mistake the criollist writer can make is to try to escape it altogether.

The fundamental difference between critical and primitive criollism, between a criollism that accepts its chains and the one that tries to bolt them, can be expressed in terms of the opposition between "originality" and "aboriginality." The primitive criollist believes in aboriginal achievement; thinking that he has the strength, in William Carlos Williams's phrase, to throw away the rotted names, he maintains that it is possible to begin from scratch, *ab origine*. The critical criollist has a less ambitious but more realistic aim: he wants to inflect, rather than efface, European culture. Thus he seeks a relative, relational "originality" rather than an absolute, pristine "aboriginality." In the sense in which I use the terms, "aboriginality" designates the (in my view) illusory ambition to shed Europe's learned fetters altogether, while "originality" designates the ability to make music with their clanging. The former defines primitive criollism; the latter defines critical criollism. One is a foundational enterprise, the other is a translational enterprise.

There is an additional, related sense that I should like to give to the notion of critical criollism. As is shown by my earlier reference to Ortiz's *ajiaco*, Cuban criollist writers not only engaged in translational performances but also theorized about them in colorfully local ways. I would say, in fact, that one of the distinguishing marks of criollism in Cuba is its theoretical flavor. Not only Ortiz, but also Juan Marinello, Félix Lizaso, and Jorge Mañach theorized about the criollist project. I have wanted to do justice to the theoretical component in Cuban criollism by integrating some of these "native" concepts into my own critical vocabulary. So that, even if my conceptual starting point is writing-as-translation, an idea that is certainly common coin in today's critical exchanges, one of the goals of my discussion is to find a vernacular vocabulary with which to discuss the same range of textual phenomena. As my title suggests, this book is itself an exercise in translation, and in reading works by Ortiz, Loveira, Nicolás Guillén, and others, I have attempted to translate their home-grown and sometimes half-baked vocabulary into a context and a language that makes it serviceable for literary analysis. Two of Ortiz's notions, in particular, will play a prominent part in my discussion: *transculturación*, Ortiz's term for the translational displacements that generate vernacular culture; and *ajiaco*, his metaphor for the outcome of these displacements. During the course of my discussion I will repeatedly return to these two concepts, which will be the dominant ingredients in my own critical stew.

This attempt to elaborate a "native" critical vocabulary is the other meaning of critical criollism, a phrase which thereby names both my discourse and the texts to which it refers. As a critical criollist, however, I have no illusions about aboriginal utterance, and I have not hesitated to include foreign ingredients in my recipe. Implicit in my argument is a double dialogue. On one level, I will study the dialogical relation between Cuban criollist works and their Spanish and European antecedents; on another level, I will myself establish a dialogue between such terms as *transculturación* or *ajiaco* and concepts currently in use (prominent among which is "dialogue" itself). My juxtaposition of epigraphs from Jacques Derrida and Juan Marinello at the beginning of the book is intended as a foretaste of this second, metadialogical level.

Readers familiar with my earlier work will recognize that the relation between Cuban literature and its peninsular antecedents is a subject that I first broached in *Literature and Liminality*. Although the argument of the present study stands on its own, I have attempted here to analyze more fully some of the texts and topics that I touched upon in the Cuban chapters of my earlier book. Because of its combination of Spanish and Spanish-American texts and because of my stress on the scatological elements in those texts, *Literature and Liminality* was something of an *olla podrida*. It pleases me to think that *The Cuban condition*, with its concentration on things Cuban and its indulgence in oral metaphors, has something of the flavor of an *ajiaco criollo*. But then as now, my fundamental interest lies in the complicated intercourse between New World and Old World culture, and more particularly, in how Cuban texts rewrite some of the masterworks of the Spanish and European literary tradition. Thus, I hope that my discussion will be of use not only to students of Cuban literature but also to those interested in the broader issues of national and continental identity. For this reason, although I have not made any effort to be comprehensive, I have tried to give my readings a certain exemplariness, in both substance and method.

My focus on Cuban literature is, then, partly the result of limitations of space and competence; but it also stems from non-professional (if such there be) considerations. As a "native" Cuban who has spent all of his adult life away from the island, the notion of a "Cuban" voice is for me as alluring as it is problematic. A Cuban voice is what I wish I had, and what I may never have. In the essay which I quoted earlier, Jorge Mañach makes the striking observation that, in Cuba, for the reasons that I have already mentioned, the nativist project is beset by anxiety – "las angustias a que todo nativismo se había de sentir vocado en nuestra isla" (p. 116). Mañach's words, in which the vexing questions of voice and vocation converge, apply to my own situation. The constituent anxiety of Cuban criollism is all the more pronounced when, as in my case, the writer's own standing as a *criollo* is uncertain. Contemplating Cuban culture at a distance – geographically and linguistically – I am myself an "impassioned spectator," and thus an instance of Marinello's notion of interested contemplation. One way in which I have tried to come to terms with this crux is by concluding my examination of critical criollism with a reading of Alejo Carpentier's *Los pasos perdidos* (1953), a novel whose protagonist and narrator is a Cuban expatriate who lives in North America. Carpentier's novel, an autobiographical memoir written in a language that cannot be

Spanish but refuses to be English, summarizes the Cuban criollist enterprise as well as my own stake in the subject matter of this study.

While I was writing this book, it often occurred to me that its underlying theme was scriptive survival. My discussions of Ortiz or Guillén or Florit or Loveira are, in a deep sense, inquiries into how these authors survived as writers. For the criollist writer, this survival generally entailed a merging of his personal voice with the *vox patriae*; this kind of writer typically looked upon himself as a sort of bard, a translator of the nation's muffled or inarticulate voice. He was – or presumed to be – a spokesman, a *vocero*. For me, this solution to the problem of scriptive survival clearly will not do; nonetheless, my desire to demonstrate the centrality of translation in Cuban criollist literature cannot but reflect an attempt to legitimize and place my own work. By trying to define the tone and timbre of a certain Cuban voice, I am trying also to define my own voice, to explore my own means and possibilities of survival as a writer, and even as a Cuban writer. It is not only the criollist author who, as Marinello put it, exists through a language that is not his own. But this should not be surprising: the fate of the critic (like that of the translator) is always to find himself in others' words.

I

Mr. Cuba

Fernando Ortiz may seem an odd choice as the subject of the first chapter of this study, since he is not generally regarded as a writer of "literature." Sometimes called Cuba's third discoverer (after Columbus and Humboldt), Ortiz is esteemed above all for his seminal contributions to the understanding of the "transcultura-tion" of African customs in Cuba. But although Afro-Cuban folklore was Ortiz's principal interest, he also found the time to write about a plethora of other subjects ranging from dactiloscopy to international law. During his long and productive life, Ortiz acquired and dis-played the kind of knowledge that is usually characterized as "encyclopedic."[1] Unlike other writers whose work or bent of mind is so described, however, Ortiz filled his encyclopedia with infor-mation about one country, Cuba. Even though foreign references are by no means absent from his texts, almost all of his reasearch dealt with Cuba, and particularly with what he once called "the ebony heart" of Cuban culture. Ortiz's vast erudition was certainly not limited to things Cuban, but knowledge of foreign cultures interested him inasmuch as it helped elucidate national customs, and he typically used his erudition to show the underlying affinities between apparently idiosyncratic or unintelligible elements in Cuban culture and universal customs or mythology. Thus he points out, for example, that certain *ñáñigo* rituals bear striking similarities to Greek tragedy, or that the sigmoid patterns in Indo-Cuban sculptures find parallels in the folk art of many nations.[2]

Because of Ortiz's long and productive attention to Cuba, any serious discussion of his work engages issues that define the very nature of what it means to be Cuban. There is a kind of "legend" surrounding Ortiz, a legend according to which the author of *Contrapunteo cubano* is something like the quintessential *criollo*, the very paradigm of *cubanidad*: Liborio with reading glasses and index cards.[3] Ortiz's mastery of all facets of Cuban culture made him "Cuba's Third Discoverer," "Cuba em pessoa," or "Mister Cuba";[4] he personified and distilled, in his life and his work, the essential lineaments of the Cuban ethos. Nicolás Guillén, for one, has said that Ortiz laid the foundations for the cultural integration of the Cuban people.[5] And Ortiz himself invested his career with symbolic value by interpreting the gradual acceptance of his research into Afro-Cuban folklore as a reflection of the history of race relations in Cuba.[6] No man is an island – except Ortiz, whose life and work are synonymous with Cuba.

Nonetheless, Ortiz's insularity has made him a relatively unknown figure. In addition, the specialized nature of some of his writing has created the impression that his work is of interest primarily to social scientists. After all, Ortiz is not a "writer" but a "scientist" – and you can pick the discipline: ethnology, sociology, dialectology, criminology, anthropology, or musicology, among others. Especially in the critical literature that has emerged from Cuba in the last twenty-five years, Ortiz's work is valued primarily for its substantive, conceptual content.[7] Hence the honorific title of "discoverer," given to him by Juan Marinello, one of the intellectual gurus of the Cuban revolution. As a result, little has been said about Ortiz as a writer, about the status of his works as texts. And yet, to my mind, there is no doubt that Ortiz is a crucial and representative figure in modern Spanish-American literature, a writer whose works address many of the same issues tackled by better-known poets and novelists.[8] Mr. Cuba's representativeness, in my view, extends to his textual labors, to the language and form of his multi-faceted books and essays.

What is more, if we continue to look upon Ortiz primarily as a "scientist," his importance will surely wane, since many of his conclusions are based on incomplete data or mistaken assumptions. In point of fact, and although this assertion will rankle with some, by conventional scientific standards of precision and objectivity, Ortiz was never a very good scientist. Although his works display monumental and nuanced erudition, they also have qualities that distance them from the detached, impersonal prose of scientific inquiry. Take, for example, the following entry from his lexicon of Cuban words, *Un catauro de cubanismos* (1923):

Guayabo – El árbol que produce la guayaba, dice el Diccionario de la Academia. ¿Pero por qué añade: 'En francés: *goyavier*'? ¿Quiere decir con esto que es un galicismo? ¿Sí? Pues no es verdad; como no lo es *guayaba*, tampoco lo es *guayabo*. ¿No? ¿Pues qué, acaso en cada otra papeleta del Diccionario se trae a colación la traducción francesa de cada vocablo? ¡Fuera, pues, el *goyavier*! Esa etimología, si se propone como tal, *no vale una guayaba*, para decirlo en criollo. Recuérdese, en cambio, alguna de las veintidós acepciones y derivados de *guayaba*, traídas por Suárez, que, como *guayabal, guayabera, guayabito*, harían mejor papel en el diccionario caste-llano que esta inexplicable etimología gabacha. ¡Que no nos venga la Academia con guayabas!, y consignemos así, de paso, otro cubanismo.

[*Guayabo* – The tree that produces the *guayaba*, according to the Dictionary of the Academy. Why does it add: 'In French: *goyavier*'? Does it mean to suggest that it is a gallicism? Really? Well, does the Dictionary by any chance provide the French translation of every word? No? Then out with the *goyavier*! The etymology, if that is what is being proposed, is not worth a *guayaba*, as we say. Let's recall, instead, some of the twenty-two accepta-tions and derivatives of *guayaba*, cited by Suárez, that, like *guayabal*, *guayabera, guayabito*, would look better in the Castilian dictionary than that inexplicable Frenchified etymology. This *guayaba* is just too hard to swallow!, and let us thus note, in passing, another cubanism.]   (p. 43)

This entry, which is typical of the style of the *Catauro*, lacks the neutrality of tone and flatness of diction of modern dictionaries. Never an impartial or innocent bystander, Ortiz has a difficult time maintaining the impassive stance of the disinterested observer. His prose is exuberant, tendentious, and even fruity. Even when compil-ing a dictionary – a singularly dry and restrictive enterprise, one would think – he cannot refrain from spicing his text with all sorts of "literary" material – etymological fantasies, jokes, puns, self-conscious similes, and more than one *guayaba*. Ortiz does not discuss language with the detachment of the philologist but with the zest, the *embullo*, of the writer, and especially, of the Cuban writer.

More generally, passages like this one attest to Ortiz's rejection of the separation between the vehicle and the object of inquiry. Begin-ning with the title, which substitutes a Cuban word, "catauro," for the "diccionario" or "tesauro" of other collections, Ortiz's wordbook is very much a Cuban text. As yet another instance of the

Cuban way with words, the *Catauro* is inseparable from its matter; the book explains *en criollo* what it means to speak *en criollo*. Like the entry for *guayaba*, Ortiz's dictionary is both instance and explanation, with the result that the non-Cuban reader – the one who, presumably, would find the volume most useful – has a difficult time making sense of some of the explanations. How many readers of the Royal Academy's dictionary, for example, would understand that final *guayaba* that Ortiz slings at the venerable Spanish institution?[9] What happens in the *Catauro*, as in Ortiz's work in general, is that the distance between instance and explanation, or that between object and subject, collapses. When Mr. Cuba speaks about Cuba, the result is pasty tautology.[10]

This collapse of distance, even as it diminishes the scientific contribution of Ortiz's books, immeasurably complicates, and hence enriches, their textual fabric. Looking upon Ortiz primarily as a scientist is somewhat like looking upon Dante primarily as a theologian – not a fruitless perspective, to be sure, but undoubtedly a limiting one. Ortiz's inmixture of subject and object, of observer and observed, may reduce the weight of his lexicographical or scientific contributions; but one can also argue, as I will, that his writerly excesses place him on a different scale – a scale calibrated to the weights and measures of artistic achievement: a scale for *guayabas*. Without an appreciation of the role of fictional or literary artifice in his works, one cannot accurately gauge Ortiz's achievement; in order to do him justice, one needs to develop a taste, and perhaps a talent, for the *guayaba*. More than a purveyor of facts, he is a peddler of *guayabas*, using this term in a non-derogatory sense as a Cuban shorthand for the dense, devious, and savory textuality of literary discourse. Ortiz is most fruitful when he is most fruity, and it is to the literary fruits of his labors that I would like to attend here.

Although Ortiz wrote no novels like Carlos Loveira or poems like Nicolás Guillén, he is Cuba's most important criollist writer. Indeed, were it not for his seminal work on black folklore, much of the Afro-Antillean literature of the third and fourth decades of this century is unimaginable. Ortiz's research helped create the climate that produced such works as Nicolás Guillén's *Motivos de son* (1930), Alejo Carpentier's *Ecue-Yamba-O* (1933), or Emilio Ballagas's *Cuaderno de poesía negra* (1934), to name only three of the better-known titles in this canon. What makes Ortiz's criollism noteworthy, though, is his conviction that it was not possible – or, if possible, not desirable – to study Cuban culture apart from its European and African antecedents. Ortiz's whole career is nothing but a sustained examination of how the exogenous roots of Cuban culture took hold, grew, and changed in the island. In spite of his superficial resemblance to some of the "primitives," Ortiz has no illusions about aboriginal achievement. Indeed, he insistently pointed out Cuba's lack of an aboriginal culture. Like other writers of a "critical" bent, he believed that whatever originality there was to achieve, it had to emerge from the judicious – and even malicious – manipulation of imports. Unlike some of his followers and students, he is far from being a naive purveyor of supposedly native cultural products.

His work, therefore, offers an initial example of what I have termed "critical criollism." Even while stressing the autonomy of Cuban culture, he remained aware that, especially in Cuba, cultural autonomy is a difficult and problematic notion, and that it cannot be achieved by short-sighted concentration on the picturesque or idiosyncratic. In an important essay, "Problemática de la actual novela latinoamericana," Alejo Carpentier points out that the blind spot of many a criollist was the belief that national or regional customs had no exogenous antecedents or correlates (pp. 10–11). This was never one of Ortiz's shortcomings. Like Carpentier, Ortiz recognized the relation between the indigenous and the foreign; more importantly, he recognized equally that, at least in Cuba, the indigenous is nothing more than a certain inflection of the foreign. Although not a "creative" writer in the usual sense, Ortiz in his works embodies that relational consciousness advocated by Carpentier for the Spanish-American novelist.[11] Indeed, it seems clear from Carpentier's examples that this is a lesson that the Cuban novelist learned, at least in part, from Ortiz, who could not look at a given element in Cuban culture without keeping one eye trained on that element's foreign antecedents or analogs.[12]

Ortiz's critical criollism is already evident in his coinage of the term transculturación.[13] True to its meaning, this neologism is itself a transculturation of the hegemonic word, "acculturation"; in the very definition of the mechanism that generates Cuban culture, the dialectic of originality and derivativeness that constitutes the mechanism comes into play. Just as literature emerges from the translation of foreign elements, the term that designates these translations is itself a translation. This kind of recursive twist is common in Ortiz, whose texts invariably practice what they theorize. Some of his best-known essays are themselves refashionings, recontextualizations, of foreign models. This makes his work doubly significant: as the theorist of transculturation, he gives us an "autochthonous" concept with which to discuss the problem of autochthony; as its practitioner, he illustrates some ways in which the concept operates.

The neologism emerges from Ortiz's desire to correct the terminological imprecision of the word then in use.[14] According to Ortiz, "acculturation" is imprecise because it highlights only one aspect of a complicated, multi-faceted phenomenon. Acculturation names the acquisition of a new culture by an outsider or newcomer; but this is only part of what happens when, as in Cuba, different cultures come into contact. The phenomenon of culture contact actually has three phases: "deculturation," or the shedding of certain elements from the culture of origin; "acculturation," or the acquisition of elements of another culture; and "neoculturation," or the new cultural synthesis created by the merging of elements from the old and new cultures. In the case of the black population of Cuba, deculturation involves the extinction of African culture as a signifying totality; acculturation involves the acquisition of fragments of the white man's culture; and neoculturation is the synthesis of the African with the European. Of the three stages, only the last can be said to designate a vernacular or native culture, and one of the difficulties of "acculturation" is its ethnocentrism, since the term assumes an already-existing cultural matrix into which outsiders are received. Instead, Ortiz stresses the creative leap, the quantum of novelty inherent in cultural shifts; it is not a matter of entering a stable, already existing culture, but of creating a different cultural configuration altogether. By replacing "acculturation" with "transculturation," he means to find a more comprehensive and therefore more exact label for this phenomenon: "En conjunto, el proceso es una *transculturación*, y este vocablo comprende todas las fases de su parábola" ["Considered as a whole, the process is a *transculturation*, and this word covers all the phases of its parabola"] (p. 135).

It is questionable, however, whether the new word is adequate to the New World. As Gonzalo Aguirre Beltrán pointed out some years later, *transculturación* etymologically denotes, not the phenomenon of culture contact as a whole, but only the moment or phase of passage from one culture to another (*El proceso de aculturación*, pp. 10–11).[15] Ortiz's claims notwithstanding, the term is no more "comprehensive" than acculturation, and the catchy neologism cannot be justified on purely theoretical grounds. But, in point of fact, "Del fenómeno social de la 'transculturación' y de su importancia en Cuba" is not predominantly a theoretical essay, since the amount of theoretical discussion is minimal, being limited to the brief three-step analysis of the process of culture contact. The second part of the title correctly indicates that the bulk of the essay is an account of the kinds of transculturation peculiar to Cuba, and the new word is explicitly linked to the Cuban context: "Hemos escogido el vocablo *transculturación* para expresar los variadísimos fenómenos que se originan en Cuba por las complejísimas transmutaciones de culturas que aquí se verifican" ["We have chosen the word *transculturation* to express the highly diverse phenomena that originate in Cuba because of the very complex cultural transmutations that take place here"] (p. 129).

The validity of the neologism, therefore, is empirical and local rather than abstract and theoretical, since the word emerges from the specific circumstances of cultural interaction in Cuba. Now according to Ortiz, the outstanding feature of this interaction is its unfinished state. Echoing Mañach's view that Cuba is "una patria sin nación" ["a nation without nationhood"], Ortiz claims that culture contact in Cuba has not ripened into a national synthesis. As he put it on another occasion: Cuban culture is "un concepto vital de fluencia constante" ["a vital concept of constant fluidity"] rather than "una realidad sintética ya formada y conocida" ["a synthetic reality, already formed and known"] ("La cubanidad y los negros," p. 4). Cuban culture, therefore, has not reached the stage of neoculturation; its distinctive feature is its imperfective, processual aspect. The following passage explains the rationale for this view:

No hubo factores humanos más trascendentes para la cubanidad que esas continuas, radicales y contrastantes transmigraciones geográficas, económicas y sociales de los pobladores; que esa perenne transitoriedad de los propósitos y que esa vida siempre en desarraigo de la tierra habitada, siempre en desajuste con la sociedad sustentadora. Hombres, economías, culturas y anhelos todo aquí se sintió foráneo, provisional, cambiadizo, "aves de paso" sobre el país, a su costa, a su contra y a su malgrado.

[There were no more transcendental factors in the formation of *cubanidad* than those continuous, radical, and contrasting geographical, economic, and social transmigrations of its inhabitants; that perennial transitoriness of purpose, that way of life always uprooted from the land it inhabited, always at odds with the society that sustained it. Human beings, economies, cultures, desires – everything here felt foreign, provisional, changeable, like "migratory birds" crossing the country at its expense, against its wishes, and to its detriment.]

("Del fenómeno social de la 'transculturación,'" p. 133)

What characterizes Cuban culture is mutability, uprootedness. Indeed, given this state of affairs, it might not even be appropriate to speak of a Cuban "culture," since the term implies a fixity of configuration that is belied by the fluidity of the Cuban situation. Note the number of words with the *tras-* or *trans-* prefix in this passage: *trascendentes, transmigraciones, transitoriedad*. In the rest of the essay, this processual particle continues to appear with some frequency: *tránsito* (pp. 129, 130), *transmutación* (p. 129), *transplantación* (pp. 130, 132, 134), *transmigrar* (pp. 131, 132), *transitivo* (p. 134), *transición* (p. 135), *traspasar* (p. 133), *trance* (pp. 130, 134). In this light, it is not surprising that Ortiz would prefer "transculturation" over "acculturation." The crucial difference is that his prefix underscores the processual, imperfective aspect of culture contact, and hence it is more apposite for Cuba. More than a comprehensive rubric for the sum or result of culture contact, transculturation is the name for the collision of cultures, for that interval between deculturation and neoculturation that defines a vernacular culture in its formative phase. Although at one point Ortiz states that transculturation names the "synthesis" of cultures (p. 130), the word properly designates the fermentation and turmoil that *precedes* synthesis. For this reason "transculturation," a coinage that denotes transition, passage, process, is the best name for the Cuban condition.

A look at another of Ortiz's essays will make clearer this processual view of Cuban culture. The opening words of the passage quoted above allude to another well-known essay, "Los factores humanos de la cubanidad," also published in 1940. Here Ortiz makes essentially the same argument as in the essay on trans- culturation, but employing a different vocabulary and style of argument. The two essays, however, contain some of the same material, sometimes repeating entire paragraphs verbatim, a not uncommon practice for Ortiz, who was constantly rehashing his ideas. Instead of anchoring his analysis in a theoretical coinage, in "Los factores humanos de la cubanidad" he proposes a homey metaphor, the *ajiaco*; for Ortiz, this stew of Amerindian origin is the culinary emblem of Cuba. He justifies the metaphor in a number of ways. First, since the *ajiaco* is made by combining a variety of meats and vegetables (whichever ones happen to be available), it conveys the ethnic diversity of Cuba. Second, the *ajiaco* is agglutinative but not synthetic; even if the diverse ingredients form part of a new culinary entity, they do not lose their original flavor and identity. So it is with Cuba, where the mixture of cultures has not led to a neoculturative synthesis, where each ethnic or cultural component has retained its identity. Third, an *ajiaco* is indefinitely replenish- able, since new ingredients can be added to the stew as old ones are used up. In this respect, this dish symbolizes the continuing infusion of new elements into the Cuban cultural mix, those "continuous transmigrations" that he had mentioned in the other essay. Lastly, *ajiaco* is itself an onomastic *ajiaco*, since it combines the African name of an Amerindian condiment, the *ají* or green pepper, with a Spanish suffix, *-aco*.

As an edible emblem of *cubanidad*, the *ajiaco criollo* gives concrete shape to the abstract notion of *transculturación*. "Transculturation" is the theoretical name; "ajiaco" is the corresponding image. Compare now the following statement from "Los factores humanos de la cubanidad" with the other essay's emphasis on the processual:

Acaso se piense que la cubanidad haya que buscarla en esa salsa de nueva y sintética suculencia formada por la fusión de los linajes humanos desleídos en Cuba; pero no, la cubanidad no está solamente en el resultado sino también en el mismo proceso complejo de su formación, desintegrativo e integrativo, en los elementos sustanciales entrados en su acción, en el ambiente en que se opera y en las vicisitudes de su transcurso.

Lo característico de Cuba es que, siendo ajiaco, su pueblo no es un guiso hecho, sino una constante cocedura. Desde que amanece su historia hasta las horas que van corriendo, siempre en la olla de Cuba es un renovado entrar de raíces, frutos y carnes exógenas, un incesante borbor de heterogéneas sustancias. De ahí que su composición cambie y la cubanidad tenga sabor y consistencia distintos según sea catado en lo profundo o en la panza de la olla o en su boca, donde las viandas aún están crudas y burbujea el caldo claro.

[Perhaps it will be thought that one must seek *cubanidad* in that new and synthetically succulent sauce formed by the fusion of the human lineages dissolved in Cuba. Not at all: *cubanidad* lies not only in the result but also in its complex formative process, desintegrative and integrative, in the substances that enter into it, in the environment in which it happens, and in the changes it undergoes along the way.

The characteristic thing about Cuba is that, being an *ajiaco*, it is not a finished dish but a constant cooking. From the dawn of its history to the present, the Cuban pot has always been renewed by the addition of exogenous roots, fruits, and meats, by an incessant simmering of heterogeneous substances. From this it follows that its composition changes and that *cubanidad* has a different flavor and consistency depending on whether one tastes the stew by taking from the bottom or by skimming from the top, where the ingredients are still raw and the liquid is clear.]

("Los factores humanos de la cubanidad," p. 169)

With Cuban culture the operative term is not *fusión* but *cocción*. In this passage Ortiz makes Cuba's imperfection a distinctive feature of its culture. He is not simply regurgitating the commonplace that, because of the youth of the Latin-American republics, cultural syntheses have not *yet* taken place.[16] His position, I believe, is closer to that of the Venezuelan philosopher Ernesto Mayz Vallenilla, who has defined Latin-American culture as indefinite deferral, as a "no-ser-*siempre*-todavía" (*El problema de América*, p. 63). It is not only that at the time Ortiz was writing Cuba was in a stage of cultural and political ferment, but that this "stage" is actually a permanent, defining condition. As he puts it: *cubanidad* is to be found not only in the "result," but also – and I would add, predominantly – in the "process." Cuba is not only *fusión* but also *cocción*; its culture is a non-synthetic mixture of heterogeneous substances – a concoction, in the literal sense of the word.

In its original (and yes, aboriginal) version, the *ajiaco* was prepared by making a hole in the ground, putting in whatever ingredients were available, adding the condiments, and letting the whole thing bake in the sun; as the contents of the hole became depleted, new and perhaps different ingredients were added. As a symbol, the *ajiaco* signifies less a particular substance or combination of substances than a certain openness or receptivity to multiple and unpredictable ethnic and cultural permutations. Ortiz's point is not unrelated to Mañach's when he labelled Cuba a "patria sin nación."[17] By describing Cuba in this way Mañach intended to designate a condition of social and political incoherence; Ortiz, in his formulations, provides the anthropological basis for that incoherence. Because of a peculiar combination of historical circumstances, Cuba is fated to suffer – or enjoy – a never-ending state of ferment that manifests itself in all spheres of Cuban society. As Ortiz says in the essay on transculturation, Cuban forms of life have always been "provisional," "changeable," "migratory." A few years later, in "Los negros y la transculturación" (1951), he uses even more emphatic language: Cuban culture is "inconexa" ["unconnected"], "esquizoide" ["schizoid"], "convulsa" ["convulsed"] (p. 38). The essence of Cuba lies in not having one; it lies in that "constante cocedura," in the incessant simmering of the *ajiaco*, an image that denotes the lack of a stable, enduring core of cultural indicia. Cuba is always cooking. Cubans are always cooking. Occupying a liminal zone or "impassioned margin" where diverse cultures converge without merging, Cuba lives in a *trans-*, in a trance. In Cuba, transience precedes essence. In Cuba, the raw and the cooked give way to the half-baked.

If one motivation for these coinages is empirical, a second motivation is, in a broad sense, political. As Ortiz mentions, his theoretical neologism is intended to replace "la voz anglo-americana" ["the anglo-american word"] (p. 135). Underlying this statement are the related questions of cultural autonomy and explanatory privilege. Ortiz's implicit claim is that Cuban phenomena are best explained by Cuban words, that Cuba can speak for itself. The coining of the neologism, therefore, is an antiauthoritarian, anticolonial gesture. When he substitutes transculturation for acculturation, Ortiz replaces a foreign term with a "native" one, and by implication calls into question the authority of Anglo-American anthropology. In this respect, and notwithstanding the obvious differences, this essay grows out of the same complex of motivations that produced *Un catauro de cubanismos*. As I tried to show in *Literature and Liminality* (chapter 6), Ortiz's *Catauro* is as much a political tract as a lexicographic document, for the author's intent is to validate Cuban Spanish before its peninsular counterpart. The same might be said about Ortiz's theoretical coinages. Like the cubanisms registered in the *Catauro*, they are instruments in the service of cultural autonomy. The issue, as Ortiz suggests in the theoretical essay, is finding or founding a vernacular *voz*, in both senses: a vernacular word and a vernacular voice.

This same issue arises in "Los factores humanos de la cubanidad." Ortiz's advocacy of a home-grown metaphor for transculturation is also an anti-colonial gesture, since the *ajiaco* replaces the current metaphor, that of the melting pot or *crisol*:

Se ha dicho repetidamente que Cuba es un crisol de elementos humanos. Tal comparación se aplica a nuestra patria como a las demás naciones de América. Pero acaso pueda presentarse otra metáfora más precisa, más comprensiva y más apropiada para un auditorio cubano, ya que en Cuba no hay fundiciones en crisoles, fuera de las modestísimas de algunos artesanos. Hagamos mejor un símil cubano, un cubanismo metafórico, y nos entenderemos mejor, más pronto y con más detalles.

[It has been said repeatedly that Cuba is a human melting pot. This comparison applies to Cuba just as it applies to the other American nations. But perhaps there is a more precise, more comprehensive, and more appropriate metaphor for a Cuban public, since in Cuba there are no real foundries outside of the very modest ones of some artisans. It is preferable to make a Cuban simile, a metaphorical cubanism, and we will understand each other better, more quickly and precisely.]   (p. 167)

This Cuban simile is the *ajiaco*. Here again, although the coinage is made partially in the name of "comprehensiveness" and "precision," the determining criterion is what Ortiz calls "appropriateness." In fact the meaning of the new metaphor is close to that of the old one; but *ajiaco* is a "native" word, one that grows out of the environment it describes, whereas *melting pot* is a term imposed from without. The substitution of *ajiaco* for *crisol* is a political and rhetorical stratagem as much as a scholarly or scientific one. Here also the intent is to replace an "Anglo-American word," as becomes transparently clear in the opening sentences of a somewhat different version of the same essay:

Se dice con frecuencia que América, toda la América, es un crisol, un *melting pot*. Acaso sea buena esta metáfora para la América que tiene fundiciones metalúrgicas, donde el símil puede ser comprendido hasta por el vulgo. Pero los americanos del Caribe podemos emplear una semblanza más apropiada. Para nosotros *América, toda América, es un ajiaco*.

[It is often said that America, all of America, is a *crisol*, a melting pot. Perhaps this metaphor will work for that part of America that has metal foundries, where the simile can be understood even by the common people. But the Americans from the Caribbean can employ a more appropriate comparison. For us *America, all of America, is an "ajiaco."*]

("América es un ajiaco" [1940], p. 20; italics in the original)

Ortiz is saying, in so many words: let's speak for ourselves. Indeed, to call Cuba a "melting pot" is not only an act of onomastic colonialism but also an ironic reminder that the lack of precious metals was precisely one factor that transformed the Caribbean basin into a melting pot. Ortiz responds to North-American colonialism with a colonialism of his own: *all* of America is an *ajiaco*, even though this metaphor is as inappropriate for the continent as a whole as that of the melting pot is for the Caribbean.

It is useful to situate these coinages in relation to Ortiz's work on what he termed the "special languages" of Afro-Cuban secret societies. As part of his research into "el hampa afro-cubana" ["the Afro-Cuban underworld"], Ortiz intended to write a book about *los negros curros, pícaro*-like characters in the black underworld of colonial Cuba.[18] Although this book was never completed, Ortiz did publish a long article in *Archivos del Folklore Cubano*. A substantial segment of this essay is given over to defining theoretically, and illustrating with many examples, the "special language" of the *curros*. What is pertinent for us is Ortiz's emphasis on the tactical value of this jargon: "Estos lenguajes especiales son necesariamente *defensivos*, pues la especialización social del grupo que los emplea necesita del lenguaje como un arma de defensa" ["These special languages are necessarily *defensive*, since the social specialization of the group that employs them needs language as a defensive weapon"] ("Los negros curros" [1928], p. 172); or:

Todo lenguaje especial de un grupo social es defensivo en tanto en cuanto tiende a solidarizar a los que lo hablan, a hacer exacta, propia, más íntima, fácil y constante la comunicación de sus ideas, también especiales. El lenguaje especial viene a ser a un grupo social diferenciado, lo que el idioma a una nación.

[Every special language of a social group is defensive insofar as it tends to bond together those who speak it, to make exact, familiar, more intimate, easy, and constant the communication of their ideas, which are also special. A special language is to a differentiated social group what a language is to a nation.]   (ibid., p. 173)

The analogy that closes this passage makes clear the significance of these remarks for our discussion. Ortiz's onomastic ploys – his theoretical and metaphorical cubanisms – need to be understood as "defensive weapons" in the struggle for cultural autonomy; they are insulating mechanisms, barriers that establish and secure Cuba's cultural borders. At the level of language, these words create that "insular consciousness" advocated by Mañach. Like some of his contemporaries, Ortiz realized political and cultural independence could not be achieved without linguistic autonomy. Unlike some of his contemporaries, however, he did not respond to this challenge only by recording and cultivating the more colorful or idiosyncratic items in the Cuban vernacular. Recognizing the importance of explanatory privilege, Ortiz tried to develop an insular theory to explain insular practices. His lexical and semantic neologisms – *transculturación, ajiaco*, and others I have not yet mentioned – are the building blocks of that theory; they are the core vocabulary of a special language that guarantees, on the theoretical level, the integrity of insular life.

But I have not yet mentioned the most encompassing neologism in Ortiz's work, which also makes its debut in "Los factores humanos de la cubanidad," an essay that is probably Ortiz's most succulent statement – meaty as well as fruity – on the distinctive features of Cuban culture. Written in his prime, and at about the same time as his masterpiece, *Contrapunteo cubano del tabaco y el azúcar*, Ortiz distilled into these pages many years of research and reflection. His subject, he says at the outset, is nothing less than the quiddity of Cuban soul, the "condición de alma" of the Cuban people (p. 165). The accepted term to designate this condition was *cubanidad*; nonetheless, for Ortiz the word is insufficient because it speaks primarily to accidents of birth or civil status. In order to be authentically Cuban, in order to possess true *cubanidad*, it is not enough to be born in Cuba or to have a Cuban passport. There is an additional, almost ineffable, criterion that sets the Cuban apart:

La cubanidad plena no consiste meramente en ser cubano por cualesquiera de las contingencias ambientales que han rodeado la personalidad indi-

vidual y le han forjado sus condiciones; son precisas también la conciencia
de ser cubano y la voluntad de quererlo ser.

[Full *cubanidad* does not consist merely in being Cuban because of any of the
environmental contingencies that have surrounded and shaped the individual personality; the consciousness of being Cuban and the will to want
to be Cuban are also necessary.]   (p. 166)

Never one to be bothered by tautology, Ortiz defines a Cuban
simply as someone who wants to be Cuban: Cuban is he who is
aware and desirous of his *cubanidad*. What does bother Ortiz,
however, is the *name* of this "plenitud de identificación ética y
consciente con lo cubano" ["plenitude of conscious ethical identification with what is Cuban"] (p. 166). Since the usual word, *cubanidad*, is too bland for his taste, he cooks up a new, spicier morsel –
cubanía, which is a self-conscious, willed *cubanidad*, a feeling of deep
and pervasive identification with things Cuban. He distinguishes
between *cubanidad*: "condición genérica de cubano" ["the generic
condition of being Cuban"]; and *cubanía*: "cubanidad plena,
sentida, consciente y deseada; cubanidad responsable, cubanidad
con las tres virtudes, dichas teologales, de fe, esperanza y amor"
["complete, felt, conscious, and desired *cubanidad*; responsible
cubanidad, *cubanidad* with the three so-called theological virtues, faith,
hope, and charity"] (p. 166). Unlike *cubanidad*, which is essentially a
civil status, *cubanía* is a spiritual condition, but a spiritual condition
identified by an act of the will, one that is fundamentally a desire, a
wanting. As the product of deliberate desire, *cubanía* is given to those
who want it; but this means, also, that it is given to those who don't
have it, those who want it in the other sense of the verb, since desire
always presupposes an absence or lack (hence the double meaning
of "want"). To want *cubanía* is already to possess it.

This neologism, therefore, covers some of the same semantic
ground as the other two. Like *transculturación* and *ajiaco*, *cubanía*
denotes a state of incompletion or imperfection. For Ortiz Cuban
culture *is* wanting: both in that it has not produced a neoculturative
synthesis and in that, in order to belong to it, you have to want it.
Perhaps the clearest example of what Ortiz means by *cubanía* is
simply his invention of the word. If *cubanía* is defined by will and
wile, by an intense and deliberate desire to be Cuban, what better

evidence of this desire than the creation of a word to designate it? Indeed, what would *cubanía* be without the name? Like *ajiaco* and *transculturación*, this neologism does what it says. In matters of cultural independence, Ortiz was very much a nominalist; for him, the road to independence was paved with dictionaries. Not content simply to redefine *cubanidad*, he confects a new word to match his volitive and cognitive criteria, and since 1940, when it was introduced, *cubanía* has become an accepted and often-used item in the Cuban vocabulary.[19] What is at stake in this essay, again, is the discovery of a vernacular *voz*, of a native idiom. Such apparently disparate texts as "Del fenómeno social de la 'transculturación,'" "Los factores humanos de la cubanidad," and *Un catauro de cubanismos* are all part of the same overriding project. If *ajiaco* is a "metaphorical cubanism" and *transculturación* is a "theoretical cubanism," then the words indexed in the *Catauro* are literal cubanisms and *cubanía* is the cubanism for "Cubanness" itself. The issue for Ortiz is whether Cuba is going to speak for itself, in all possible senses of the expression. If it is going to do so, then one must find substitutes for the hegemonic terms – *transculturación* for acculturation; *ajiaco* for melting pot; *catauro* for dictionary; *cubanía* for *cubanidad*.

One of Ortiz's important lessons, I believe, is this awareness that one of the most insidious types of colonialism is the onomastic or conceptual, the situation that arises when the originality or distinctiveness of the home-grown is explained and rationalized using foreign categories, as if we could grow the guavas but needed someone else to package the paste. Ortiz realized that it is not enough to study vernacular phenomena if these studies are innocently couched in others' words. We need also a vernacular "theory" with which to articulate the results of research into the vernacular. And I put "theory" in quotations to indicate that Ortiz's theoretical discourse may not accord with our sense of what theory is. But this is precisely because Ortiz's theories (if that's what they are) are inseparable from his practices. At least in Mr. Cuba's case, this inmixture, I believe, is deliberate, appropriate, and salutary. In linguistic terms, "scientific detachment" involves a switch in verbal registers. This switch is formally expressed as the distinction between a "language" and a "metalanguage," between the language that is the object of study and the language that speaks about this object. In Roland Barthes's scheme, a metalanguage materializes when the plane of content and the plane of expression constitute two separate semiotic systems (*Writing Degree Zero and Elements of Semiology*, pp. 89–94). But Ortiz's terminological inbreeding is such that it is difficult to wrench content and expression apart. The proof is in the *ajiaco*, an all-purpose sauce that appears on both planes, thereby collapsing the distinction between object and subject, and between language and metalanguage. The *ajiaco* is a part of the object of Ortiz's analysis as well as the conceptual category with which this object is analyzed. Realizing that it did no good to claim a vernacular culture if that claim was spoken in a foreign tongue, Ortiz is intent on examining Cuban ways in a Cuban way.[20] His words to those who would insist on objectivity and detachment might well be: "¡Que no nos venga la Academia con guayabas!" ["That guava is too hard to swallow!"]. The liability of this approach, of course, is that it makes his work inaccessible to a readership impatient or unacquainted with its "special language." The asset that outweighs the liability is that, if you want to understand Ortiz, you cannot but do it in his own terms. You don't have to read him, but if you do, he makes you eat his words.

Having said this much, I should reiterate that Ortiz's desire to write about Cuba as a Cuban did not make him susceptible to the pitfalls of "primitive" criollism. Absent from his linguistic thinking is the Adamic notion of the pristine, aboriginal name. As all of his coinages attest, Ortiz was very much aware of the "dialogical" slant in his vernacular voice. None of his coinages claim aboriginal status; *transculturación* is based on "acculturation"; *ajiaco*, word and recipe, has a mixed Amerindian, Spanish, and African ancestry; and even *cubanía* is only Cuban by naturalization, since Ortiz acknowledges that this coinage was inspired by Unamuno's analogous distinction between *hispanidad* and *hispanía* ("Los factores humanos de la cubanidad," p. 166). Ortiz's neologisms always entail a translation, in either the linguistic or the topographical sense, of already existing terms. His is a home-grown vocabulary that clearly displays its foreign roots: others' words that have been made one's own. This is why Ortiz's criollism is critical rather than primitive, original rather than aboriginal.

In Ortiz's best work, Marinello's hermeneutic feat becomes a hermeneutic feast. Ortiz keeps his distance, as Marinello suggested, but he is not afraid to meddle, to *meter la cuchareta*. Ever the impassioned spectator, he has his *ajiaco* and eats it too. But one would not expect anything less from Mr. Cuba, whose very nickname has it both ways, lacing the foreign with the autochthonous. In the two chapters that follow we will prolong this line of inquiry by studying how Ortiz, a man for all seasonings, applied his translational talent not only to the preparation of lexical morsels but also to the confection of whole texts.

2

The politics of enchantment

Ortiz concludes his essay on transculturation by appealing to the "unimpeachable authority" of Bronislaw Malinowski:

Sometido el propuesto neologismo, transculturación, a la autoridad irrecusable de Bronislaw Malinowski, el gran maestro contemporáneo de etnografía y sociología, ha merecido su inmediata aprobación. Con tan eminente padrino, no vacilamos en lanzar el neologismo susodicho.

[Having been submitted to the unimpeachable authority of Bronislaw Malinowski, the great contemporary master of ethnography and sociology, the proposed neologism, transculturation, won his immediate approval. With such an eminent godfather, we have no hesitation in launching the aforesaid neologism.]

("Del fenómeno social de la 'transculturación' y de su importancia en Cuba," p. 135)

The choice of language is revealing. The Cuban ethnologist "submits" to the "unimpeachable authority" of the "great master" in hopes of receiving his "approval." Ortiz may be the father of the neologism, but Malinowski is the "godfather." Without him, lexical baptism cannot occur. Anxious to give the phenomenon of culture contact a new and better name, Ortiz seeks Malinowski's blessing and patronage, a blessing that the master bestows in a prologue that accompanies all editions of *Contrapunteo cubano*. The *voz* of the amateur requires the endorsement of the voice of the master.

Coming at the end of the essay, in the place where an author normally leaves his signature, the appeal to Malinowski divides the responsibility for the coinage. It is as if the essay were subscribed, in the double sense of the word, by both Ortiz and Malinowski; hence, in the prologue, Malinowski declares that he intends to "appropriate the new expression" (p. 6). Ortiz's deferential gesture captures his typical stance as an author. In Ortiz's work one encounters none of that "magisterial rhetoric" so characteristic of the Spanish-American essay.[1] Never much given to speaking *ex cathedra*, Ortiz usually avoided the authoritative pose that one associates with the essays of a Rodó or a Paz. The Cuban's pose and prose are resolutely antimagisterial; his attitude is not that of the master but of the apprentice, the *pinche de cocina*. Better still, his attitude is that of the *cook-calambé*, the savage cook who, almost by magic, conjures up ingenious indigenous delicacies.

But Ortiz's submissiveness is not simply or primarily a sign of intellectual timidity. His deference to authority has a sly, roguish dimension, for by putting his word in the mouth of the master, Ortiz again has it both ways: he concocts a "native" vocabulary that is underwritten by a foreign agency. This behavior is best understood, I think, as a ruse, as another "defensive weapon" in his rhetorical arsenal. More concretely, Ortiz's deferential gesture bears comparison to the behavior of the *vivo*, the Cuban equivalent of the Spanish *pícaro*. As we know, the *pícaro*'s deviousness extends to his scriptive deportment. Lázaro is never more sly, never more cunning, than when composing his crafty letter for "Your Grace." Ortiz's submissiveness, I want to argue, is not unlike Lázaro's. Lázaro, the Spanish *pícaro*, relies on epistolary skill to plead his case; Ortiz, the Cuban *vivo*, relies on his rhetorical wiles to disguise the anticolonial, antiauthoritarian thrust of his theoretical pronouncements.

But what, exactly, is a *vivo*? In the most fundamental sense, the *vivo* is simply a survivor, someone who manages to stay alive, *vivo*, in difficult circumstances; in another, complementary sense, the *vivo* is someone who survives by dint of his wit, his *viveza*; in still a third sense, the *vivo* is someone whose wit allows him to live at others' expense – his so-called *vivío*. And when the *vivo* finds a *vivío*, he becomes a *vividor*, a kind of leech or "ingenioso parásito callejero" ["ingenious parasite of the streets"], in the words of Raimundo Lazo.[2] In Cuban folklore, the *vivo*'s antitype is the *bobo*. As Ortiz himself points out in *Entre cubanos*, for the average (male) Cuban, *bobo* is that which one must not be at any cost.[3] The habitual ripost, "No seas bobo," encapsulates the reluctance to be thought anything less than wily, astute, in the know. As a parasite, the *vivo* feeds off the *bobo*. In fact, part of the *vivo*'s *viveza* lies in playing the fool, in having the ability to "hacerse el bobo," as the saying goes. In the Cuban version of the master–slave dialectic, the two terms of the mutually implicated binomial are *vivo* and *bobo*. The *vivo* is he who sponges off the *bobo*; the *bobo* is he who lets himself be exploited by the *vivo*. If one is not *vivo*, one is *bobo*. *Vivo* or *bobo*? – in Cuba, *that* is the question.

Ortiz's stance as an author is best understood as a scriptive translation of the behavior of the *vivo*. So as to insure his scriptive survival, Ortiz plays out linguistic and rhetorical tricks that are forms of *viveza*. Indeed, the posture of the translator, of the native refashioner of foreign terms and texts, is already a kind of parasitism that might well come under the heading of a *vivío*.

One of the best examples of this textual *vivío* in Ortiz's output is an early and little known "essay" entitled *El caballero encantado y la moza esquiva*. Originally published in several installments in the *Revista Bimestre Cubana*, this work is actually a paraphrase, with comment and interpolations, of Benito Pérez Galdós's penultimate "novela española contemporánea" ["contemporary Spanish novel"], *El caballero encantado* (1909). From the full title of Ortiz's work – *El caballero encantado y la moza esquiva (Versión libre y americana de una novela española de D. Benito Pérez Galdós)* [*The Enchanted Gentleman and the Haughty Maiden (Free American Version of a Spanish Novel by D. Benito Pérez Galdós)*] – one can begin to form some idea of Ortiz's intentions in producing this "version" of the Galdosian novel. These intentions begin to surface in the subtitle, where the adjective "libre" ["free"] carries a double sense, political and literary. Ortiz's version is "free" because its author does not hesitate to depart from his original. As an intralingual translator, Ortiz realizes that he must take substantial liberties with Galdós. An intralingual translation is "free," or it does not exist at all. In this case the translator's liberties include the invention of several characters and of an epilogue absent from the Spanish original. These licenses, however, are part of a broader program, for "libre" must also be construed in its political sense. Appearing only a few years after Cuba's independence from Spain, Ortiz's *versión libre* is both a "free" and an "independent" rewriting, one that testifies to literary and political autonomy.

In order to understand why Ortiz decided to undertake this translation, something has to be said about the background of

Galdós's novel. *El caballero encantado*, like several of the Spaniard's late works, reflects the spiritual and material crisis provoked in Spain by the "disaster" of 1898. Along with many of the members of the Generation of 1898, the Spanish novelist realized that Spain, after the loss of its last overseas colonies, desperately needed some sort of "regeneration," to use the language of the day.[4] According to one school of thought, one avenue of regeneration lay in strengthening Spain's cultural and economic ties with its former colonies. Using the notion of "panhispanism" as a banner, the proponents of this view not only stressed the common cultural and linguistic heritage of the Hispanic world but sometimes asserted Spain's tutelary role in the perpetuation of what they regarded as "Hispanic civilization."

In *El caballero encantado* Galdós gives fictional form to the pan-hispanic agenda. The protagonist is Carlos de Tarsis, a Spanish *señorito* who, as the novel begins, is sinking deeper and deeper into debt. In order to solve his financial crisis, Tarsis courts Cynthia, a wealthy and beautiful young lady from Colombia. After Cynthia turns him down, Tarsis realizes that his interest was more than monetary. In despair, he goes to a friend's house and, after a mysterious and magical sequence of events, wakes up in the middle of a field somewhere in Castile, but with a new identity. This is the "enchantment" of the title, for it turns out that, in punishment for his dissolute ways, Tarsis has been turned into a humble peasant, Gil. This punishment is meted out by "La Madre," a personification of the "soul of the race" (p. 300). The rest of the novel is given over to the protagonist's pilgrimage across Spain, during which he comes to realize the error of his former ways. By the end of the novel, Tarsis, like his biblical namesake, has become a new man, and the enchantment is lifted. The story concludes on a hopeful note with the marriage of Tarsis and Cynthia and the birth of a son, Héspero.

It does not take great critical acumen to get the point of Galdós's allegory. Tarsis – abulic, frivolous, spiritually and materially bankrupt – is an incarnation of the Spanish nation, and particularly of its land-owning gentry; Ortiz, in his version, calls him "Don Pueblo Hispano" (p. 33).[5] La Madre represents something like Unamuno's *casticismo*, that is, a substratum of enduring Spanish values; she is, in

Tarsis's words, "nuestro ser castizo, el genio de la tierra, las glorias pasadas y desdichas presentes, la lengua que hablamos" ["our Spanish being, the genius of the earth, our past glories and present misfortunes, the tongue that we speak"] (Galdós, p. 173). Cynthia – young, wealthy, and pliant – is the symbol of Spanish America; and Héspero, product of the union of Tarsis and Cynthia, is living proof of panhispanic solidarity.

Although Ortiz essentially agrees with Galdós's analysis of the Spanish predicament, he takes exception to the Spaniard's treatment of Cynthia, and particularly to the nuptials that bring the story to a close. For Ortiz the noble sentiments and elevated rhetoric of panhispanic tracts shrouded the movement's imperialistic agenda, and the marriage of Tarsis and Cynthia was simply a reflection of panhispanism's disguised attempt at recolonization. In his collection of essays on the topic, pointedly entitled *La reconquista de América*, he puts the matter this way:

El "panhispanismo" abarca, pues, la defensa y expansión de todos los intereses morales y materiales de España en los otros pueblos de lengua española: influencia intelectual y moral, conservación del idioma, proteccionismo aduanero, privilegios económicos, legislación obrera para sus emigrantes, etc. Más no quisiera el pueblo de mayor sentimiento imperialista, salvo la directa acción política que no es lo principal ni lo necesario, como en Cuba podemos testimoniar en relación con el imperialismo norte-americano. Así, pues, aunque el panhispanismo sea por ahora intelectual y económico, no deja de ser un imperialismo.

["Panhispanism" includes, then, the defense and expansion of all of the moral and material interests of Spain into the other Spanish-speaking nations: intellectual and moral influence, the conservation of the language, trade protectionism, economic privileges, workers' legislation for its immigrants, etc. The country with the greatest imperialist sentiment could not wish for more, save direct political action, which is neither important nor necessary, as we have witnessed in Cuba in relation to North American imperialism. So, then, even if panhispanism is for the time being intellectual and economic, it does not cease to be a form of imperialism.]

(p. 8)[6]

Since Ortiz viewed the fraternal rhetoric of the panhispanic movement as nothing but imperialistic double-talk, he found it necessary to argue vigorously against its proponents. Hence his decision to publish a "free" version of Galdós's novel, a decision prompted, he says, by the desire to "interpret" the novel "from an American point of view, underscoring the principal incidents and statements and those that will be of greatest interest to the sons of Spanish America" (p. 31).

Since the symbol of Spanish America in the novel is Cynthia, most of Ortiz's attention falls on her. This emphasis is already visible in Ortiz's addendum to the original title: "El caballero encantado *y la moza esquiva*." Missing from the original title is any mention of the novel's female protagonist, an omission symptomatic of the peninsular bias of the Spanish work. The American version corrects this imbalance by giving Cynthia equal billing and suggesting that, as an evasive and haughty maiden (the two senses of *esquiva*), she will not be an easy target for the Spanish gentleman.[7] Just as Ortiz's subtitle juxtaposes the adjectives "americana" and "española" ("versión libre y americana de una novela española"), his main title also opposes qualifiers: "caballero *encantado*" vs. "moza *esquiva*." Tarsis may be enchanted, and thus docile or passive, but Cynthia is resistant to any such manipulation. Insinuating a contrast between Spanish enervation and Spanish-American vivacity, Ortiz's free version keeps Tarsis in the role of the dupe but liberates Cynthia from playing the fool. Moreover, since evasiveness is one of the principal weapons in the arsenal of the *vivo*, in Ortiz's version Cynthia is not only *esquiva* but *viva*. For Galdós, Cynthia is more or less a *dama boba* – passive, compliant, without a mind of her own. Ortiz restores Cynthia's alertness, thereby stressing Spanish-America's recalcitrance to neocolonialistic *boberías*. In the American version Tarsis is the only one who is enchanted, *embobado*.

Ortiz, therefore, disputes Cynthia's enchantment. In Galdós's novel, while Tarsis is wandering about Castile, he meets a peasant girl named Pascuala, who turns out to be Cynthia under a spell. Ortiz rejects the identification of Cynthia and Pascuala. His first objection is that, if one accepts the narrator and La Madre's opinion that enchantment is punitive, Cynthia's spell is unwarranted, since the novel makes no mention of her sins. Clearly Tarsis's enchantment is retribution for his lethargy (*bobería* for *bobería*), but what are Cynthia's corresponding sins? Galdós does not say. His other objection has to do with Cynthia's expatriation. Why should Cynthia, asks Ortiz, be living in Castile? Even if hypnotized, Tarsis remains on home ground, but Cynthia is not only enchanted but transplanted.

Tarsis, al fin, de noble trocóse en gañán, pero pisó en una u otra encarnación el suelo duro de Castilla y sintió el sabor de una misma tierruca con una misma alma; pero Cintia, la pobre americana, pareció cambiada en hija de Matalebreras, su riqueza fue sólo ¡un título de maestra de escuela española! y su persona espiritual tan distinta, como lo fue el ambiente.

[Tarsis, in the end, was transformed from a nobleman into a peasant, but in one or the other incarnation he trod the hard soil of Castile and he felt the flavor of the same earth with the same soul; but Cynthia, the poor American, appeared changed into a daughter of Matalebreras, her riches were only a degree to teach in Spanish schools! and her spiritual person was as different as her environment.]   (p. 150)

Ortiz concludes that either Tarsis mistakes Pascuala for Cynthia (once *bobo* always *bobo*) or that "there was a cruel injustice on the part of the sorcerers" (Ortiz, p. 150).

   Weighing these alternatives, he finally decides that Tarsis (and, by implication, Galdós or the narrator) were hallucinating when they identified Pascuala with Cynthia. That is to say, the enchantment that befalls the characters runs deeper than first appears, afflicting even the novel's narrator and author. This opinion is expounded primarily in an epistolary epilogue where Cynthia and her younger sister, "Juanita Antilla" (Juana, of course, is another name for Cuba), discuss Tarsis's situation. Presented in the guise of a conclusion to the novel, Cynthia and Juanita's correspondence provides Ortiz's allegorical reply to the Spaniard's allegory. According to Cynthia, who signs herself "América Andina," she is *not* Pascuala, Tarsis's mistake being "el despropósito más extraordinario y elocuente de su delirio" ["the most extraordinary and eloquent absurdity of his delirium"]. Moreover, Pascuala, who is a teacher, is actually the symbol of "the liberty of modern culture." Cynthia then adds that her marriage to Tarsis never took place, and that she has decided to spurn both of her suitors, Tarsis and "Samuel Johnson."

   The epilogue clearly illustrates the double sense of Ortiz's phrase, "versión libre." In a political sense, the freedom of Ortiz's version is transmitted by the sisters' resolve to remain unattached, independent from both Spain and the United States. In a literary sense, the translation's freedom manifests itself in the contrivance of an epilogue for which no precedent exists in the original. Since the epilogue summarizes the novel from the point of view of Cynthia, the mouthpiece of Spanish America, it is here that one perceives most clearly Ortiz's "American" interpretation and that the "moza esquiva" of the title is justified. By means of the letters, Cynthia and Juanita not only convey the American point of view, but they do so in their own words. Ortiz makes the same point that underlies his linguistic coinages: Cuba, Spanish America, can speak for themselves.

Coming at the end of *El caballero encantado*, after the events in Galdós's plot have played themselves out, the epilogue also serves to *place* New World culture. As the sequence in Ortiz's title already indicates, New World culture occupies an epigonic position: just as "la moza esquiva" follows "el caballero encantado," the New World inscribes itself "after" the Old World. However, this belatedness does not imply cultural or political subservience, for in the American version Cynthia has the last word. Having read Galdós's novel, she proceeds to reconstrue its plot from her own perspective, pointing out the "equívocos" ["ambiguities"] and "despropósitos" ["absurdities"] in the Spanish text. The point of the epilogue is twofold: American letters begin where Spanish stories end, and these letters are largely concerned with reinterpreting those stories.

Ortiz's anticolonial posture thus translates into a certain hermeneutic stance. His rewriting bears out Marinello's view that the Spanish-American writer occupies a position of interpretative privilege with respect to Old World texts. In the "Translator's prologue," Ortiz states that *El caballero encantado* is a novel "que debe leerse dos veces, una al correr de la vista sobre las páginas, otra más pausada y entre líneas toda ella" ["that has to be read twice, first quickly skimming over the pages and then more slowly, reading between the lines"] (p. 31). Since his version provides that second, interlinear reading, the "translation" is simply an interested, impassioned gloss. Ortiz continues:

Sirva esto de explicación a los que no vean claro el espíritu de las páginas de esta fantástica historia, que el traductor no puede aclarar más de lo que estuvieren, para no ser traidor de otra traición que la que le hace al aviso de su prudencia, de dejar intacto el original en espera de una mejor pluma americana que pueda refundirla con más respetos al lenguaje del Maestro y más holgura de los lectores.

[Let this serve as explanation to those who do not see clearly the spirit of the pages of this fantastic story, that the translator cannot clarify more than they already are, so as not to commit another treason beyond that which he commits against the warning of his prudence, which says that he should leave the original untouched and wait for a better American pen to recast the story with greater respect for the language of the Master and the greater enjoyment of its readers.]   (p. 31)

Ortiz's claim that he does not clarify the sense of the original so as not to betray Galdós is immediately belied by the pages that follow. The whole purpose of the translation, he says, is to clarify, to make explicit what remains half-hidden in the Galdosian original; his intention has been only to present the novel "monda y lironda, sin los afeites y colores que le diera el esclarecido ingenio de su primer narrador" ["plain and bare, without the embellishments and colors that the genius of its first narrator gave it"] (p. 31). And yet the differences between original and translation become evident as soon as one turns the page, since in a footnote appended to the title of the first chapter, Ortiz reveals that neither the chapters of his translation, nor its titles, "correspond" to those in the Spanish original (p. 32). This lack of correspondence between original and translation, which extends much further than the chapter divisions and titles, culminates in the letters of the epilogue – another sort of "correspondence" without correspondence in the original, and one whose subject, furthermore, is Cynthia's refusal to correspond to Tarsis's advances.

The issue, then, is what sort of correspondence should exist between translation and original. Since Ortiz does a great deal more than restate the novel in other words, his notion of "correspondence" does not entail a one-for-one equivalence. Even when he seems to follow his original most faithfully, that is, even when he quotes Galdós, the distance between texts is evident. In fact, in some ways Ortiz's most licentious act as translator is his decision to *quote* Galdós. A translator does not quote, for a quotation supposes a relation of non-identity between the quoted text and the quoting context, and this is the distinction that a translator strives to erase. In the optimal translation, the new text would be indistinguishable from the original, the translator becoming no more than an invisible conduit for the author's words. But by encircling Galdós's words in quotation marks, Ortiz takes his distance from his predecessor. The use of quotation marks can then be seen as another of the insulating mechanisms available to the intralingual translator. That "great distance" that Marinello discussed is here reduced, but not diminished, to a typographical notation. The quotation marks that pepper the translation, and that have no equivalent in the original, show that Ortiz is a poor correspondent, that he refuses to follow Galdós word for word, letter for letter.

But Ortiz not only quotes. He also comments, rearranges, supplements. The result, again, is a recreative rather than repetitive translation. Instead of trying to narrow the distance between the two versions, Ortiz flaunts his unfaithfulness. *El caballero encantado y la moza esquiva* enacts a kind of "secession," textual and political, which frees Spanish America from the Spanish metropolis. Spanish America, *la moza esquiva*, is what exceeds or falls outside *El caballero encantado*; hence Cynthia and Juanita's liminal placement in an epilogue missing from the original. In Galdós's novel Cynthia has no place; the American version, from the title on, gives her a place of her own. What Ortiz adds to his Spanish original is *conciencia de isla*, insular consciousness, an awareness of the New World's separateness from Europe.

The other important issue here has to do with the suitability of the term "translator" to describe the linguistic activity of someone working within one language. What does it mean to translate from Spanish to Spanish – or is it from "Spanish" to "Cuban"? In what sense can it be said that Ortiz is transposing Galdós's Spanish into a different tongue? As I already mentioned in the last chapter, the relationship between the Cuban vernacular and its foreign antecedents is one of Ortiz's persistent themes. Although *El caballero encantado y la moza esquiva* contains little that one could identify as "Cuban" Spanish (indeed, the diction of Ortiz's addendum to Galdós's title, "la moza esquiva," is anything but Cuban), by labelling his text a translation Ortiz nonetheless posits the distinctness of a vernacular idiom. Time and again Ortiz pauses to make the point that Cuban and Castilian Spanish are not equivalent. Thus, certain incidents in the Spanish novel are "untranslatable": "También quisiéramos contar lo que allí ocurrió y las cosas que se dijeron y hablaron, pero son intraductibles al americano, y sólo en la lengua de Castilla pueden leerse si se quiere comprender su espíritu" ["We would also want to tell what happened there and the things that were said and spoken, but they are not translatable into American, and if one wants to understand their spirit, one has to read them in the language of Castile"] (Ortiz, p. 158). Although it will be left to other works in Ortiz's bibliography to itemize these differences, his assumption of the role of translator implicitly makes the claim of linguistic autonomy.

Since one of the crucial planks of the panhispanic program was linguistic solidarity, this is an important claim. According to the advocates of panhispanism, the Spanish language was the corner-stone of Hispanic civilization, the indissoluble bond that tied together all of the different nationalities within "la inmensa His-pania."[8] As La Madre says at one point, she "dominates" because of her language: "Allá, como aquí, domino por mi aliento, *sicut tuba*; por la vibración de mi lenguaje, que será el alma de medio mundo" ["There, as here, I dominate through my breath, *sicut tuba*; through the vibration of my language, which will be the soul of half the world"] (Galdós, p. 154; Ortiz, p. 145). Rodríguez-Puértolas has recently attempted to explain, and explain away, the transparent ethnocentrism of this and similar statements, but without success.[9] The imperialistic thrust of Mother's tongue is difficult to blunt. The issue is not fraternity but domination, and the instrument of domi-nation, as Nebrija had recognized centuries earlier, is language. When La Madre speaks, half the world listens.

Or does it? In some parts of the world at least, La Madre needs a translator, who in this instance is none other than Mr. Cuba. Her voice may carry, *sicut tuba*, but her meaning does not. Ortiz's adoption of the mask of translator is a way of shattering the postulated linguistic unity underpinning the plea for panhispanic solidarity. If Galdós needs a translator, then Spain and Spanish America are divided by a common language. The label of "trans-lator," like the adjective "libre" of the subtitle, joins political and literary considerations, and one of the lessons of Ortiz's texts is the inseparability of the political and the literary. From the literary standpoint, the label is significant because it suggests that Cuban texts emerge from the translation of Iberian originals. From the political standpoint, the label serves to underscore the cultural autonomy of Spanish America with respect to Iberian culture.

Ortiz's stated deference to Galdós, the "Master," needs to be seasoned, therefore, with a grain of salt and a sliver of *ají*. The end of the translator's prologue is reminiscent of the conclusion to "Del fenómeno social de la 'transculturación,'" which also closes with a nod toward another *maestro*, Malinowski. We should not overlook the similarities between these two essays, so obviously different in other ways. As we have already seen, the theoretical essay is also an exercise in translation; and when Ortiz states that he will interpret Galdós's novel "from an American point of view" (p. 31), this declaration of intent fits the theoretical essay just as well. If the notion of transculturation can help us make sense of *El caballero encantado y la moza esquiva*, Ortiz's "translation" of the Spanish novel can help us understand what he is really up to in the theoretical essay.

These similarities point to an important fact: in spite of the impressive diversity of Ortiz's production, his writings as a whole exhibit a remarkable uniformity of tone and purpose. This uniformity emerges from what I have termed his "hermeneutic stance," that is to say, from his view that vernacular *voces* will always resonate with foreign echoes. When the sobriquet of "Cuba's third discoverer" is applied to Ortiz, one tends to overlook that, novel though his writings may be in their substantive content, they devolve from other texts, from other discourses. As cultural artifacts, his texts are marked by their place of origin; the secessionist translation of *El caballero encantado* furnishes an extreme example of what is in fact a general tendency in his work. It is no exaggeration to say that one of Ortiz's most important "discoveries" is having devised a textual strategy for distancing himself from the master texts of Western culture, be they "literary" or "scientific."

Ortiz's performance as translator must finally be seen as a strategy of evasion, as a kind of *viveza* or *esquivez*. Cynthia, who also writes, is a fitting symbol for Ortiz's scriptive shiftiness. As author, Ortiz is no less evasive, no less haughty than Cynthia herself. The label of "translator" is a cover, a mask that tends to dissemble the extent of his tampering with the original. As we have seen, the dominant motif in the plot of *El caballero encantado* is the change of identity, a fate that befalls every character including La Madre. But Ortiz also changes identity, though deliberately so. And his metamorphosis from author to translator entails a congruent metamorphosis in the text itself, which changes from *El caballero encantado* into *El caballero encantado y la moza esquiva*. In the deft hands of Ortiz, the Spanish novel changes complexion, but only in order to reveal its true aspect. And Ortiz himself, in the end, must be seen for what he really is: the author of an "original repetition" of Galdós's novel.[10]

During the course of one of her fulminations against Spanish society, La Madre says to Tarsis that Spaniards have let their language get the better of them: "el vicio capital de los españoles de tu tiempo [es] que vivís exclusivamente la vida del lenguaje, y siendo éste tan hermoso, os dormís sobre el deleite del grato sonido" ["the capital vice of the Spaniards of your day (is) that you live exclusively the life of language, and since language is so beautiful, you are lulled to sleep by the delights of that pleasant sound"] (Galdós, p. 150; Ortiz, p. 142). She then admonishes Tarsis that "los hechos son varones, las palabras son hembras" ["deeds are male, words are female"] (ibid.). By accepting the feminine Cynthia as the emblem of Spanish America, Ortiz comes down on the side of language, but he rejects La Madre's separation of word and deed. Realizing that the "life of language" is a form of political action, Ortiz provides an object lesson in how to do political things with words. For this reason, the Cuban *caballero* offers a telling illustration of the relation between Cuban culture and its Iberian antecedents. Without being a great literary achievement, perhaps precisely because it is not, this work displays with particular clarity some of the principal issues involved in the New World's search for literary and linguistic autonomy. The critical criollist, as I have argued, is a translator, and the texts he produces are refashionings of foreign models. Ortiz's text demonstrates this simply and clearly. In the following chapter we will study a more complicated and, in many ways, more successful transculturation. But the issues Ortiz raises in *El caballero encantado y la moza esquiva* are crucial, and he raises them so starkly that one cannot help feeling a little bewitched by his performance.

3

Cuban counterpoint

From one of Ortiz's least-known works let us now move to what is undoubtedly his best-known essay, *Contrapunteo cubano del tabaco y el azúcar*. First published in 1940 and subsequently reprinted several times, *Contrapunteo cubano* shows Ortiz's virtues as an essayist to best advantage: it is written in a lively, often humorous, and sometimes lyrical style, the documentation is casual but copious, and the subject has implications that extend far beyond the economic plane.[1] In the impact of tobacco and sugar on the history of Cuba Ortiz found a subject on which he could exercise his relational talent to best advantage. The contrasts between tobacco and sugar are both determining and representative. They are determining inasmuch as the peculiarities of the two industries have done much to shape the course of Cuban history; and they are representative because the counterpoint of the two products symbolizes many of the defining features of the Cuban character. The impulse to allegory evident in *El caballero encantado y la moza esquiva* surfaces here once again: for Ortiz sugar and tobacco are the leading actors in an allegorical drama that plays out the dominant characteristics of Cuban culture.

The book's argument is set up by means of a by now familiar stratagem. Ortiz begins by evoking his "literary precedent," which in this case is the dispute between Carnival and Lent in the *Libro de Buen Amor*, and asserting his inability to live up to this model:

Acaso la célebre controversia imaginada por aquel gran poeta [Juan Ruiz] sea precedente literario que ahora nos permitiera personificar el moreno tabaco y la blanconaza azúcar, y hacerlos salir en la fábula a referir sus contradicciones. Pero careciendo nosotros de autoridad, así de poeta como de clérigo, para sacar personajes de la fantasía y hacerlos vivir humanas

47

pasiones y sobrehumanos portentos, diremos tan sólo, sin versos y en prosa pobre, los sorprendentes contrastes que hemos advertido entre los dos productos agrarios fundamentales de la historia económica de Cuba.

[Perhaps the celebrated controversy imagined by that great poet can be the literary precedent that now permits us to personify brown tobacco and white sugar and make them appear in the fable to relate their contradictions. But since we lack authority, both as poet and as cleric, to take characters from our imagination and endow them with human passions and superhuman portents, we will only state, without verses and in meager prose, the surprising contrasts that we have noticed between the two fundamental agrarian products in the economic history of Cuba.] (p. 17)

Ortiz situates himself with respect to Juan Ruiz much as he had situated himself with respect to Pérez Galdós. He acknowledges the influence of the model, which acts upon him with the force of an "authority," but concedes his creative inferiority. In *El caballero encantado y la moza esquiva*, this inferiority was embodied both in the assumption of the secondary role of translator and in the assertion that his translation was only a provisional, makeshift version of the novel, which awaited "a better American pen" to do it justice (*El caballero encantado y la moza esquiva*, p. 31). In *Contrapunteo cubano* he issues similar disclaimers: lacking the talent of "poet" or "cleric" (scriptive professions both), Ortiz will redact his work, not in verse or artistic prose, but only in "prosa pobre" ["meager prose"].[2] No attempt will be made, therefore, to create an imitation worthy of the model; instead, Ortiz will content himself with mere jottings, prolegomena, source materials for some future poet worthy of the task, a poet not himself.

El contrastante paralelismo del tabaco y el azúcar es tan curioso, al igual que el de los personajes del diálogo tramado por el arcipreste, que va más allá de las perspectivas meramente sociales para alcanzar los horizontes de la poesía, y quizás un vate quisiera versarnos en décimas populares la *Pelea de Don Tabaco y Doña Azúcar*. Al fin, siempre fue muy propio de las ingenuas musas del pueblo, en poesía, música, danza, canción y teatro, ese género dialogístico que lleva hasta el arte la dramática dialéctica de la vida. Recordemos en Cuba sus manifestaciones más floridas en las preces antifonarias de las liturgias, así de blancos como de negros, en la controversia erótica de la rumba y en los contrapunteos versificados de la guajirada montuna y de la currería afrocubana.

[The contrasting parallelism of tobacco and sugar, like that of the characters in the Arcipreste's dialogue, is so curious that it goes beyond the merely social to reach the realms of poetry, and perhaps some bard will want to give us in popular *décimas* the *Battle Between Don Tabaco and Doña Azúcar*. After all, it was always very typical of the ingenuous muses of the people, in poetry, music, dance, song, and theater, to express themselves in that dialogical genre that gives artistic form to the dramatic dialectic of life. Let's remember in Cuba its most attractive manifestations in the antiphonal prayers of the liturgies of blacks and whites, in the erotic controversy of the rumba, and in the versified counterpoints of the country-dwelling farmers and the Afro-Cuban rogues.] (p. 18)

From reading the essay it becomes clear, however, that the future poem is simply Ortiz's text. Not for nothing did he label it a "contrapunteo" – even if there are no verses, the essential ingredients are all here, since he does personify the protagonists and play out contrasts. The account even ends in an appropriately fictional fashion with the "marriage" of tobacco and sugar and the birth of an offspring – a conclusion that Ortiz himself likens to that of a "fairy tale" (p. 127). His "meager prose" notwithstanding, Ortiz *is* that popular bard who sings the virtues and vices of Don Tabaco and Doña Azúcar.

In rhetorical terms, the first paragraphs of *Contrapunteo cubano* constitute a kind of paralepsis, the trope that disclaims what one says even as one says it.[3] This ploy is not unusual in Ortiz, who typically presented his *finished* texts as preliminary sketches, rough drafts, notes, or progress reports. This was even the case with books like *El huracán* or *Contrapunteo cubano del tabaco y el azúcar*, where their author's painstaking care is evident on almost every page. It is not simply that Ortiz's modesty made him downplay his accomplishments or that he sometimes did not finish what he started (though both of these things are true enough); the point is rather that Ortiz's habit of looking upon his writings as preliminary or tentative shapes their rhetorical protocol, the way they present themselves to the reader. Whatever their actual state, Ortiz's works typically adopt a rhetoric of incompletion. Time after time, he makes disclaimers similar to those in *Contrapunteo cubano* or *El caballero encantado y la moza esquiva*. His first, voluminous book on Afro-Cuban folklore, *Los negros brujos* (1906), was subtitled "Apuntes para un estudio de etnografía criminal." This sense of writing "notes" for a future study, a study that perhaps never materialized, stayed with Ortiz throughout the rest of his career.

Typical in this respect is the description of *Un catauro de cubanismos* as "simples apuntaciones de un mamotreto lexicográfico" ["simple notes from a lexicographical tome"] that will pave the way for a "definitive" arrangement of materials: "Pensamos, si el porvenir no nos es ingrato, preparar pronto una edición de este mamotreto con las papeletas ordenadas alfabéticamente, con algún mejor aliño, y enmiedas y adiciones" ["We intend, if our fate allows us, to prepare soon an edition of this tome with the entries arranged alphabetically, with a better appearance, and with corrections and additions"] (p. vii). Typical also is the presentation of his masterful study of African elements in Cuban music, *La africanía de la música folklórica de Cuba*:

El campo de nuestro estudio es en realidad sobradamente extenso e inexplorado, como selva virgen o manigua espesa, y este trabajo, pese a su extensión, es sólo un ensayo, en el sentido literario de este vocablo; pues no pasará de una simple exploración preliminar en el monte firme, trazando ciertos arrumbamientos iniciales y abriendo a machetazos algunos trillos y trochas para que otros con más competencia puedan cruzar por esas veredas iniciales y llevar a buen término la explanación completa.

[The field of our study is in reality inordinately broad and unexplored, like a virgin jungle or a dense thicket, and this study, in spite of its length, is only an essay, in the literary sense of the word, since it will not be more than a simple preliminary exploration into the thick of the jungle, marking a few initial directions and clearing with our machete a few trails so that others with more competence can traverse these initial paths and finish the explanation.]   (p. vii)

Nearly all of Ortiz's works are "essays" in this sense. An essay, in one fundamental sense, is an approximation, a tentative or preliminary grappling with a subject that awaits more sustained or polished treatment. According to Walter Pater, in language reminiscent of Ortiz's, the essay "does in truth little more than clear the ground, or the atmosphere, or the mental tablet."[4] In Spanish the preliminariness of the essay is reinforced by the word's theatrical meaning, since an *ensayo* is also a rehearsal, a dry run. In this respect also essays are non-definitive, preparatory, preambular. An essay is indeed a *mamotreto* in the strict sense, that is, a sort of memory-book or file for future use – "apuntes para," in Ortiz's phrase. There is always in the essay this anticipation – whether real or rhetorical – of a future definitive work for which the present assemblage of materials serves as preparation. Hence the heterogeneity and discursiveness typical of the form.

My point is that this roughness, this preliminariness are the *definitive* characteristics of Ortiz's texts. Resorting once again to Mayz Vallenilla's terminology, one can say that the "no-ser-todavía" of Ortiz's works is actually a "no-ser-*siempre*-todavía." (Significantly, the revised edition of the *Catauro* was published only posthumously, fifty years after Ortiz announced it, and then only with the aid of an editor who "ordered" the entries.) Irrespective of their author's actual intentions, Ortiz's works customarily sell themselves short, issuing disclaimers that are often contradicted by the works themselves. As in *El caballero encantado y la moza esquiva* and *Contrapunteo cubano*, Mr. Cuba's writings say one thing and do another. If the former rewrites Galdós's novel while pretending only to furnish an "abbreviated translation" (*El caballero encantado y la moza esquiva*, p. 259), the latter stages the dispute between tobacco and sugar while presuming only to gather materials for some eventual *mise en scène*.

In light of this, it is not inaccurate to say that the dominant genre of Ortiz's *oeuvre* is the "work-in-progress." Ortiz offers his writings as rough drafts for studies that will require, as he put it in *El caballero encantado y la moza esquiva*, "a better pen." In a literal sense, this preliminary, unfinished quality of his work is nowhere more evident than in his research into Afro-Cuban folklore. Ortiz's first important published work in this area was *Los negros brujos*, which appeared in Madrid in 1906. This was to be the first part of an ambitious multivolume study of the Afro-Cuban "underworld" on which Ortiz labored throughout most of his life, but which he never completed; indeed, it is both moving and a little pathetic that, at the time of his death in 1969, Ortiz was still working on the fourth volume in the series, *Los negros curros*, which he had begun well over sixty years earlier. Adding up to several books and dozens of articles, the *Hampa afro-cubana* (the project's collective title) may serve as an emblem of the constitutive incompleteness of Ortiz's completed works. The paraleptic paradox of his production is his disclaimer, against all evidence, of conclusive achievement. But, as we have already seen, Ortiz never liked to speak *ex cathedra*. If he generally looked upon his published writings as work-in-progress, he regarded himself as a sort of "author-in-progress." His stance as a writer was never that of the self-assured investigator fully in control of his material. Just the opposite: he saw himself as a neophyte, a beginner, and hence he saw his works as nothing more than "essays." Of the *Glosario de afronegrismos* he said that it was "un ensayo vacilante y lleno de temores, como el niño que en busca de nidos de cotorras intenta penetrar en monte firme, *casimboso* y lleno de temblores" ["a vacillating and timid essay, like the child who searching for parrots' nests goes into a deep forest that is full of water-holes and swamps"] (*Glosario de afronegrismos*, p. xv). In rhetorical terms at least, Ortiz is that scared but not timid child who ventures into uncharted territory.

This rhetorical strategy has important implications for our understanding of Ortiz's ideas about Cuba. As "work-in-progress," his writings make a close fit with his conception of Cuban culture, whose definitive feature is also an abiding imperfection – the "constant cooking" of the *ajiaco*. Just as Cuban culture subsists in a transitional, imperfective stage, Ortiz's texts, faithful products of the culture, also fall short of finality. Like Cuba, Ortiz is always cooking, and his work never does reach a neoculturative synthesis. When he asserts that the "deferral of consolidation" is a characteristic of Cuban culture ("América es un ajiaco," p. 24), the phrase applies equally to his own texts, which also defer consolidation. Cuba's cultural incompletion is asserted and explained in texts that are themselves incomplete, rhetorically or substantively. Once again, Ortiz's discourse is one with its object of study. Reading Ortiz, one is never sure whether one is reading "about" Cuba or whether one is experiencing Cuban culture first hand. In this narrow but significant sense, Ortiz is indeed "Mr. Cuba."

Because paralepsis opens a gap between intention and performance, it is a trope of rhetorical duplicity, another sort of *viveza* or *esquivez*. The typical paraleptic gesture is to affirm by denial, to say one thing and do another, or, more exactly, to say one thing even as one says its opposite. The textbook examples of this trope are statements on the order of "I do not mention that you have taken monies from our allies" (from the *Ad Herennium*), where the main clause denies the very thing the subordinate clause accomplishes. Borrowing from the terminology of speech act theory, one might call such an utterance a "counterperformative", since it counters – but does not cancel – its own performance. Since a paraleptic utterance fulfills what it forbids, it is never identical with itself. Paralepsis creates a counterpoint between affirmation and negation, acknowledgment and disavowal, identity and non-identity. The notion of trance, which Ortiz used apropos of Cuban culture, is apposite here: a paraleptic work like *Contrapunteo cubano* exists in a trance, trance being the interval between self-identity and self-difference. On either end of the interval the antinomy is dissolved: either Ortiz's essay is that folk-poem evoked in its opening paragraphs, or it is not. But since paralepsis simultaneously affirms exclusive propositions, it holds these two alternatives in a trance. Ortiz dramatizes the contrasts between tobacco and sugar while stating that he does not. Although, as Malinowski notices in the prologue, the *Contrapunteo* is indeed the "epic of tobacco and sugar" (p. 8), Ortiz disclaims any such feat. The paraleptic pose is held to the very end. Even after bringing off his brilliant *tour de force*, Ortiz does not stop downplaying his own accomplishment; as he says in the conclusion, "Acaso canten un día los vates de Cuba cómo el alcohol [...]" ["Perhaps one day Cuban bards will sing of how alcohol (...)"] (p. 128).

This attitude is carried through to the very last sentence of the essay, which continues in the paraleptic mode: "Y con el alcohol en las mentes terminará el contrapunteo" ["And with heads filled with alcohol the counterpoint will come to an end"] (p. 128). In this sentence the future tense is a rhetorical contrivance rather than a logical necessity. Even though this assertion actually marks the termination of Ortiz's own essay, the reference is to a text not yet in existence. With the last word – "contrapunteo" – the essay names itself but pretends to be addressing another. As a result, the essay has a double identity; it is both a preliminary assembly of information and its definitive artistic arrangement; it is both rehearsal and performance, anticipation and fulfillment.

As an act of ontological duplicity, paralepsis is a useful instrument for dealing with the preemptive authority of "literary precedents." Precursors affect a writer in two ways. On the one hand, they can facilitate new work by making available a stock of forms, themes, and expressive resources; Ortiz alludes to this enabling function of precedents when he states that the *Libro de Buen Amor* "permits" him to personify tobacco and sugar ("Acaso la célebre controversia imaginada por aquel gran poeta sea precedente literario que ahora nos permitiera personificar el moreno tabaco y la blanconaza azúcar"). On the other hand, a precursor or a tradition – tradition being the congress of precursors – can also have a disabling influence, since the earlier work might appear as a hindrance to creation. From the perspective of the "ephebe,"[5] every uttered word may appear to reduce the supply of available utterances. If the author-to-be arrives on the scene late enough, he may form the impression that nothing remains to be said because his precursors have said it all. In the first instance tradition is an invitation to speech; in the second, it is an inducement to silence.

The duplicity of paralepsis allows Ortiz to manage these incompatible pressures. Occupying a halfway point between speech and silence (the exemplary "I do not mention that..." of the handbooks), a work written in the paraleptic mode exploits inherited resources while presuming not to. When Ortiz tells us that he will not attempt to emulate his illustrious predecessor, he is casting off the onus of imitation; having thus excused himself, he can proceed with impunity to write his own version of the dispute of Carnival and Lent. Ortiz employs paralepsis in order to clear some ground for himself, to establish that "distance" that Marinello discussed in "Cubanismo y americanismo literarios." As a verbal *viveza*, as a form of rhetorical *picardía*, paralepsis allows him to negotiate the twin but contrary imperatives of tradition. When I said earlier that Ortiz saw himself as an "author-in-progress," I was thinking of this duplicitous authorial stance, according to which a writer simultaneously avoids and assumes the responsibilities of authorship. The trick is to exploit the precursor and yet keep one's distance, to become, again in Marinello's terms, an impassioned spectator. As a rhetorical combination of rapport and detachment, paralepsis provides another instrument with which to accomplish this end.

Thus, the most fundamental counterpoint in *Contrapunteo cubano* is the ontological counterpoint between identity and difference. But this is not the only instance of counterpoint in the essay, which employs this motif on several different levels. Indeed, one of the essay's salient features is the consistency with which Ortiz carries through the contrapuntal motif. On one level, it provides the framework for Ortiz's analysis of the dialectic of tobacco and sugar; on a second level, it describes *Cuban Counterpoint*'s relation to itself, the doubleness of a paraleptic utterance; and on a third level, the "contrapunteo" describes also the relation between Ortiz's essay and its literary precedents. Since I have already touched upon the second of these levels, let me now turn back to the most fundamental level of contrast, that between sugar and tobacco, and then go on to analyze the intertextual counterpoint between Ortiz's essay and the *Libro de Buen Amor*.

On the most basic level, Ortiz's contrapuntal mechanism serves to make intelligible the connection between tobacco and sugar. *Contrapunteo cubano* consists of a long sequence of striking contrasts – literal and figurative – between these two products: sugar is white, tobacco is dark; sugar is female, tobacco is male; sugar is prudent, tobacco is a curse of the devil, and so on. Of the many differences that Ortiz discovers, four are noteworthy here. The first and most fundamental is that tobacco is a native product while sugar is an exogenous one.

El tabaco es un don mágico del salvajismo; el azúcar es un don científico de la civilización.
El tabaco fue de América llevado; el azúcar fue a la América traído. El tabaco es planta indígena que los europeos llegados con Colón descubrieron, precisamente en Cuba, a comienzos de noviembre del año 1492; la caña de azúcar es planta aquí extranjera y lejana que del Oriente fue llevada a Europa y a las Canarias y de allí trajo Colón a las Antillas, en 1493.

[Tobacco is a magic gift of savagery; sugar is a scientific gift of civilization.
Tobacco was taken from America; sugar was brought to America. Tobacco is an indigenous plant discovered by the Europeans who came with Columbus, precisely in Cuba, at the beginning of November of that year 1492; cane sugar is here a foreign and distant plant that was taken from the Orient to Europe and from there to the Canary Islands, from where it was brought by Columbus to the Antilles, in 1493.] (p. 71)

In Ortiz's allegorical scheme, sugar represents the invasion of Cuba by a "white," exogenous culture. Although he recognizes sugar's claims to naturalized *cubanidad*, his discussion clearly tips the balance in favor of tobacco. Unlike sugar, tobacco is dark and native, and represents the indigenous substratum, "lo más indígena

y autóctono que nos queda" ["the most indigenous and autochthonous thing we have left"].[6] The counterpoint of tobacco and sugar
thus embeds the dialectic of foreignness and autochthony that
produces vernacular culture. The issue, once more, is Cuba's "insularity," its economic, cultural, and political independence. Will
the island be overrun by white, foreign-born sugar? Or will it retain
the native flavor of indigenous tobacco? In spite of the obvious
differences between *El caballero encantado y la moza esquiva* and *Contra-*
punteo cubano, the issues that underlie this work are the same ones
that motivated the translation of Galdós, since here also Ortiz is
concerned with the question of Cuba's cultural integrity.

Related to this is a second contrast of a topographical order: as
befits a product brought in from the metropolis, sugar is "central."
The "culture" of sugar (understanding the term in both its agricultural and social senses) is centripetal, monopolistic. The instal-
lations where the sugar cane is processed are called "centrales"; the
fields where it is grown are called "colonias." Moreover, since the
sugar industry as a whole tends toward the *latifundio*, that is, the
accumulation of land in a few hands, it is the agricultural equivalent
of empire. The culture of sugar reproduces, on a small, sweet scale,
the relation between the exploitative metropolis and the exploited
colonies.[7]

The culture of tobacco, by contrast, is decentralizing, individual-
ist, centrifugal. The *vegas* or tobacco plantations, which are often
located on the "margins" of rivers, are not subordinated to any
central organization (p. 52). Each *vega* is an autonomous entity.
There is a certain dehumanized, mechanical quality about the
production of sugar, where the entire organization of the plantation
is designed to provide the largest amount of raw material for the
"jaws" of the "arachnid" machinery in the sugar mill (p. 52). Not
so with tobacco, where each cigar is produced individually by
human hands. Because of the impulse toward autonomy inherent in
the production of tobacco, it is no accident that tobacco growers
played a crucial role in the Wars of Independence, and Ortiz
recounts the anecdote (which for him has emblematic value) that in
1895 the order of insurrection for the war against Spain reached
Havana from Key West hidden inside a cigar (p. 125). The culture
of tobacco favors individualism, local control, the independent

operation of separate, small plantations. In the culture of tobacco, small is beautiful; in the culture of sugar, the bigger the better. Unlike his counterpart in the sugar industry, the tobacco grower is a minimalist, and his product is intended for the consumption of a select few.

In fact, the individual care involved in the confection of each cigar makes the culture of tobacco less an "industry" than an "art." The cigar maker revives the ancient connection between the artisan and the artist.

Bien puede, pues, decirse que en el cultivo y cosecha del tabaco en Cuba, el esfuerzo humano es el elemento de mayor valor, por la gran variedad de energías especializadas, físicas y mentales que deben ser combinadas para el mejor resultado, como si se tratara de producir una obra de arte, la maravilla de una siempre variante y armoniosa sinfonía de aromas, sabores y estímulos.

[One can well say, then, that in the cultivation and harvesting of tobacco in Cuba, human effort is the most valuable element, because of the great variety of specialized mental and physical energies that need to be combined for the best results, as if one were producing a work of art, the miracle of an ever-changing, harmonious symphony of aromas, flavours and stimuli.] (p. 53)

The task of the cigar maker is to create an art-object that harmoniously blends a variety of sensory stimuli. As the Baudelairean echoes of this passage attest, Ortiz regards the manufacture of tobacco as an indigenous art form: a Cuban cigar is a symbolist poem that goes up in smoke. As the creator of *puro* poetry, the cigar maker possesses intellectual gifts lacking in the workers involved in the production of sugar. Quoting José Martí's description of tobacco factories as "academias con su leer y su pensar continuos" ["academies with their continuous reading and thinking"], Ortiz adds: "Trabajador de hojas de tabaco y de hojas de libro. Así era el tabaquero" ["Someone who worked with tobacco leaves and book leaves. That was the cigar worker"] (p. 126).[8] The cigar worker and the writer are kindred spirits: both work with leaves, both are readers, and both produce works of art. It is no accident, therefore, that smoking cigars engenders a "contemplative ecstasy" that inspires the brotherhood of "poetas fumadores" ["poets who smoke"] (p. 25).

Because the manufacture of tobacco is an art, its product cannot be quantified. One of the most extraordinary features of the tobacco industry is the absence of precise measures: "el comercio del tabaco en rama carece de métrica" ["the commerce of tobacco leaves lacks metrics"] (p. 58). All the "measuring" in the tobacco industry is done by rough estimates without the aid of scales or other instruments. Because of this, the shrewdness of the tobacco merchant must itself be "immeasurable" (p. 60), and tobacco's units of measure – the *gavilla* and the *tercio* – do not have fixed values. A *gavilla* can have between thirty-five and sixty leaves; a *tercio* or package of *gavillas* can weigh between 120 and 150 pounds and contains a variable number of *gavillas*. By contrast, in the sugar industry precise quantification takes place at every stage, from the moment the stalks leave the field to the moment the refined sugar is given a price in the world market. As Ortiz puts it, "En el tabaco lo principal es la calidad, en el azúcar la cantidad. El ideal del tabacalero, así del cosechante como del fabricante, está en la distinción; que lo suyo sea único, 'lo mejor'; el ideal del azucarero, así del cultivador como del hacendado, está en que lo suyo sea 'lo más'" ["With tobacco the principal thing is quality; with sugar, quantity. The ideal of the tobacco worker, grower or manufacturer, lies in the distinctiveness of his product, which he wants to be unique, 'the best'; the ideal of the sugar worker, farmer or owner, lies in having his product be 'the most'"] (p. 44).

In general, sugar signifies order, measure, central organization, uniformity. It is a meaningful coincidence that the sugar mill is called an *ingenio*, for the sugar industry relies on the rational exploitation of natural resources. Tobacco, on the contrary, relies less on reason than on intuition. Sugar is Apollonian; tobacco is Dionysian. Hence the qualities associated with tobacco are nonconformity, inexactness, diversity, individualism, license – in a word, *relajo*: "el azúcar alardea de orden y al tabaco se le achaca relajación" ["sugar boasts of orderliness and tobacco is accused of laxity"] (p. 61). Being the "weed of the devil," tobacco is the agricultural equivalent of *choteo*, and both are linked to the same constellation of attributes. There is even in tobacco, as there is in *choteo*, an excremental dimension: "El tabaco es cosa hombruna. Sus hojas son vellosas, como trabajadas y oscurecidas al sol, y su color el de la suciedad" ["Tobacco is a manly thing. Its leaves are coarse, cured and darkened by the sun, and its color is that of filth"] (p. 31).[9]

Ortiz's characterization of the "art" of cigar-making can be referred to his own literary practice. Not surprisingly, Ortiz is also of the devil's party, and the *Contrapunteo*, from the title on, bears witness to the *relajación*, the lack of measure, of the tobacco industry. As we already know, Ortiz's texts are never tidy, measured, well-made. They are uneven like a *gavilla*, hybrid like an *ajiaco*. This is certainly true of *Contrapunteo cubano*, with its heterogeneous mixture of statistics, anecdotes, quotations, and hermeneutical flights of fancy. The untidiness of the work comes to the fore especially in the twenty-five "complementary chapters" that supplement the titular essay. Ranging in subject matter from the technical ("De las semillas del tabaco") to the literary ("De la copla andaluza sobre el tabaco habano") to the political ("De la remolacha enemiga"), and varying in length from one brief paragraph to more than a hundred pages, the complementary chapters (the first of which is a complementary chapter on the phenomenon of complementary chapters) supplement the main essay with a bewildering array of facts and figures. In the definitive 1963 edition, the titular essay occupies the first one hundred pages, while the complementary chapters take up the remaining four hundred. As the years went by, Ortiz kept adding ingredients to his original mix and in the end produced a sprawling, mammoth, nearly indigestible work.

The bipartite structure of the book, with the general principal essay balanced by the more detailed additional chapters, offers a further textual parallel to the thematic counterpoint of tobacco and sugar. The complementary chapters, which are keyed to different parts in the main essay, provide a centrifugal, dispersive counter to the centripetal, centralizing impetus of the principal argument. The main essay is the equivalent of the large, agglutinative *central*; the complementary chapters, of the discrete, autonomous *vegas*. Going through the book, the reader is forced into a kind of textual counterpoint as he goes back and forth between the main essay and the aleatory chapters.

Having said this much, we can now superimpose these intra-textual counterpoints on the intertextual counterpoint between *Contrapunteo cubano* and the "Pelea que ovo Don Carnal con la

Quaresma." Ortiz's text, even as it examines the counterpoint of tobacco and sugar, and even as it displays the contrapuntal structure in its own organization, is itself engaged in a contrapuntal relation with the medieval genre of the allegorical debate, and specifically with the dispute between Don Carnal and Doña Quaresma in the *Libro de Buen Amor*. The Cuban counterpoint will be yet another "free American version" of a peninsular text. In fact, since the contrapuntal format appears in all sectors of vernacular culture – among white as well as blacks, in the city as well as in the countryside, in religious rituals as well as in secular celebrations – this "dialogical genre" is a staple of Cuban culture, something "muy propio de las ingenuas musas del pueblo" ["very typical of the ingenuous muses of the people"] (p. 18). In weaving his counterpoint, Ortiz is simply following a deeply rooted national tradition, one that has its precedents not only in European culture but in African practices as well.

By invoking the medieval precedent and then enumerating its vernacular variants, Ortiz presents the Cuban *contrapunteo* as yet another example of "transculturation," of the translation and transformation of elements from foreign cultures. Not only this: the Cuban *contrapunteo* furnishes another name for the phenomenon itself. Like *ajiaco* and *transculturación*, *contrapunteo* will be a vernacular name for the process that gives rise to vernacular culture. Like the other terms we have encountered so far, it is a "theoretical cubanism," a native term that designates the emergence of the native. As we have seen, *transculturación* and *ajiaco* draw attention to the imperfection and heterogeneity of Cuban culture. Now in *contrapunteo* we have a word that highlights the contestatory or oppositional aspect of vernacular culture. More clearly than either of the other two terms, *contrapunteo* serves to underscore the fact that Cuban culture merges from a "conversation" or "dialogue" between the home-grown and the foreign. A counterpoint designates a relation of at least two terms in which the second term answers or "counters" the first. In a literary context, that first term is the "literary precedent" that enables and gives meaning to the work of the successor. Without the initial "point," there is no counter-point; and without a European *contrapunto*, there is no Cuban *contrapunteo*, word as well as genre.

The debate between Carnival and Lent in the *Libro de Buen Amor* is the point to Ortiz's counterpoint. Thus, the essay is peppered with references to and quotations from the Arcipreste. If Ortiz begins by invoking the figure of the "genial presbítero" ["talented priest"] (p. 17), he concludes in like fashion by remembering "aquel arcipreste apicarado" ["that roguish archpriest"] (p. 127). Between beginning and end, Juan Ruiz is used repeatedly as an authority: "Ya decía el desenfadado arcipreste de Hita" ["As the loose-tongued archpriest of Hita used to say"] (p. 93); "Vuelven a la memoria las agudezas satíricas del gran poeta de la Edad Media hispana" ["One is reminded of the satirical wit of the great poet of the Spanish Middle Ages"] (p. 111); "como escribiera el mismo perspicaz arcipreste en uno de sus versificados análisis sociales" ["as the same perspicacious archpriest wrote in one of his versified social commentaries"] (p. 109). The first obvious effect of the insertion of the Arcipreste's verses into Ortiz's text is to establish a counterpoint between his own "meager prose" and Juan Ruiz's literary verse. One of the characteristics of tobacco is the absence of metrics; one of the differences between Ortiz's prose and the Arcipreste's alexandrines is, also, the former's lack of "métrica." In the Arcipreste's *cuaderna vía*, where each stanza contains four rhyming lines of fourteen syllables each, measure reigns.[10] But Ortiz's prose is immeasurable. His text evinces a metrical *desmesura* that is but one element in a larger pattern of disorder.

By resorting to Juan Ruiz as his authority, Ortiz practices his usual self-effacement. However, Mr. Cuba finds other ways of establishing his autonomy. To begin with, the relevance of Juan Ruiz's work is limited by the fact that the Spanish poet did not know tobacco. The Arcipreste was familiar with sugar, of course, and sang its praises in a stanza quoted in *Contrapunteo cubano* (p. 34); but tobacco, which originated in America, was unknown in Europe in the fourteenth century.

La Edad Media de los pueblos blancos no conoció el tabaco, pero sí el azúcar. El Arcipreste de Hita pudo hartarse de golosinas azucaradas ... Pero el travieso eclesiástico no supo del tabaco ni del fumar.

[Sugar was familiar to white people in the Middle Ages but not tobacco. The Archpriest of Hita could fill himself up with sweet titbits ... But the mischievous ecclesiastic did not know of tobacco or smoking.] (pp. 34–35)

Ortiz's first claim to originality, to literary independence, will reside in the content of his counterpoint. He will introduce into the tradition of the allegorical debate a new dialogical pair, tobacco and sugar. By fabricating new protagonists, he will also alter the traditional tenor of the *débat*. Unlike the Arcipreste, who used the dialogical format in order to debate religious and ethical questions, Ortiz will use the genre for the discussion of social and economic issues. The Arcipreste's debate is a vehicle for religious doctrine; Ortiz's counterpoint will be a vehicle for secular concerns.

Tales contrastes no son religiosos ni morales, como eran los rimados por aquel genial presbítero ... Tabaco y azúcar se contradicen en lo económico y en lo social, aun cuando los moralistas rígidos se han preocupado un tanto de ellos a lo largo de su historia, mirando con iracundia al uno y con benevolencia a la otra.

[Such contrasts are not religious or moral, as were those set to verse by that talented priest ... Tobacco and sugar contradict each other economically and socially, even though rigid moralists have discussed them throughout history, looking with ire upon one and with benevolence upon the other.]
(p. 18)

In the prologue to *El caballero encantado y la moza esquiva*, Ortiz had already employed religious formulas to express his relation to Galdós; appealing to "his own good faith" and "the easy reparation of his sacrilegious daring" as extenuating factors, he excused himself for his "profanation" of the Spaniard's "holy book" ("relicario libro," *El caballero encantado y la moza esquiva*, p. 31). Ortiz's revision of the terms of the Arcipreste's debate may also be labelled a "profanation" of the religious allegory of the Arcipreste, for Ortiz ignores altogether the Lenten strain in the medieval text. In the *Libro de Buen Amor* the dispute between Don Carnal and Doña Quaresma separates into three distinct episodes. The first one narrates the battle proper, which ends when Carnal's armies are routed and Carnal is imprisoned; the second episode consists of Carnal's repentance and confession while in jail; and the third episode, which relates Carnal's escape from jail and Quaresma's exile, ends with Carnal's triumphant return to town escorted by Don Amor. Although critics are divided as to the overall meaning of these incidents, there is no doubt, at least, that Juan Ruiz gives Quaresma her due, since her ultimate defeat signifies less a wholesale rejection of spiritual values than a recognition of the cyclical nature of Lenten observance.[11]

Unlike Juan Ruiz, Ortiz has no place for Quaresma. In Ortiz's debate the contending parties do not symbolize the contrast of spirit and flesh, abstinence and indulgence, but two different modes of indulgence. Although tobacco and sugar differ in that they cater to different senses, both are vehicles for sensual pleasure and thus delegates of Don Carnal. Just as he misreads Galdós, Ortiz "misreads" the Arcipreste, spinning his Cuban allegory from only one of the terms in the original counterpoint. Ignoring the moral and religious dimensions of the medieval poem, Ortiz stages his counterpoint in the name of the flesh. But this means that the Cuban counterpoint is not an authentic *estrif*. As Ortiz mentions, in the Cuban counterpoint there are "contrasts" but there is no "conflict" (p. 127). The real enemy of Cuban sugar is not tobacco but beet-sugar, "la remolacha enemiga" (p. 371); and the real enemy of Cuban tobacco is the foreign leaf. Because of their underlying affinities, sugar and tobacco are ultimately compatible. Hence the Cuban counterpoint concludes not with vanquishment but with reconciliation. At the end, combat turns into courtship:

No hay, pues, para los versadores de Cuba, como habría querido aquel arcipreste apicarado, una "Pelea de Don Tabaco y Doña Azúcar," sino un mero discreteo que debiera acabar, como los cuentos de hadas, en casorio y felicidad. En la boda del tabaco con el azúcar. Y en el nacimiento del alcohol, concebido por obra y gracia del espíritu satánico, que es el mismo padre del tabaco, en la dulce entraña de la impurísima azúcar. Trinidad cubana: tabaco, azúcar y alcohol.

Acaso canten un día los vates del pueblo de Cuba cómo el alcohol heredó del azúcar las virtudes y del tabaco las malicias; cómo el azúcar, que es masa, tiene las energías y el tabaco, que es selecto, la inspiración; cómo el alcohol, hijo de tales padres, es fuego, fuerza, espíritu, embriaguez, pensamiento y acción.

Y con el alcohol en las mentes terminará el contrapunteo.

[Against what that beloved roguish archpriest would have wanted, for Cuba's versifiers there is no "Battle between Don Tabaco and Doña Azúcar," but only a discreet courtship that should end, as in fairy tales, with marriage and happiness. With the wedding of tobacco and sugar. And with the birth of alcohol, conceived, in the sweet womb of most impure sugar, by deed and grace of the satanic spirit who is tobacco's very father. The Cuban trinity: tobacco, sugar, and alcohol.

Perhaps one day Cuban bards will sing of how alcohol inherited from

sugar its virtues and from tobacco its faults; how it inherited energy from
bulky sugar and inspiration from select tobacco; how alcohol, as the child
of such parents, is fire, force, spirit, drunkenness, thought and action.
    And with heads filled with alcohol the counterpoint will come to an end.]

(pp. 127–128)

Less an *estrif* than a *dialogo d'amore*, Ortiz's counterpoint concludes
with the festive reunion of the two antagonists. Since tobacco and
sugar both serve Don Carnal, our lord of the flesh, they are finally
compatible. In the battle between Carnival and Lent there was no
possibility of reconciliation, and the dispute had to end with the
banishment of one of the combatants; but in the Cuban version the
conclusion is a harmonious wedding. Appropriating in his own way
the alliance between Carnal and Amor, Ortiz takes his distance
from Ruiz. Not only does he diverge from what the Arcipreste
"would have wanted" ("No hay, pues, para los versadores de Cuba,
como habría querido aquel arcipreste apicarado"), but he brings in
a disconcertingly different generic model, that of the fairy tale or
cuento de hadas. The last point in his counterpoint is generic: aban-
doning the adversarial genre of his earlier exposition, his dé-
nouement is actually a tying of the knot that descends from a
different set of generic conventions.
    The "profaneness" of Ortiz's rewriting becomes obvious in these
sentences. To believe Ortiz, the marriage of tobacco and sugar was
made in hell. In his Cuban trinity – "tobacco, sugar, and alcohol" –
the Holy Spirit has been replaced by unholy spirits: the "espíritu
satánico" slips into the role of the "espíritu santo." Moreover, the
description of the birth of alcohol parodies the doctrine of the Virgin
Birth. Instead of the spotless virgin conceiving through the agency
of the Holy Spirit, the "impurísima azúcar" ["most impure sugar"]
conceives through the evil offices of the devil of tobacco. (In Ortiz's
antitheology, only cigars are *puros*.) And the fruit of her womb is not
Christ but Bacardi. This frenzied finale is itself a mesmerizing
transculturation of diverse religious doctrines. Perhaps inspired by
those same unholy spirits, Mr. Cuba conflates the doctrines of Holy
Family and the Holy Trinity, projecting the familial structure of the
former – father, mother, son – onto the gnostic structure of the latter
– father, son, spirit. As a result, his Cuban Trinity is nothing less
than a devilish hodgepodge or an unholy *ajiaco*.

The implied setting for this passage is a wedding celebration where alcohol runs free and abstinence goes up in smoke. In this Cuban epithalamium, consummation leads to conception, conception leads to consumption, and consumption engenders a sort of poetic frenzy. The essay, which had begun soberly enough by acknowledging its author's limitations, concludes with a scene of bacchic – and even "tobacchic" – excess. At the beginning, Ortiz was all modesty and measure. But by the time he reaches the end of the essay, the measured allegory of his earlier disquisitions has been consumed. Because allegory is based on a sequence of reasoned equivalences, it is a "sober" form. Like the production of sugar, allegory requires an *ingenio*, for its author as well as its reader. But Ortiz's conclusion, with its intoxicating conflation of symbols, with its unholy trinity and its confounding conception, enacts a scene far removed from the theater of allegory. It is impossible to read the end of *Contrapunteo cubano* as the appropriate epilogue to an allegory, especially one whose precedent is the medieval *débat*. Even if Ortiz originally declared a doctrinal and didactic aim,[12] at the end he has something different "in mind" – alcohol: "Y con el alcohol en las mentes terminará el contrapunteo" ["And with heads filled with alcohol the counterpoint will come to an end"]. As befits a work built on the paraleptic model, Ortiz's peroration undoes his exordium. Cuban counterpoint: from decorum to delirium, from sobriety to excess.

My discussion of *Contrapunteo cubano* and other works by Ortiz has had two ends in view: first, to establish the terms of my argument (*transculturación, ajiaco, cubanía, contrapunteo*), and second, to provide some illustrations of how these terms apply to Ortiz's own textual practice. But because Mr. Cuba, creative writer though he was, did not write novels or poems, I have thus far only dealt with texts situated just outside the canon of Cuban literature. In the chapters that follow we will get into the canon by examining works by Nicolás Guillén, Eugenio Florit, Carlos Loveira, and Luis Felipe Rodríguez. But once again I will be arguing that these writers' works approach the question of a vernacular expression by recasting foreign models. I will be primarily interested, therefore, in how a poem by Guillén or a novel by Loveira "transculturate" Spanish or European texts.

Thus, although Ortiz's works will figure only tangentially in the rest of the book, his example will flavor all of my subsequent analyses. Without first having savored Ortiz's spicy contribution to critical criollism, we would be unable to appreciate the taste of the other ingredients in the stew.

4

Nicolás Guillén between the *son* and the sonnet

Nicolás Guillén, best-known as a composer of *sones*, has also favored the sonnet. Although the fame of the author of *Sóngoro cosongo* (1931) rests primarily on his innovative nativist verse, from his earliest poems Guillén has also shown a marked predilection for traditional poetic forms, and particularly for the sonnet. Indeed, almost half of the poems written before *Motivos de son* (1930) are sonnets. His first collection, *Cerebro y corazón*, completed in 1922 but not published until 1965, already contains twenty-two of these compositions. In Guillén's literary career, the sonnet preceded the *son*; the mature *sonero* grew out of the juvenile sonneteer. Beginning with *Motivos de son* sonnets appear less frequently in his work, but they never disappear altogether. One finds sonnets in *West Indies, Ltd.* (1934), in *Cantos para soldados y sones para turistas* (1937), in *Elegía a Jacques Roumain* (1948), in *La paloma de vuelo popular* (1958), in *Tengo* (1964), and in *Poemas de amor* (1964). In his recent poetry, Guillén has continued to resort to this form with some frequency; *La rueda dentada* (1972) includes eight sonnets, and there are sonnets also in *El diario que a diario* (1972), and *El corazón con que vivo* (1975).

In spite of Guillén's persistent use of the sonnet and other classical forms, the critical consensus seems to be that Guillén's "learned" poetry is less significant than his vernacular verse. Ezequiel Martínez Estrada, for one, does not find much interest in the Guillén of the sonnets:

El poeta conoce y maneja con maestría el verso regular; usa de la rima y escande como cualquier aventajado escolapio de la Poética Didascálica. Ha compuesto, a veces, intercalados con piezas vernáculas y aborígenes, impecables sonetos, silvas, romances, madrigales y hasta tercetos a la manera de Dante. No es ésa, naturalmente, la poesía que nos interesa de él, pues aunque de méritos artísticos incomparablemente más altos, carece de otros valores que no acierto a calificar mejor que con dos palabras griegas de expendio libre: *ethos* y *ethnos*, en que reside su fuerte personalidad humana y poética.

[The poet knows and handles with mastery regular verse forms; he uses rhyme and he scans like any bright student of Didactic Poetics. At times he has composed, interspersed among his vernacular and aboriginal works, impeccable sonnets, *silvas*, madrigals and even tercets in the manner of Dante. But, obviously, this is not the poetry that interests us, since although it has incomparably higher artistic merits, it lacks other values that I can only describe with two Greek words freely interpreted: *ethos* and *ethnos*, in which Guillén's strong human and poetic personality resides.]

(*La poesía afrocubana de Nicolás Guillén*, p. 65)

Martínez Estrada's strict separation of artistic merit and vernacular content is puzzling; if Guillén's sonnets and madrigals are only schoolboy exercises, it is difficult to see how one can claim for them "superior artistic merit." In my view, the interest of these poems *fechos al itálico modo* lies precisely in that they demonstrate how *ethos* and *ethnos* can exist in traditional forms like the sonnet or the madrigal. Guillén's sonnets, some of which I will study in this chapter, and his madrigals, which I will discuss in the next, are worthy of attention because they mark the point of intersection between his "white" literary formation and his attempt to develop a vernacular literary idiom. Indeed, one could say that Guillén's project of creating a poetry with "Cuban color" (as he puts it in the famous prologue to *Sóngoro cosongo*) finds its definitive challenge in genres like the sonnet and the madrigal. To write a mulatto madrigal or a mestizo sonnet is to transform, to transculturate, two of the "whitest" literary forms, two genres whose whiteness extends even to their conventional content, the stylized portrait of a limpid *donna de la mente*. Guillén's achievement is to add color, and even local color, to the pallid outlines of this conventional figure.

The Nicolás Guillén who will appear in these pages, therefore, is neither the social reformer nor the practitioner of onomatopoetic, incantatory verse. I am interested in a more elusive Guillén, one who does not quite fit the image of Cuba's "black Orpheus."[1] I am interested in the poet who, alongside such poems as "Sensemayá" and "Canto negro," composed sonnets and madrigals. But Guillén's "white" verse is undoubtedly the least studied aspect of his poetic production, and one that – as happens in Martínez Estrada – is sometimes denigrated. Although a great deal has been said about Guillén's "mulatto" poetry, this discussion has generally drawn attention to the black ingredient in the mix. And yet, as Nancy Morejón once said (not without exaggeration perhaps), Guillén "es el más español de los poetas cubanos" ["the most Spanish of Cuban poets"].[2]

Guillén's use of the sonnet is not only persistent but varied. He has written sonnets in hendecasyllables, in alexandrines, and in free verse. At times he employs consonance (with varying rhyme schemes), at other times, assonance. In the choice of subject matter, also, there is considerable diversity. His sonnets deal with a whole gamut of topics, from the political to the prandial. One memorable instance of the latter, which will remind us of Ortiz's gastronomic *gusto*, is a sonnet entitled "Al poeta español Rafael Alberti, entregándole un jamón," in which Guillén reaches heights of sybaritic indulgence worthy of Baltazar de Alcázar. It begins:

> Este chancho de jamón, casi ternera,
> anca descomunal, a verte vino
> y a darte su romántico tocino
> gloria de frigorífico y salmuera.
>   Quiera Dios, quiera Dios, quiera Dios, quiera
> Dios, Rafael, que no nos falte el vino,
> pues para lubricar el intestino,
> cuando hay jamón, el vino es de primera.

> [This vast ham, almost the size of a calf, came to see you
> and give you its romantic bacon,
> the glory of refrigerators and salt.
>   May God, may God, may God, may
> God, Rafael, provide us with wine,
> since, when there's ham, the intestines
> need to be lubricated with a fine wine.]   (II, p. 256)[3]

As I have already indicated, Guillén's earliest sonnets appear in *Cerebro y corazón*. Nearly all of the poems in this volume demonstrate Guillén's debt to the poetry of the *modernistas*, making plain the young poet's apprenticeship in the works of Darío, Silva, Casal, Nervo, and other figures of the turn of the century. A typical example of this youthful poetry is a sonnet entitled "Tú."

> Eres alada, y vaporosa, y fina:
> hay algo en ti de ensueño o de quimera,

como si el alma que te anima fuera
la musa de Gutierre de Cetina.
    Tu piel es porcelana de la China;
tus manos, rosas de la Primavera
y hay en la gloria de tu voz ligera
un ruiseñor que, cuando cantas, trina ...
    Un torrente es tu loca cabellera,
y tu cuerpo magnífico de ondina
bambú flexible o tropical palmera ...
    Y eres alada, y vaporosa, y fina
como si el alma que te anima fuera
la musa de Gutierre de Cetina.

[You are winged, and vaporous, and refined:
there's something dreamlike or chimeric about you,
as if the soul that animated you
were Gutierre de Cetina's muse.
    Your skin is Chinese porcelain;
your hands are Spring roses;
and in your glorious, light voice
there's a nightingale that trills ...
    Your wild hair is a torrent;
your magnificent, undine body
is a flexible bamboo or a tropical palm.
    And you are winged, and vaporous, and refined,
as if the soul that animated you were
Gutierre de Cetina's muse.]   (pp. 34–35)

The author of "Sensemayá" is nowhere to be found in these vaporous and vapid verses. The one vernacular note is the passing reference to the "tropical palm," though even this insinuation of the poet's real-life environment is vitiated by being predicated of a woman with the body of a water nymph, a creature that has never graced the fauna of Cuba. Rather than a flesh-and-blood woman, the lady of the poem is only a tissue of descriptive clichés that, as the references to Gutierre de Cetina suggest, go back to Renaissance Petrarchism. More than a *mujer*, she is a *mujer-cita*. As the speaker himself recognizes, this lady is nothing but a chimera – an entity built from disparate scraps and thus lacking a distinct identity. Even though the sonnet begins as a straightforward definition ("Eres ..."), with the adjectives that follow – "alada, y vaporosa, y fina" – it becomes clear that the woman's insubstantiality precludes further specification. In fact, all of this lady's attributes lead *away* from her: her skin comes from China, her hands belong to the Spring, her voice is like a nightingale's, she has the body of a water nymph, and her soul belongs to Gutierre de Cetina, her spiritual daddy. By the end of the enumeration, "tú" has been emptied of any individualizing content, and the word itself is less a "personal" pronoun than an impersonal marker of Guillén's debt to a certain literary tradition and its attendant conception of woman. What Guillén "addresses" in this poem is simply a constellation of commonplaces.

Using "Tú" as a term of comparison, let us now take a look at the first sonnet of Guillén's mature work, "El abuelo," which appeared in *West Indies Ltd.* (1934).

> Esta mujer angélica de ojos septentrionales,
> que vive atenta al ritmo de su sangre europea,
> ignora que en lo hondo de ese ritmo golpea
> un negro el parche duro de roncos atabales.
> Bajo la línea escueta de su nariz aguda,
> la boca, en fino trazo, traza una raya breve,
> y no hay cuervo que manche la solitaria nieve
> de su carne, que fulge temblorosa y desnuda.
> ¡Ah, mi señora! Mírate las venas misteriosas;
> boga en el agua viva que allá dentro te fluye,
> y ve pasando lirios, nelumbios, lotos, rosas;
> que ya verás, inquieta, junto a la fresca orilla,
> la dulce sombra oscura del abuelo que huye,
> el que rizó por siempre tu cabeza amarilla.
>
> [This angelic lady with septentrional eyes
> who lives attentive to the rhythm of her European blood,
> does not know that in the depths of that rhythm
> a black man beats the taut skin of hoarse drums.
> Beneath the outlines of her small nose,
> her mouth, with its delicate contour, traces a brief line,
> and there is no crow to stain the solitary snow
> of her skin, which glows tremulous and naked.
> Oh, my lady! Look into your mysterious veins;
> travel in the living water that flows inside you;
> watch the lilies, nelumbiums, lotuses, roses passing by;
> and you will see, restless, by the cool shore,
> the sweet dark shadow of your fleeing grandfather,
> the one who left his mark forever in your curly yellow head.]

(p. 149)[4]

There are significant affinities between this sonnet and the previous one. Both poems derive from the tradition of courtly love, a fact that shapes the appearance of the women as well as the manner of description. "El abuelo" begins by actually quoting this tradition, since "mujer angélica" is a transposition of *donna angelicata*, one of the epithets applied to the Lauras and Beatrices of Medieval and Renaissance poetry.[5] This little lady is no less a *mujer-cita* than "tú." In addition, the description in both instances follows a downward path, from the head to the torso, as was prescribed by classical rhetoric. In "El abuelo" the descending trajectory generates a fairly detailed catalog of traits. The lady, perhaps, is naked before a mirror, and we watch her as her glance inspects her physical charms, beginning with her light-colored eyes and concluding with her limpid skin.

The tradition of *amour courtois* is also present in the subtle insinuation of the motif of vassaldom, an essential element in the thematics of courtly love.[6] By addressing her as "mi señora," another transposition of a conventional formula, *midons* (as in the poems of the troubadours), the speaker adopts the conventional posture of a lover subjugated by an indifferent mistress. These connections with courtly literature are reinforced by the fact that "El abuelo" follows rather closely the structural format of the Italian sonnet, since it divides into two metrical and conceptual units (the two quartets and the sestet) separated by a *volta*, that is, a change or modulation in the course of exposition. Here the *volta* is punctuated by the exclamation with which the first tercet begins: "¡Ah, mi señora!" Upon reaching this point, the sonnet "turns" in a number of directions: the speaker modulates from a description in the third person to a direct address, from "esta mujer" to "mi señora"; he abandons the catalog of physical charms in favor of a description of her state of mind; and he brings to an end the downward trajectory in order to peer into his lady's soul. Psychological intimacy replaces physical intimacy. The speaker proposes now to accompany the woman on a journey into the innermost recesses of her being, and the two verbs of sight which appear in the tercets, "mírate" and "verás," have to do less with physical sight than with spiritual vision. In the two quartets the description had gone from top to bottom; in the tercets the direction is not down but in, from the lady's skin to her soul, from her physique to her psyche.

This movement inward is accompanied by a retrospective glance, by a kind of flashback. Since by peering into her soul the speaker discovers his lady's ancestry, looking in means looking back. Thus, the tercets are successively introspective and retrospective. They take us from the *hic et nunc* of the lady's resplendent skin to the *illo tempore* of her place of origin. As we move from her boudoir to the African jungle, the modern world gives way to the colonial epoch, and the poem as a whole modulates from inspection to introspection to retrospection: from the lady's snowlike skin to her heart of darkness to her shadowy grandfather. We should recall that in the earlier sonnet there was also a movement away from the woman's immediate physical presence, but it only led into the rarefied realm of literary convention; here the displacement takes us to very different surroundings and has a very different effect, for this is not a voyage of escape but of discovery, and even, as the reference to her grandfather suggests, of entrapment. This journey back to the source concludes with the last line of the poem, which suddenly redirects our gaze back to the body of the woman, to her "cabeza amarilla" ["yellow head"]. We return to the woman's body, and specifically to her upper body, which had been the sonnet's point of departure.

The phrasing at the end suggests, however, a marked switch in focus. In the last line of the poem the speaker employs, not the metaphorical language of amorous encomia, but the prosaic lexicon of impassive description. In "Tú" the "wild hair" of the woman had been compared, with typical hyperbole, to a torrent. At the end of "El abuelo" the hyperbolic torrents have been replaced by a "yellow head." One can summarize the argument of the poem by juxtaposing its opening words with its closing ones: "mujer angélica" with "cabeza amarilla." On one level, the two phrases are nearly synonymous, since angel-ladies are almost always blond. But these two phrases embody diverse ways of looking upon the woman's blond hair. In one instance, idealization and hyperbole; in the other, sobriety and simplicity. As happens in numberless love sonnets, this poem recounts the transformation of the poet's lady, but in a direction contrary to the traditional one, for there is no idealization or sublimation. By the end of the poem the earth-angel of the opening lines has been transformed into a flesh-and-blood woman whose blood pounds to the beat of African drums. The subject of "El abuelo" is not blanching but coloration. Guillén adds color, "Cuban color," to the *versos blancos* (as it were) of the Petrarchan sonnet.

Another point of contact between "Tú" and "El abuelo" is their attention to genealogy. "Tú" may be seen as an exploration of the protagonist's genealogy, which goes back to Gutierre de Cetina, for it turns out that this winged lady ("alada, y vaporosa, y fina") has flown in from the Renaissance. In other words, Cetina is the "grandfather" of "Tú." By the same token, "El abuelo," from the title on, makes evident its interest in the lady's ancestry, though here the regress leads back to a workhorse of a different color. A black slave now occupies the position assigned to Cetina in the other sonnet. But the claims that "Tú" makes for Cetina's influence on the lady are similar to the claims made on behalf of the black ancestor. In both instances the forebear infuses his descendant with vital breath; just as Cetina "animates" the protagonist of "Tú," the black ancestor determines the very pulsations in the veins of his granddaughter, whose apparent whiteness is revealed as mere illusion, as an *engaño de los ojos*. With his typical wit, Fernando Ortiz once remarked that there were Cubans so light-skinned that they could pass for white. He must have been thinking of someone like this angelic woman, mulatto in hair and heart but white everywhere else. At any rate, the mixed heritage of the lady is crucial not only because it symbolizes Cuba's mestizo culture, but also because it marks the spot where Guillén transculturates the literary tradition that animates his own poem. The intrusion of that dark, fleeing shadow represents what one might term the "barbaric" moment in the poem, the point at which Guillén has grafted foreign matter – be it lexical or, as in this case, racial – onto the European family tree. In "Tú" there is no question of barbarism, since this poem prolongs or perpetuates tradition in a pure, unproblematic way; but in "El abuelo" Guillén departs from his earlier sonnet as well as from its models by injecting into the poem a "barbaric" ancestry.

The transculturation of the angel-lady into a Cuban mulatto entails important alterations in the rest of the sonnet. One of the dogmas of formalist criticism is that by changing one element in a system, one alters the system as a whole. Something of this sort happens in "El abuelo," where the transfiguration of the lady transfigures other elements as well. Foremost among these is the motif of vassaldom. Once it has been translated from the nevernever land of courtly literature to Cuban territory, this conventional gesture acquires a profoundly human dimension, since it can now be construed as a reference to the institution of slavery. What appeared initially as a deference to literary usage now becomes a reference to a deplorable historical reality. As a result, the speaker's exclamation, "¡Ah, mi señora!," acquires an unsuspected pathos.[7] As by anamorphosis, the entire scene suddenly changes complexion: no longer does a suitor address a fickle lady, but a slave addresses his mistress. Seen from this perspective, "El abuelo" enacts one of the paradigmatic scenes in Cuban literature (and in Cuban history as well), the scene depicting an interracial romance. Moreover, by insinuating a link between the speaker of the poem and the enslaved grandfather, Guillén suggests that, if the suitor is being spurned, the reason lies perhaps in the lady's aversion to her own black background.

The lady's mixed ancestry also alters the place of this poem in the tradition of the sonnet. As its name indicates, the sonnet was initially a musical form; a *sonetto*, literally, is a brief song, or – *hablando en criollo* – a brief *son*. As the paronomasia suggests, the Cuban *son* and the Italian sonnet are distant relatives, for both have musical roots. The *son* is Cuba's native sonnet, or the sonnet is Italy's native *son*. Now in the first stanza the speaker states that in the depths of this woman one can hear the sound of African drums; but this percussive beating constitutes, of course, one of the most important antecedents of the Cuban *son*.[8] Those drums are beating out the rhythms of an ancestral *son*, a chant whose echo is perhaps audible in the assonance of *hondo* and *ronco* in lines three and four. What the angel-lady carries within her is the deep beat of a *son*. What a sonnet carries within itself, also, are the vestigial echoes of a "sonetto," a *son*. By referring to the lady's origins in musical terms, Guillén has collapsed her geneaology with that of the sonnet. Just as the woman travels back to her African home, the sonnet itself may be said to travel back to its acoustic origins.

Because of the role of music in the poem, "El abuelo" is perfectly compatible with Guillén's "folkloric" poetry. In fact, this poem may be read as an italianate rendition of Guillén's well-known "Canción del bongó." Both poems make the same point, that all Cubans are mulatto, if not racially ("cueripardos"), then spiritually ("almiprietos"). Therefore all Cubans, regardless of social class, are susceptible to the call of the African drums.

Esta es la canción del bongó:
– Aquí el que más fino sea,
responde, si llamo yo.

[This is the song of the bongo drums:
"Here even the most refined person
answers, if I call."]   (p. 116)

The essential subject of "El abuelo" is the angel-lady's belated
response to the sound of the bongo drums, represented in the sonnet
by the atavistic *atabales*. In spite of superficial differences (and let's
not forget that the theme of "El abuelo" is the deceptiveness of
surfaces), "Canción del bongó" and "El abuelo" are cognate works
– the sonnet is a "white" version of what the *son* renders in mulatto.
In more general terms it may be said that the *son* and the sonnet are
the two opposite but mutually implicated poles of Guillén's poetry,
the two terms in his own Cuban counterpoint. Just as in the case of
the *son* he needs to impose poetic form on African rhythms, to turn
the beat of the bongo drums into a "canción," in the case of the
sonnet he needs to infuse a traditional form with indigenous vitality,
to bring out the "son" in the sonnet.

   If we listen a little longer to what may now be called "el son de la
dama," we will notice that the first stanza is not the only place where
the distant *atabales* resound. The densest, most charged word in the
poem is the adjective "inquieta," in the first line of the closing tercet:

que ya verás, *inquieta*, junto a la fresca orilla
la dulce sombra oscura del abuelo que huye,
el que rizó por siempre tu cabeza amarilla.

[and you will see, *restless*, by the cool shore,
the sweet dark shadow of your fleeing grandfather,
the one who left his mark forever in your curly yellow head.]

This word, marking the precise spot of the lady's anagnorisis, and
accenting it with the choking sound of a plosive consonant, summarizes the poem's trajectory, since it brings about the reunion of
granddaughter and grandfather. At first glance *inquieta* seems to
modify the *tú* implicit in *verás*. The woman feels restless, perturbed,
upon discovering that she is mulatto, and the adjective underscores
her disquieting realization. But it is equally plausible to read
"inquieta" as a description not of the woman but of her grandfather,

the fleeting and fleeing shadow that moves across the last lines. The sense would now be: "que ya verás [la sombra] inquieta ... del abuelo que huye" ["and you will see [the] restless [shadow] ... of the grandfather who flees"]. The lady is restless because of her impending realization; the grandfather is restless because of his flight from the slave traders. Separated by centuries and circumstances, granddaughter and grandfather join in a common anxiety, albeit one with very different roots. This second reading of *inquieta*, of course, supposes that the adjective is displaced, distanced from the noun it modifies. This hyperbatonic placement is not inconsistent with the poem's meaning. Hyperbaton names the separation of sentence parts that normally go together; it is a form of syntactical displacement, of grammatical dislocation. But displacement and dislocation are precisely what the sonnet is about. What does the poem describe if not the black grandfather's own dislocation, his enslavement and exile? The dislocated syntax functions as an analogue of his historical dislocation. Or, to reverse the analogy, exile itself is a sort of hyperbaton, an existential dislocation that shatters the concinnity of self and surroundings. Just as the hyperbaton disjoins adjective and noun, slavery disjoins the grandfather and his African home.

The adjective "inquieta," therefore, has an ambiguous referent, as it applies both to the woman and her grandfather. This ambiguity is another way of saying that the black slave and the white lady, in a profound sense, are indistinguishable.[9] "Inquieta" joins the grandfather with his granddaughter, both grammatically and affectively.[10] From this arises a certain ironic parallelism between the lives of the two relatives: the granddaughter, like her ancestor, tries to escape; but that from which she flees is her grandfather. There is a double, failed flight in the sonnet: the grandfather attempts to flee from the slave trader but, as the lady's curls attest, he does not succeed; the girl attempts to avoid her black origins but, as the grandfather's manes attest, she also does not succeed. If he is enslaved by a white man, she is "trapped" by her black ancestor.

I would suggest that the poem contains yet another foiled escape. Although in modern Spanish *inquieta* only means restless or perturbed, etymologically the word has an acoustic root, as is shown by *quieto*'s etymological doublet, *quedo*. *Quieto* goes back to *quietare*, to silence, to make quiet. In its phonic sense, *inquieto* means noisy, not silent. That is to say: the word resonates with the beating of the *atabales* of the opening stanza. "Inquieta" marries sound and sense, *son* and sense, sound and sonnet. Although the sonnet as a genre has all but forgotten its musical origins, in "El abuelo" these origins are synoptically retrieved. Much like the poem's protagonist, the genre resuscitates its own ancestry. Guillén's transculturated sonnet is actually closer to the source, more "primitive," than its predecessors.

This means, also, that *inquieta* not only links grandfather and daughter, but makes explicit the figurative bond that unites them – the sound of the *atabales*. In this voluble word the poem voices the acoustic conceit with which it began (the equation of the lady's negritude with the beating of the African drums). In order to ascertain Guillén's revisionary use of the sonnet form in "El abuelo," it is enough to remember that in "Tú" the "light voice" of the girl had been likened to a "nightingale that trills."[11] By comparing the girl's voice with a nightingale's song, Guillén is still working with the metaphorical commonplaces of Western love poetry. However, by substituting the percussive drums for the melodious nightingale, he is incorporating into this network of imagery an entirely *un*common place (Africa), a place foreign to the tradition of the sonnet as a whole but very much a part of this sonnet's genealogy. Those African drums also mark the spot of Guillén's deviation from tradition, his literary barbarism. In fact, the drums are "barbaric" in the genuine sense of the term, for the messages they send are surely unintelligible to the girl. Like the girl's mulatto-ness, of which they are the phonic metaphor, the *atabales* bear loud witness to Guillén's daring, noisy intervention in the Western literary tradition.

"El abuelo" demonstrates that Guillén's "learned" poetry does not lack, as Martínez Estrada claimed, *ethos* and *ethnos*. "El abuelo" is an "ethnic" sonnet, as it were, a sonnet *con ton y son*. Even when he begins from a constellation of received attitudes and themes, like the stylized portrait of an ethereal woman, Guillén knows how to give it a sound and sense all his own. A more accurate way of looking at Guillén's poetry, it seems to me, is contained in the following statement by Juan Marinello, which accurately conveys the significance of Guillén's combination of the popular and the learned:

Hay en el poeta de *West Indies* una milagrosa capacidad para insuflar su potencia natural en moldes de la mejor calidad tradicional. El perfecto maridaje entre el soplo primitivo y la expresión culta de viejas sabidurías es la clave del valor de estos poemas. Nunca, en nuestra lírica, la voz múltiple de la masa ha encontrado vestiduras como éstas, a un tiempo fieles y transformadoras.

[The poet of *West Indies* has a miraculous capacity for wedding his natural potency to the finest traditional moulds. In the perfect marriage between primitive breath and old and learned forms of expression lies the key to the worth of these poems. Never before in our lyric poetry has the multiple voice of the people found vestments like these, at once faithful and transforming].[12]

"El abuelo" fits this description well: it is both traditional and innovative, both faithful and transforming – as if Gutierre de Cetina had also played the *bongó*.

5

Mulatto madrigals

It is a curious but little noticed fact that in the early poetry of Nicolás Guillén the adjective "white" occurs with notable persistence. Guillén's work before *Motivos de son* includes a whole panoply of white objects that range from poetic "espumas blancas" ["white foam"], "olas blancas" ["white waves"], and "blanco marfil" ["white ivory"], to prosaic "vestiduras blancas" ["white clothes"] and "sábanas blancas" ["white sheets"]. Given Guillén's early admiration for *modernista* and *fin de siècle* literature, still very much the fashion in Cuba in the early 1920s, this preference is not surprising. More intriguing, though probably traceable to the same origins, is the use of "white" as a term of artistic or literary value. One striking example appears in a sonnet dedicated to Amado Nervo, where Guillén praises the Mexican poet for having transmuted the "black roses" of life into "white rhymes" (p. 74).[1] Although it may be difficult to determine exactly what Guillén means by a "white rhyme," the general sense of the poem is clear: artistic creation is a kind of blanching or sublimation; Nervo's rhymes are white because they have turned formless pain into structured language. Through poetry, one passes from disorder to order, from murkiness to intelligibility, from a black funk to what Guillén elsewhere calls a "white harmony" (p. 9). In art, in poetry, life's impurities, its dark roses, are sublimated or clarified. For the Guillén of *Cerebro y corazón*, all art aspires to the condition of whiteness.

Another early poem, this one dedicated to Rubén Darío, confirms this nonchromatic sense of "white":

Yo he visto en mis delirios tus pálidos jardines

y he oído el coro ilustre de líricos violines
que desgranaba en ellos sus ritmos de cristal.

Señor Rubén Darío: por eso es que mi lira
también tiene en sus cuerdas la cuerda que suspira
con el temblor alado de un blanco madrigal.

[I have seen in my deliriums your pale gardens
and I have heard the illustrious choir of lyrical violins
that scattered in them its crystal rhythms.

Master Rubén Darío: that is why my lyre
also has among its strings the string that sighs
with the winged tremor of a white madrigal.]   (p. 62)

It is somewhat odd that Guillén chooses the "white madrigal" as the
symbol of Darío's poetic manner, for in the Nicaraguan's voluminous output there are only a couple of madrigals, and these are
minor, occasional pieces.[2] But here "white madrigal" is simply a
synecdoche for poetry itself, an equivalence corroborated by the fact
that this poem is not a madrigal but a sonnet.[3] Since Guillén's
youthful artistic goal was creation of a poetry devoid of historical
concerns and oriented toward previous poetic practice, his initial
inspiration came from what once he called "la urgente musa del
madrigal" ["the urgent muse of the madrigal"] (p. 82).[4]

Beginning with "Negro bembón," the startling initial poem in
Motivos de son (1930), he will of course abandon these *versos blancos* in
favor of a poetry with "Cuban color." Significantly, the adjective
"white" will appear only rarely in Guillén's subsequent work, and
then usually with pejorative connotations, as in the following lines
from "Velorio de Papá Montero": "carne prieta y viva / bajo luna
muerta y blanca" ["dark and living flesh / under a white and lifeless
moon"] (p. 124 – where whiteness equals death and darkness
equals life). Nonetheless, Guillén never did abandon his madrigal
muse completely, for *Sóngoro cosongo* contains two madrigals, and
West Indies Ltd. adds a third. What did happen to Guillén's madrigals is that, like his sonnets, they changed complexion: the "white
madrigal" of his juvenile verses turned mulatto, in both content and
form.

As we might expect, Guillén's mulatto madrigals are different
from the excerpts quoted above in some of the ways in which "El

abuelo" is different from "Tú." Still, the mulatto madrigals raise a supplementary set of issues that will form the subject of this chapter. I will begin with some additional remarks on "El abuelo" that will help establish a context for my discussion.

The bipartite structure of "El abuelo" extends to its forms of address. Whereas the quatrains describe the angel-lady in the third person, in the sestet the speaker switches to a direct address, a transition marked by the conventional apostrophic interjection, "¡Ah, mi señora!" Coming where it does, at the beginning of the flashback, this interjection has an incantatory function, since it beckons or brings back to life the black grandfather, that shade that lurks in the lady's past. The speaker, even as he turns away from the poem's implied readers (an apostrophe, literally, is a "turning away"), asks the lady to turn toward herself, to look inward and homeward so as to retrieve her black ancestry. This retrieval is conveyed by the embedding of a second apostrophe inside the first. There are *two* apostrophes in the poem, one within the other, for the speaker's apostrophe contains a request to listen to another summons: the beating of the African drums. As the percussive metaphor for her mulatto-ness, the drums are also an address; their pounding is another apostrophe directed to the lady, an apostrophe that she, at the beginning of the sonnet, elects to disregard. If with her outer ear the lady is asked to listen to the speaker's words, with her inner ear she is asked to listen to the beating of the drums.

This use of apostrophe is very much in tune with the essential nature of the trope. Exploiting the deep-rooted belief in the creative power of names, apostrophe animates the inanimate or makes the absent present. By naming something or someone, it makes it come alive, gives it a shape and a location. As Jonathan Culler has remarked, apostrophe demonstrates "the power of poetry to make something happen."[5] Hence the centrality of apostrophe in "El abuelo," a poem that strives to present, and to make present, the protagonist's mulatto-ness by resurrecting her grandfather. In terms of the poem's imagery, this resurrection is expressed by the contrast between the "solitary snow" of the second quatrain and the "living water" of the first tercet: the solitary snow connotes death and inertness, but living water – a metaphor that also animates the inanimate – suggests just the opposite, since it applies both to the lady's life-blood and to the flowing water of the African river. The passage from solitary snow to live water enacts a rite of seasonal and personal renewal: in the transition from the deserted Arctic wastes to the lush tropical jungle, the grandfather is born again and the granddaughter discovers her true color. Rhetorically these rebirths are made possible by the apostrophe. The speaker's exceedingly direct address melts down the lady's icy exterior to reveal the mixed blood pulsating within.

If we now turn toward the madrigals, we find that all three of Guillén's mulatto madrigals adopt the form of an apostrophe. These apostrophes, however, are directed not to an angel-lady but to an "hembra elemental" (p. 136), a sort of earth-goddess who personifies the life-affirming values of the "living water" of the sonnet. Absent from the madrigals, therefore, is the pre-apostrophic moment, that wintry season of cognitive blankness that spreads over the first half of the sonnet. Because "El abuelo" traces a curve that goes from Europe to Africa, one can read this sonnet as a parable of the evolution in Guillén's career from the early *modernista* poetry to his vernacular verse. (One might even read the line, "y ve pasando lirios, nelumbios, lotos, rosas," as an invitation to transcend the decorative excesses of *modernista* poetry.)[6] The angel-lady, white like a madrigal, is the muse of *Cerebro y corazón*, a collection which is full of ethereal women. In her pre-apostrophic phase, she can be regarded as an emblem of Guillén's poetic whiteness, as the source and subject of his early poetic exercises. What happens in the sonnet, though, is that, in the middle of the poem, and as a result of the apostrophe, the angel-lady changes colors. This parallels the evolution in Guillén's poetry: as it became attuned to the percussive rhythms of Cuba's African heritage, it also changed complexion, and the European rhythms of the sonnet became transfused with the African beat of the *son*. The "turning away" of apostrophe would then signify Guillén's rejection of his youthful *modernismo* and the espousal of the criollist aesthetic evident in *Motivos de son* and subsequent works.

This allegorical dimension makes the depiction of the lady's anagnorisis in acoustic or musical terms all the more pertinent. If she is indeed a cipher of Guillén's career, one can hardly think of a better metaphor for the return of the native than her attentiveness to the sound of the *atabales*, especially given the currency of the metaphor to describe Afro-Cuban poetry in general. Discussing the origins of the Afro-Cuban movement, Fernando Ortiz put the matter this way: "Por 1928 comienzan los tambores a retumbar en la lírica cubana" ["Around 1928 the drums begin to beat in Cuban lyric poetry"].[7] These are the same drums that beat in "El abuelo," a poem which can then be regarded as a poetic record of this modulation in lyrical taste.

Now in the madrigals the drums are heeded from the first: the sonnet's climax is the madrigals' point of departure. Here Guillén *begins* from the apostrophe. This means that, in aesthetic terms, the madrigals fulfill what the sonnet only foretells. Unlike the angel-lady, the madrigals unambiguously assume Cuba's black heritage. If the apostrophes in "El abuelo" looked back toward the past, the apostrophes of the madrigals look to the present and the future. If the sonnet's tone was hortatory – "boga," "mírate," "que ya verás" – that of the madrigals is assertive: the evanescent, fugitive shadow has become an accepted fact of life. Typical in this respect is the madrigal in *West Indies Ltd.*:

> Sencilla y vertical,
> como una caña en el cañaveral.
> Oh retadora del furor
> genital:
> tu andar fabrica para el espasmo gritador
> espuma equina entre tus muslos de metal.

> [Simple and straight,
> like a cane stalk in a cane field.
> Oh, you who provoke genital
> fury:
> your gait fabricates for the screaming spasm
> equine foam between your metal thighs.]   (p. 140)

Like "El abuelo," this poem separates into two parts divided by an apostrophe (lines 1–2; lines 3–6). Unlike the sonnet, however, the transition from one part to another does not involve a brusque shift or reversal. There is no migration from the cold north to the warm tropics; there is no melting of frozen snow into live waters. By carrying over the rhyme of the initial couplet into the fourth and sixth lines, Guillén underscores that the poem's structural partitions do not correspond to any divisions within the protagonist herself. Being of one piece – "sencilla y vertical" – this woman has neither the complexes nor the complexities of the angel-lady. Hence the speaker does not display any of the reticence evident in "El abuelo," whose convoluted syntax echoes the quandaries of the protagonist. Like its protagonist, the poem is itself simple and straightforward: it begins with a nominative phrase, goes on to the apostrophe, and closes with a declarative sentence.

Like Guillén's other madrigals and an additional poem, "Mujer nueva," to which they are closely related,[8] this poem is usually read as a loving, celebratory description of the beauty of the black woman, a popular theme in Afro-Antillean poetry.[9] But it has also been said that these poems caricature black woman by portraying her as little more than "a sexual animal without thought or feeling."[10] Rather than take part in this debate, I will shift the ground of the discussion by drawing attention to these poems' involvement with the issue of poetic language; I want to argue, specifically, that these poems are important not because they give away the author's *machismo*, but because the woman they portray – the woman they invent – is Guillén's vernacular muse, the source and sometimes the subject of his mulatto verses. In other words, the madrigals are significant precisely *because* they create a stereotype, a fictional being that bears little relation to any flesh-and-blood woman, but one who validates and empowers Guillén's mulatto poetry. We have already seen that, in "Tú," the "spirit" that "animated" the lady was Gutierre de Cetina's muse. In my opinion, the woman in the madrigals is the "spirit" that will similarly "animate" Guillén's vernacular verse. The "elemental woman" reveals the post-apostrophic face of the angel-lady.

Since Guillén's madrigals are "performative" rather than "descriptive," their apostrophic form is crucial. Apostrophes are performative: they bring into being the entities they invoke. Thus, by addressing this "new woman," Guillén creates an entity who will act as the source of his indigenous inspiration. One should not overlook the circularity of the procedure. Guillén animates a muse who will in turn animate his poems. There is a symbiotic relation between poem and subject whereby one validates the other; the two are mutually implicated fictions, the grounds for each other's existence. It is obvious that Guillén's "new woman" is every bit as much a fiction, a text-effect, as the angel-lady of courtly literature. Guillén has simply switched stereotypes, replacing the traditional idealization of woman with a different kind of idealization.

The distinction between originality and aboriginality comes into play here. Guillén's mulatto muse is an aboriginal fiction. Her function is to establish an alternative foundation, a native mythology for Cuban-color poetry. Even the titles of the poems demonstrate, however, that Guillén is aware of the connection between his vernacular muse and the Western poetic tradition. That is why I stress the fictional status of Guillén's earth-goddess. In the poetry of Guillén, aboriginality is a ploy, a trope, a metaphor intelligible only in relation to that which it replaces or defers. Guillén's native muse, to put it in different terms, has rhetorical rather than ontological force. Guillén is too shrewd to make ontological claims for the aboriginal. Especially in Cuba, where indigenous culture is all but missing, the idea of the "aboriginal" can be proposed only as a useful, perhaps a necessary, fiction.

The poetic function of this fiction comes to the fore in the second stanza of "Mujer nueva."

> Coronada de palmas
> como una diosa recién llegada,
> ella trae la palabra inédita,
> el anca fuerte,
> la voz, el diente, la mañana y el salto.
>
> [Crowned with palms
> like a newly arrived goddess,
> she brings the unpublished word,
> the strong haunch,
> the voice, the tooth, the morning, and the leap.]   (p. 120)

Of the panoply of things that the new woman brings, the most important is the first mentioned, "la palabra inédita" ["the unpublished word"]. In a narrow sense, this phrase names the numerous cubanisms, barbarisms, and *jitanjáforas* (often of African origin) that spice Guillén's poetry. The paradigmatic example is perhaps *sóngoro cosongo*, two unpublished words that were published for the first time in *Motivos de son*. But *sóngoro cosongo*, of course, is not only an euphonious *jitanjáfora* but the title of a book of poems. In a broader sense, the "unpublished word" is Guillén's vernacular poetry as a whole, including of course "Mujer nueva," the poem that contains the justification for this poetics of the neologism. One finds here the same mutual implication of subject and poem that appears in "Tú" and similar poems: angel-ladies do not exist, most probably, except in poems like "Tú"; but were it not for the availability of this woman as grist for the poet's mill, the poem itself would not exist. By the same token, "Mujer nueva," itself a *palabra inédita*, bears witness to what it portends. Guillén's poems are not self-consuming artifacts but self-fulfilling prophecies. The "new woman" brings what "Mujer nueva" puts into practice, in the most pertinent sense of the expression: that is, inserts into the poetic practice of the West.

Since I have just referred to a "poetics of the neologism," it is appropriate to reflect for a moment on the differences between Guillén and Ortiz, whose texts also propound and practice a similar poetics. When Ortiz substitutes foreign words with theoretical and metaphorical cubanisms, he is performing the same gesture that Guillén repeats in his poems, with their reliance on "unpublished words." But although the intent in both cases is to create a native voice, a vernacular expression, each author goes about it in a different way. The difference can be summarized in the contrast between Guillén's apostrophes and Ortiz's paralepses. These two rhetorical figures have opposite effects: apostrophe does what it says; paralepsis denies what it does. In the hands of Ortiz and Guillén, both are weapons against hegemonic cultural and literary forms, but one might say that paralepsis is a "defensive" weapon, while apostrophe is an "offensive" one. If the paraleptic utterance allows Ortiz to keep tradition at a distance, Guillén's apostrophes create an entity that will be the source, support, and subject of an alternative tradition. The reference to "fabrication" in the madrigal quoted above – "tu andar fabrica para el espasmo gritador / espuma equina entre tus muslos de metal" ["your gait fabricates for the screaming spasm / equine foam between your metal thighs"] – insinuates the founding power of this woman. Even if the context is erotic rather than literary, one can still perceive the woman's generative power as the stimulus for the poet's fabrications. If Ortiz, in his use of paralepsis, exhibits the cautious wiles of the *vivo*, Guillén, in his use of apostrophe, displays the assertive ostentation of the *guapo*, a character who is certainly not absent from *Motivos de son* or *Sóngoro cosongo*. Ortiz dissembles, hedges, hits and runs. Guillén undertakes a frontal assault. By invoking his black goddess – "Oh retadora del furor genital" – he issues a taunt or *guapería* aimed at the Western poetic tradition, the objects of whose invocations are goddesses of a rather different hue. If Ortiz's essays give us the writer as *vivo*, Guillén's poems give us the bully as bard.

Having said this much, I should now like to read the madrigal that follows immediately after "Mujer nueva."

> Tu vientre sabe más que tu cabeza
> y tanto como tus muslos.
> Esa
> es la fuerte gracia negra
> de tu cuerpo desnudo.
>
> Signo de selva el tuyo,
> con tus collares rojos,
> tus brazaletes de oro curvo,
> y ese caimán oscuro
> nadando en el Zambeze de tus ojos.
>
> [Your womb knows more than your head
> and as much as your thighs.
> That
> is the strong black grace
> of your naked body.
>
> Yours is the sign of the jungle,
> with your red necklaces,
> your bracelets of curved gold.
> and that dark caiman
> swimming in the Zambezi of your eyes.]   (pp. 121–122)

What happens in this poem can be described as a process of grounding. I intend with this term to signify two related phenomena: first, grounding designates a reduction of the spiritual to the material; the ground, in this sense, is simply the realm of the telluric, the material or natural world. In the second sense, the ground designates the origins. In criollist literature, these two senses often converge: the ground, in the physical sense, is also the ground, in the philosophical sense. Hence the intent, in criollist writing, to achieve an ever closer link with *la tierra*, regarded as the matrix of individual and national identity.

When Guillén speaks of women like this one as "hembras elemen-
tales," he intends the adjective in an almost literal sense. These
women are elemental because they are tied to the elements, in
syntony with nature and its rhythms. What defines the "new
woman" is earthiness, materiality. As the phrase *donna angelicata*
("woman turned angel") suggests, in Western love poetry women
are normally transported from the ground to the empyrean, an
assumption whose Christian model is Mary's bodily ascent to heaven.
In Guillén's madrigals the opposite happens – not sublimation but
grounding. In all three madrigals, therefore, one sees a sustained
attempt to anchor the female protagonist in natural and even
"primitive" phenomena. The other madrigal in *Sóngoro cosongo*
begins: "De tus manos gotean/las uñas, en un manojo de diez uvas
moradas" ["From your hands, your nails/drip, like ten violet
grapes"] (p. 121). Brimming with natural juices, this woman's
body oozes nature. This poem continues:

> Piel,
> carne de tronco quemado,
> que cuando naufraga en el espejo, ahúma
> las algas tímidas del fondo.

> [Your skin,
> flesh from a burnt trunk,
> that, foundering in the mirror, smokes
> over the timid algae at the bottom.]   (p. 120)

Unlike the angel-lady, whose mirror image may be those "timid
algae" that have been smoked over, the new woman has a privileged
relation to nature. She is "supernatural" not in that she is beyond
nature but rather in that she heightens or condenses nature's
attributes. All of her features are rooted in natural objects – her skin
has the color of burnt wood, her nails are like grapes, she is erect like
a sugar-cane stalk, and so on.

This closeness to nature is concisely rendered in the line that
begins the second stanza of one of the madrigals quoted above:
"Signo de selva el tuyo" ["Yours is the sign of the jungle"]. More
than a lifelike copy of any actual class of human beings, the new
woman is a sign, a token, the condensation of values that cluster
around the notion of the jungle. Just as the description of the winged
lady in "Tú" led away from the woman's physical specificity and

toward a network of literary commonplaces, here the portrait also leads away from concrete selfhood and toward a network of highly charged attributes. Everything about this woman signifies "selva": her nakedness, her neckwear, her bracelets, the darting pupils in her eyes.[11]

This grounding mechanism is equally evident in the opening lines of this madrigal, for it turns out that this woman thinks with neither head nor heart (the traditional seats of knowledge, and also the title of Guillén's first book, *Cerebro y corazón*), but with her womb. Odder still, she also thinks with her thighs, which "know as much as her womb."[12] In the lines that follow this uterine wisdom turns into something rather different but no less incongruous, "grace": "Esa/es la fuerte gracia negra/de tu cuerpo desnudo" ["That/is the strong black grace/of your naked body"]. Even though *gracia* here means primarily "gracefulness," one cannot ignore the rich connotations of the word in both the Greco-Roman and the Christian traditions. In Spanish, additionally, *una gracia* is a *boutade*, an impertinent remark or joke. Without insisting that all of the word's semantic history figures in Guillén usage, it is undeniable that the expression "fuerte gracia negra" is something of an impertinence, a *gracia* in the Spanish sense, since the noun is surrounded by modifiers inconsistent with the word's conventional associations: "grace" should be impalpable, light, airy, not "black" and "strong." If one thinks of the word as a proper noun, the incongruity is all the more striking. Like the Greek Graces, Guillén's symbolizes beauty (and we should recall that one of the Graces, Thalia, was the muse of bucolic poetry); unlike her classical counterparts, however, she is black, she doesn't dance to the strains of Apollo's lyre, and she doesn't reside in Olympus; instead, she moves to the beat of bongo drums and she comes from the Zambezi. Black and strong, Guillén's Grace is to her mythological sisters as Cuban coffee is to ambrosia.

By grounding grace in the uterine knowledge of a robust black body, Guillén sketches an alternate mythology of poetic creation, one that serves as the support and source – in short, as the ground – of his vernacular verse. To take offense at Guillén's portrayal of black women is to err on the side of literalism, for in these poems Guillén is talking about his poetry as much as about anything else. The womb wisdom of black Grace is important because it is the fictional source, the founding myth, of Guillén's poetic practice. *Sóngoro cosongo* is the sort of uterine utterance that the new woman knows. When you think with your thighs, you speak *sóngoro cosongo*. These are the tropical fruits of her womb, the unpublished words that she vouchsafes to her poet. No less than the angel-lady of the earlier poetry, the black Grace is the poet's muse, the source of his authority, the ground of a *poesía de la tierra* that roots literary expression in native soil.[13]

One may well wonder, then, why Guillén decided to domicile his muse in the hoary shelter of the madrigal. If these are indeed new names and images, why assign them to a genre that betokens the "old," the "published" words? Like the sonnet, the madrigal circulated in the courtly setting of Renaissance love poetry, and it entered Spanish poetry in the work of the Petrarchist poet Gutierre de Cetina. In fact, although many Spanish-language poets have written madrigals, in Spanish the genre is practically synonymous with Cetina, and particularly with one poem, which begins with the well-known line, "Ojos claros, serenos" ["Clear, serene eyes"]. The comparison of these Spanish eyes with those of the new woman is enough to suggest the tension between Guillén's madrigals and literary tradition, and to give some indication of the polemical value of Guillén's use of the madrigal. But this tradition is present in these poems in less polemical ways as well, so that the link is not simply oppositional. A madrigal, according to the standard definition, is "a short *silva* on a light topic."[14] The madrigal I have been discussing (the one that begins "Tu vientre sabe más que tu cabeza") fits this definition fairly well, though not without some unintended irony when it comes to the "lightness" of the topic. Following the conventions of the *silva*, the poem is composed preponderantly of lines of seven and eleven syllables (lines 5, 6, 7, and 9 are heptasyllables; lines 1 and 10 are hendecasyllables), which alternate without a fixed pattern; in addition, all of the lines rhyme (even if only assonantally); and its length, ten lines, is exactly that of Cetina's madrigal (the usual length of sixteenth-century Spanish madrigals is between ten and twelve lines). This family resemblance, which suggests that the titling of this poem was not a casual gesture, cements the relation between Guillén's madrigals and their "white" forebears.

In order to explore this relation a bit further, consider now the primitive meaning of the word "madrigal." Edmund H. Fellowes explains its derivation as follows: "just as *lingua materna* means 'mother tongue,' so *carmen matricale*, or *cantus matricalis*, may have stood for 'mother song,' denoting the primitive and spontaneous song of the country folk, in other words, *folk-song*, and ... it came to be associated subsequently with some special class of folk song of individual character" (*The English Madrigal*, p. 27). The madrigal, it turns out, is itself a native *son*. So that, at least etymologically, it would seem an apt rubric under which to house Guillén's project of creating a vernacular poetry. Behind his adoption of this genre lies the same etymological reasoning present in his transculturation of the sonnet. As he did with the sonnet, Guillén takes the madrigal back to its source, recovering and activating the term's primitive meaning. Since he intends to give poetic voice to the "primitive and spontaneous" sounds and *sones* of Afro-Cuban culture, he adopts the form of the madrigal, a form whose name already signifies an attachment to folk culture.

A second justification for the label is disclosed by a brief comparison of the madrigal and the sonnet. Although the two forms have some similar features – both are Italian, musical in origin, and closely associated with the courtly-love tradition – they differ in two principal ways: first, the madrigal, at least throughout the Renaissance, remained primarily a musical genre. In this respect, there is a closer fit between madrigal and *son* than between *son* and sonnet. Second, the madrigal, as poetry, has no definite metrical scheme. Unlike the sonnet, which is characterized by fixed formal features, madrigals derive their identity principally from being called such. Even the *silva* pattern, flexible as it is, does not appear in every Spanish madrigal. The only comprehensive description of madrigals is that they are short lyric poems with an amorous theme (although Quevedo, for one, wrote madrigals on political subjects). But this description is too vague for purposes of generic classification. Ultimately a madrigal is a poem that its author chooses to call a madrigal. Especially with Spanish-language madrigals, which are less uniform than their Italian models, only the title marks the poem's "genre," since the poem's structure or subject does not provide sufficient grounds for classification.[15] In Spanish at least, the madrigal is a nominalist genre, since the only functional criterion for inclusion is the name itself. This is what happens with Guillén's madrigals – they are madrigals because their author tells us so. If Guillén had not entitled these poems "Madrigal," one would have little reason for citing the madrigal tradition in a discussion of these texts. Nonetheless, this does not attenuate the poem's link to the genre – just the opposite, in fact: that Guillén labeled the poems in this way indicates that, in his view, their intelligibility rested, at least in part, on their being read as "madrigals," that is, against the background of a certain corpus of works and, in the case of Spanish-language literature, most certainly against the background of Cetina's madrigal, one of the best-known poems in Spanish. Titling these poems "madrigal" is a translation gesture, since it indicates that they translate into the Cuban vernacular the traditional subjects of madrigal verse.

But given the content of Guillén's madrigals, the title not only translates but also provokes, thereby furnishing another instance of Guillén's literary *guapería*. By invoking the madrigal tradition, Guillén only underscores the extent to which his madrigals deviate from the genre.[16] The title of the poem creates a context for Guillén's revisionism; it too is a "grounding" mechanism, except that the ground so created will immediately be removed. Guillén lays the groundwork – and then switches grounds. The incongruity of including madrigals in a collection entitled *Sóngoro cosongo* is striking, but this is precisely the point. The full intelligibility of these poems depends on their being placed in a literary genealogy, even if Guillén proceeds to give his ancestors a black eye.

Thus, the image of "ese caimán oscuro / nadando en el Zambeze de tus ojos" ["that dark cayman / swimming in the Zambezi of your eyes"] is all the more powerful when read against the precedent of Cetina's "clear, serene eyes." Not only are the new woman's eyes uncharacteristically dark, but their comparison to an alligator swimming in an African river situates the description in a setting far removed from Cetina's poem. As in "El abuelo," the woman of the mulatto madrigal is an occasion for transport but not for escape, since the metaphor places us in the real and historically pertinent African landscape. Cetina is interested in the spiritual qualities of his loved one; her eyes are the windows of her soul, and the two epithets that describe them, "clear" and "serene," have as much to

do with spiritual as with physical qualities. But there is nothing
spiritual about an alligator swimming in the Zambezi, an image that
gives concrete shape to the "grace" of the opening stanza. The dark
sinuous reptile embodies strong black grace. Even the geographical
specificity of the image challenges the conventions of Occidental
love poetry, for the Zambezi river is another one of those entirely
uncommon places that one finds in Guillén's works. Like everything
else in the poem, this river is a "sign of the jungle."[17]

Signo de selva – the phrase itself is suggestive, given that the
metrical skeleton of the madrigal is the *silva*, a term that is the
etymological doublet of *selva* (in fact, in seventeenth-century usage,
silva alternated with *selva* and *sylva* as the name of the poetic form).
In one last example of grounding, Guillén takes the metrical *silva*
back to the material *selva*.[18] If Ortiz's typical gesture toward his
literary precedents is to temporize, Guillén's is to a-temporize, to
leap over his less distant precursors in search of a pristine, telluric,
and arguably more authentic tradition. Guillén himself deliberately
practices the atavism that the speaker of "El abuelo" foists on the
angel-lady. Speaking of his use of the *romance* in *Motivos de son*, he has
said that his intention was "*amulatar* el romance español, esto es,
cubanizarlo, volviéndolo a su ser pristino" ["make the Spanish
romance *mulatto*, that is, make it Cuban, returning it to its pristine
being"].[19] The paradox of a hybridization that simultaneously
retrieves pristine origins underlies Guillén's cultivation of traditional genres like the sonnet and the madrigal (and in ways more
striking than with his use of the *romance*). The claim that one would
make for these poems is simple but extraordinary: although they
were composed during the third and fourth decades of this century,
they have the freshness, the youthfulness of aboriginal creation. But
their aboriginality, as we have seen, is a calculated effect, and it does
not imply blithe disregard for poetic precedent. Guillén's originality
lies in the deft simulation of aboriginality.

6

The discourse of the tropics

Nicolás Guillén's *Motivos de son* was not the only important book of poetry published in Cuba in 1930. Within a few months of the publication of Guillén's *sones*, another slender volume of nativist poetry appeared under the title of *Trópico*. Its author was Eugenio Florit, a young Spanish-born poet who had moved to Cuba as an adolescent and who was already well-known in Cuban literary circles, having contributed poems and reviews to *Revista de Avance* and *Social*, the two most important literary magazines of the day. *Trópico* is a collection of twenty-four *décimas* preceded by an introductory poem, "Inicial," and divided into two parts of equal length, "Campo" and "Mar."[1] Florit's use of the *décima*, the genre of choice of Cuba's popular bards, is already a sign that, like *Motivos de son*, *Trópico* reflects the criollist urge to specify native realities. But unlike Guillén, whose poetry grows out of the predominantly urban experience of Cuba's black and mulatto population, Florit finds his subject matter in the white and rustic world of the Cuban *campiña*.

This contrast is sharp and significant. Traditionally Cuba has had two repositories of vernacular content – urban black and rural white. Let me make the contrast starker by reducing it to the opposition between two typical and stereotypical figures: the *diablito* and the *guajiro*.[2] Since they both represent an alternative to the values associated with modern civilized life, in some respects the *diablito* and the *guajiro* are cognate figures; both embody a more primitive and authentic existence, a life in closer touch with the realm of the telluric or the natural. Going back to Guillén's imagery, we might say that neither one uses his head: the *guajiro* thinks with his heart, and the *diablito*, like Guillén's black Grace, with his loins and his thighs. In other respects, however, the *diablito* and the *guajiro* stand for different values. Writers who focus on the *guajiro* usually want to draw attention to, or argue for, the fundamental "whiteness" of Cuban culture. The *guajiro*, a descendant of the Spanish colonizers, is modest, hard-working, monogamous, stoic, and God-fearing. In contrast, the black *diablito* is ostentatious, sensual, promiscuous, and he purveys a heterodox religious *ajiaco* of Catholic and African beliefs. He is a figure of excess, the embodiment of a life of sensual indulgence. Attention to the *diablito*, therefore, reflects a desire to highlight Cuba's non-white and non-Western heritage, what Ortiz called the "ebony heart" of the island. If the *guajiro* represents the "natural" option to civilization, the *diablito* represents the "barbaric" option. If the *guajiro*'s primitivism is Adamic, the *diablito*'s is demonic, as his name already suggests.

Although the *diablito* was a popular subject for nineteenth-century *costumbristas*, he did not become a significant part of Cuban literary culture until the early decades of this century, when Ortiz's research made him available to novelists and poets. The *guajiro*, on the other hand, was already an important figure in the literature of the romantic period, where he was often used to represent an unspoiled, pastoral existence away from the evils of civilization. In the works of poets like José Fornaris and Juan Cristóbal Napolés Fajardo (better known as the "Cucalambé"),[3] the *guajiro* becomes the spokesman for the virtues of life in the countryside, away from the vices and vexations of urban existence. Needless to say, this picture of Cuban country living did not entirely resemble the harsh realities of life in the *campiña*, and most of these writers were actually cultured men of letters who reproduced in their works the Horatian commonplaces they had learned and imitated in school.[4] In this respect Afro-Cuban poetry, its simplifications notwithstanding, was perhaps in closer touch with reality than the bucolic verses of the *siboneístas*, since poets like Guillén and Ballagas did make an effort to incorporate in their works the more sordid aspects of the life of Cuba's black and mulatto population.[5]

Eugenio Florit's *Trópico* needs to be situated in relation to this counterpoint between the *guajiro* and the *diablito*. If *Motivos de son* speaks for the *diablito*, *Trópico* speaks for the *guajiro*. Florit's poetic interest in the life of the *guajiro*, however, must be qualified and nuanced, for *Trópico* is both a continuation and a revision of the *siboneísta* tradition. The book's pedigree becomes visible from the first page, since Florit's epigraph has been borrowed from none other than Cucalambé:

> Ven, Rufina, que ya empieza
> a madurar la guayaba.
>
> [Come, Rufina, for the guava
> is beginning to ripen.]

Although identified only as a "décima popular," these lines come from one of Cucalambé's best-known poems, "A Rufina: Invitación segunda."[6] The references to Rufina, who is Cucalambé's muse in the same sense in which the black goddess is Guillén's, continue into the body of Florit's book. The dedications to the first and second parts state, respectively: "A Rufina, que nació al tiempo de la guayaba" ["To Rufina, who was born in the season of the guava"]; and "A la memoria de Rufina, muerta con el caramelo amargo de una ola" ["To the memory of Rufina, killed by the bitter caramel of a wave"]. The initial task of *Trópico*'s reader is to determine the significance of these dedications. Florit's book begins with an invocation and concludes with a eulogy. Its two parts commemorate Rufina's birth, mentioned in the dedication to "Campo," and her death, mentioned in the dedication to "Mar." To read *Trópico* is to attempt to explain Rufina's birth and death by determining the nature of Florit's relation to *siboneísmo*, which he revives and lays to rest. It is appropriate, then, that the opening epigraph takes the form of an invitation, for these lines are themselves an invitation to compare Florit's *décimas* with those by the Cucalambé.

The reasons for Florit's strange treatment of Rufina may be found in the other branch of *Trópico*'s bifurcated lineage. The *décima* or *espinela* is not only the favorite genre of Cuba's popular poets but also a popular form among some of Florit's Spanish contemporaries; during the years when Florit was composing *Trópico* in Cuba, on the other side of the Atlantic some members of the Spanish Generation of 1927 (such as Jorge Guillén and Luis Cernuda) were also writing *décimas*. In Florit's poems, this peninsular precedent is as important as the native antecedents. As Florit himself acknowledged, his book was heavily influenced by the poetry of the Generation of 1927, and

more particularly, by their revival of the work of Góngora, which cul-
minated with the celebration of the tricentenary of Góngora's death.[7]
Like Guillén's sonnets and madrigals, Florit's *décimas* integrate
foreign and autochthonous matter. Although the content of *Trópico*
links this work with nineteenth-century *siboneísmo*, Florit's specific
treatment of his subject owes a great deal to the Gongorist revival.
Even the division of the book into "Campo" and "Mar" reveals the
Spaniard's imprint, since it is reminiscent of the successive settings of
the two *Soledades*, terrestrial and aquatic.[8] What is striking is that the
Cordoban poet should appear among palm trees and thatched huts.
In *Trópico* Góngora goes *guajiro* – undoubtedly as odd a coupling as
Guillén's conflation of *son* and sonnet. By working with *décimas*, Florit
shrewdly found a genre amenable both to the exotic and the home-
grown, one that allowed him to season the criollist stew with the technical savvy of Góngora and his modern disciples.

The result is a book that establishes, once again, a fruitful tension
or counterpoint between the native and the exogenous. In Florit's
hands, the *décima* becomes a sort of *ajiaco*, the vehicle for his own free
American version of the Cuban counterpoint. Like Ortiz, and even
more than Napolés Fajardo, Florit too is a "cook-calambé," a native
chef who serves up his own nourishing brand of tropical cuisine.

The introductory poem of *Trópico* shows that Florit was aware of
the originality of his recipe. Diverging sharply from the rest of the
collection, "Inicial" is composed of quartets that, from the first
stanza, disclose the book's divided loyalties.

> Pues de la tierra, canto, agradecido,
> te revelas en clásica envoltura,
> detén el ala por mirar el nido
> y luego bebe un manantial de altura.

> [Since from the earth, song, grateful,
> you reveal yourself in classic vestment,
> still your wing to look at the nest
> and then drink in a spring from the summits.]   (p. 81)

As is the norm with criollist literature, Florit's poems emerge from
the earth; his is a song of the earth, "de la tierra." Also like criollist
literature, these lines convey a sense of inaugural achievement, as is
evident from the poem's title, which is doubly motivated: not only is
"Inicial" the first poem in the book, but the book itself is an "initial"

composition, a new kind of writing. What is more, since this composition explains *Trópico*'s design and intent, since it bears Florit's signature as a nativist poet, the poem may also be said to inscribe its author's initials. This initiatory and initializing gesture carries over into the first verb in the poem, "reveal." The telluric song of these poems will be a revelation, an original melody. When Florit says two stanzas later that he will speak with the "voz del pueblo cantor" ["voice of the singing people"] (p. 81), the strong implication is that this is a new voice, one that has not been heard before in literature of this kind.

This founding gesture is a recurring motif in criollist writing, as the initial sentences of *Sóngoro cosongo* indicate: "¿Prólogo? Sí. Prólogo ... Pero nada grave, porque estas páginas deben ser frescas y verdes, como ramas jóvenes" ["A prologue? Yes. A prologue ... But nothing solemn, for these pages should be fresh and green, like young boughs"] (*Obra poética*, vol. 1, p. 113). Since the criollist writer felt that he was the first to render native settings, characters, and customs, he often assumed the pose of the discoverer, the bearer of new knowledge, of unpublished words, green and fresh like saplings. As a consequence, the classical topos of *intellectum tibi dabo* appears often in criollist literature. It is everywhere in Ortiz, for example, and it is also an important motif in Marinello's "Americanismo y cubanismo literarios." One indication of Florit's insertion into the criollist movement is that his small collection of *décimas* shares this sense of discovery, of original achievement.

Original, not aboriginal: the language of Florit's opening also reveals that, even if these poems do contain the *vox populi*, this voice will be inflected by a foreign accent. Or better, that it will have a "double accent," to use the title of another of Florit's books – an accent at once native and foreign, homey and exotic.[9] Florit's complicated diction and elegant vocabulary immediately distance these poems from nativist verse.

It is instructive to contrast the opening of 'Inicial" with the first lines in *Motivos de son*:

> ¿Po qué te pone tan brabo
> cuando te disen negro bembón,
> si tiene la boca santa
> negro bembón?

> [Why do you get so angry
> when they call you fat-lips,
> if you have a wonderful mouth,
> fat-lips?]   (*Obra poética*, vol. 1, p. 105)

One can imagine – and some reviews of the time record – the surprise of many of Guillén's early readers upon opening the slender volume and coming across this initial poem. Although this was not the first time that the voice of Cuba's blacks had been heard in poetry,[10] "Negro bembón" still marked a sharp departure, in diction and theme, from the poetic norm of the day. The voice who speaks here is a demotic, if not a demonic, voice – that *boca santa* ["wonderful mouth"] that the poem itself names, and which it reproduces with phonetic fidelity. Florit's opening is no less alarming, but for opposite reasons, since what distinguishes "Inicial" is not the rudeness of the voice but its refinement. Although Florit professes to speak for the "pueblo cantor" ["singing people"], the vocabulary, tone, and style of his doubly accented discourse make no attempt to imitate popular speech. Coming on the heels of the epigraph from the Cucalambé, "Inicial" jars the reader into an awareness of *Trópico*'s separation from its native precursors and analogues. The epigraph creates expectations – lexical, thematic, tonal – that are immediately shattered in the poem that follows. Even if "Inicial" begins with an illative, *pues*, it breaks sharply with what went before. No longer will we enjoy the comfortable familiarity between poet, text, and reader of Cucalambé's informal invitation, "Ven, Rufina." Instead of addressing the familiar Rufina, Florit speaks to an impersonal "canto," and in the place of the straightforward syntax of Cucalambé's invocation, he inserts the typical Gongorine disjunction of noun and genitive, with the prepositional phrase, "de la tierra" placed before the noun it modifies, "canto" (or perhaps, "envoltura"):

> Pues de la tierra, canto, agradecido,
> te revelas en clásica envoltura. . . .
>
> [Since from the earth, song, grateful,
> your reveal yourself in classic vestment . . .][11]

Indeed, this hyperbaton suggests *Trópico*'s separation from his sources; even if the poet's song emanated "from the earth," it has become detached from its origins. Bracketed by commas, the *canto* stands alone; hence the claim of originality, of initial achievement.

As Marinello pointed out, the key is distance. Florit's *neo-siboneísmo* takes its distance in two directions: even as the vernacular subject matter of his book separates Florit from his peninsular models, his poetic diction distances him from his native ancestors. The newness, the *neísmo* in his *siboneísmo* emerges from this double distancing. One of the *décimas* in the collection begins:

> Vi, desde un pico de sierra
> – con mi soledad estaba–
> cómo el cielo se aprestaba
> a caer sobre la tierra.
>
> [I saw, from the summit of a mountain
> – I was with my solitude –
> how the sky was getting ready
> to fall upon the earth.]   (p. 91)

The first question posed by these lines is whether "soledad" names a book or an emotion, for Góngora is certainly Florit's constant companion in his excursion through the Cuban countryside. And one may certainly venture that, given Florit's allegiance to Góngora, what befalls *la tierra* in Florit's tropics is nothing other than the heavenly or tempestuous (depending on how one interprets *cielo*) rhetoric of Gongorist poetry. But what I want to stress here is the speaker's positioning, which is more assuredly emblematic. Because the countryside is observed from a summit, "desde un pico de sierra," Florit's tropics will lack the intimacy or familiarity of the landscapes of the *siboneístas*, who wrote from the down-to-earth perspective of the "rústico y pobre guajiro" ["rustic and poor *guajiro*"].[12] Florit will view the tropics perched on a cliff, and this location will shape what he is able to see and render.[13] That promontory is the Cuban equivalent of an ivory tower, the emblem of Florit's separation from palpable, lived experience.

From this distancing follows what is perhaps Florit's most radical departure from the tradition of *siboneísmo*. As we have already seen, one of the dominant characteristics of nativist literature is its cultivation of vernacular *voces*, in both senses of the *voz*. One cannot stress enough the extent to which the criollist project is onomastic. Quite often, the search for *cubanía* issues in a search for *cubanismos*, and the literary quest for a vernacular poetic voice resolves itself into a lexicographical search for a linguistic vernacular. Indeed, as Marinello perceptively pointed out, one of the pitfalls of criollism is the belief that the former will follow from the latter, that it is enough to "secrete criollisms" ("Americanismo y cubanismo literarios," p. 49) in order to find a Cuban voice. Nonetheless, this nominalism is deeply rooted in the criollist movement, and most works of this persuasion participate in it to some degree. Even the term *criollismo* betrays nominalist thinking, since this word is one of those local expressions registered in regional dictionaries.

This onomastic fervor, which Lezama Lima has aptly labeled a "júbilo nominal,"[14] has deep roots in Cuban literature, going back to Silvestre de Balboa's *Espejo de paciencia*, a seventeenth-century epic whose *octavas reales*, rather incongruously, catalog the Indian names of local flora and fauna.[15] It appears again in the work of later writers like Manuel de Zequeira y Arango, the neo-classical poet best known for his paean to the pineapple, and reaches an almost delirious extreme in the poems of the *siboneístas*, which are sometimes little more than chaotic enumerations of exotic names. Two examples: the first, a *sextina* by Franciso Poveda (or Pobeda), known in his day as "El trovador cubano" ["The Cuban troubadour"]; the second, one of the stanzas from "A Rufina," the poem that Florit cites in his epigraph.

POVEDA: Aquí nacen con presteza
el piñipí y abey,
el espino, el jamagüey,
la chirimoya, el anón,
el serení, el marañón,
el cubainicú y yarey.[16]

NAPOLÉS: Tengo, Rufina, en mi estancia,
Paridas matas de anones,
Cuyos frutos ya pintones
Esparcen dulce fragancia:
Hay piñas en abundancia
Dulces así como tú;
Hay guayabas del Perú
Y mameyes colorados,
Que comeremos sentados
Bajo el alto sabicú.

[I have, Rufina, on my farm,
Trees full of *anones*,
Whose ripe fruits
Spread a sweet fragrance:
There's an abundance of pineapples
Sweet like you;
There are guavas from Peru
And red *mameyes*,
That we'll eat while we sit
Under the tall *sabicú*.]   (*Poesías completas*, p. 123)

Not only is the poetic voice of *Rumores del Hórmigo* or *Cantos del Siboney* that of the humble peasant who renders the scenes, sights, and sounds of life in the *campiña*; more important, this endeavor is carried out, to a considerable degree, by seeding the poems with the names of native fauna and flora.

This lexicographical criollism, some of whose modern manifestations are word-hoards like Ortiz's *Un catauro de cubanismos* (1923) or Suárez's *Diccionario de voces cubanas* (1920), is almost completely absent from *Trópico*. There are very few local words in Florit's lexicon, and even these are of fairly generalized usage – *sinsonte*, *manigua*, *ceiba*. Since the onomastic fervor of criollist literature also manifests itself in a penchant for picturesque toponyms (like that in the title of Cucalambé's collection), it is equally significant that there are no place names in *Trópico*. His stark titles – "Trópico," "Campo," "Mar" – are already symptomatic of the book's lack of lexical specifity.

A good example of Florit's avoidance of vernacular names is the following stanza from "Campo":

Brillan luces voladoras
tan sueltas sobre la casa,
como luminosa masa
partida en tenues auroras.
Entre las brisas sonoras
son átomos de diamante.
Alza un brazo el caminante
al cruzar por la arboleda
y presa en la mano queda
una chispa titilante.

[Flying lights shine
so loose above the house,

like a luminous mass
broken up into tenuous dawns.
Among the sonorous breezes
they are diamond atoms.
The wayfarer raises an arm
as he goes by the trees
and catches in his hand
a titillating spark.]   (p. 95)

After reading these lines it is not immediately obvious that this is actually a description of the Cuban firefly, the *cocuyo*, even though the *cocuyo* is an ever-present item in the "descriptive system" of Cuban criollism.[17] *Siboneísta* poetry is luminous with *cocuyos*, the appeal of whose Indian name is compounded by the metaphorical uses of the insect's light. So, for example, José Fornaris likens his loved one's eyes to *cocuyos*, thereby playing a regional variation on a traditional image:

Miel de abejas son tus labios,
Son llamas los ojos tuyos,
Cual los brillantes cocuyos
Lucen tus ojos mi bien.

[You have lips of honey,
your eyes are flames,
like glowing fireflies
your eyes shine, my love.][18]

More pertinent to our purposes, the *cocuyo* provides the opening image for one of the Cucalambé's best-known poems, "Hatuey y Guarina":

Con un cocuyo en la mano
Y un gran tabaco en la boca,
Un indio desde una roca
Miraba el cielo cubano.

[With a firefly in his hand
And a great cigar in his mouth,
From a rock an Indian
Was watching the Cuban sky.]
(*Poesías completas*, p. 151)

This stanza is typical of *siboneísmo*'s onomastic exploitation of the picturesque. Each of these four lines names the native in a different way: the first line lights the way with the *cocuyo*; the second lights up a different way with another home-grown name for another luminous reality, the *tabaco*; and the third presents the native himself, the Indian. The fourth line, in a recapitulatory gesture, provides the generic adjective for what has preceded – *cubano*. The firefly, the cigar, the Indian, the Cuban skies – all are signifiers of *cubanidad*, tokens that tell the reader, in effect: "this is a nativist poem."

If we now return to Florit's handling of the *cocuyo*, we notice at once the double accent of his criollism. Florit's *décima* clearly follows in the tradition of poems like the Cucalambé's; indeed, one may even regard Florit's description as an expansion of the first line of "Hatuey y Guarina," "Con un cocuyo en la mano," which would then be the "hypogram" that generates the poem. What *is* unusual in Florit's poem, however, is the studied avoidance of the picturesque name. Although the nativist poet is easy prey to the onomastic temptation of *cocuyo*, Florit succeeds in resisting this temptation. His *décima* is a carefully wrought exercise in onomastic restraint.

Because Florit refuses to say "cocuyo," the firefly appears in his poem, but in other words. This avoidance of the native name is, of course, an instance of the mechanism of "alusión y elusión" that Dámaso Alonso described in a famous essay on Góngora's poetry.[19] Instead of naming the object, Florit puts together a complicated sequence of periphrases in which the native name is replaced by metaphorical equivalents, all of which highlight the *cocuyo*'s luminosity: "luces voladoras" ["flying lights"], "luminosa masa" ["luminous mass"], "tenues auroras" ["tenuous dawns"], "átomos de diamante" ["diamond atoms"], "chispa titilante" ["titillating spark"]. These metaphors suggest that the poem does strive to "name" the object, but in a different, perhaps more enlightening, way. One might say that Florit's criollism is euphemistic rather than onomastic, for he is less interested in the picturesque cubanism than in the poetic euphemism.

What lends force to these comparisons is the fact that the action of the poem mirrors the purpose of the euphemisms, which is to capture the *cocuyo* poetically, to hold it "presa en la mano." Semantically, the poem moves from dispersion to concentration, from plurality to singularity. At the beginning the insects are a dispersed luminous mass – "luces voladoras / tan sueltas sobre la casa" ["flying lights / so loose above the house"]; at the end, the focus has

narrowed to one spark of light, which is now "presa" rather than
"suelta": "y presa en la mano queda/ una chispa titilante" ["and
(he) catches in his hand/a titillating spark"]. Especially since the
last lines echo the title of one of the sections of Jorge Guillén's
Cántico, "Pájaro en mano," it is difficult not to read this grasping as
the act of poetic apprehension. The tacit theme of this poem is
Florit's manner of apprehending vernacular reality. Traversing the
Cuban countryside, he is content to grasp one small shining facet of
it, in this instance the luminosity of the *cocuyo*, an appropriation that
does not culminate in, or even include, the object's name.

The contrast with that other Guillén, Nicolás, is instructive once
again. We can think of a poem like "Acana," which takes exactly the
opposite approach to apprehending native phenomena. This poem
consists almost entirely of the insistent, incantatory repetition of a
name, with hardly any descriptive elaboration or metaphorical
overlay:

> Allá dentro, en el monte,
> donde la luz acaba
> allá en el monte adentro,
> ácana.
>
> Ay, ácana con ácana,
> con ácana;
> ay, ácana con ácana ...
> Con ácana.
>
> [Deep inside, in the woods,
> where the light goes out,
> deep inside the woods,
> *ácana*.
>
> Ah, *ácana* with *ácana*,
> with *ácana*;
> ah, *ácana* with *ácana* ...
> With *ácana*.]   (*Obra poética*, vol. 1, p. 254)[20]

Suárez, in his *Diccionario de voces cubanas*, defines *ácana* as follows:
"Arbol indígena y silvestre de tronco recto, que alcanza unos diez
metros, de hojas ovales, rígidas, coriáceas, que produce una fruta
sustanciosa más pequeña que el zapote, y cuya madera es una de las
más estimadas en Cuba para construcciones rústicas y navales, por
su incorruptibilidad y dureza, a cuyas cualidades se une las de la

sonoridad, notable peso y color rojizo hermoso" ["A wild indigenous tree with a straight trunk, that grows to about ten meters, with
coriaceous, rigid oval leaves, which produces a nutritious fruit
smaller than the *zapote*, and whose wood is valued in Cuba for rustic
houses and shipbuilding, because of the wood's durability and
hardness, qualities enhanced by its sonority, weight, and beautiful
reddish color"] (p. 4). Realizing that there is poetry enough in the
bare sonority of the name, which echoes the rich sonority of the
material, Guillén abstains from amplification. By simply repeating
"ácana," he takes an epistemological shortcut and relies on the
name to evoke the thing. Florit, on the contrary, takes the long road,
electing to bypass the name and instead placing the object itself in a
new light. His poem is no less reiterative than Guillén's, but it is a
semantic rather than an onomastic reiteration, synonymy rather
than anaphora. Thus he repeatedly names not the insect but its
shining attribute. Guillén wants to make you hear: "ácana con
ácana con ácana." Florit wants to make you see: "presa en la mano
queda/una chispa titilante."

It is not coincidental that these varying approaches to specifying
native reality are associated with the diverging senses of sound and
sight. At the outset of "Acana," Guillén establishes that there is
nothing to be seen, since we are going inside the jungle, "where the
light goes out." The only sensory appeals, therefore, will be acoustic: the haunting repetition of *ácana*. This emphasis on the phonic at
the expense of the visual is consistent with what we know of Guillén.
The loud point of "El abuelo," after all, is that visual appearances
may deceive, but phonic realities do not. Even Guillén's treatment
of the sonnet accentuates its acoustic component. His message
seems to be that, if one wants to reach the heart of Cuba, one has to
listen, for the essence of Cuba is oral and aural – what Marinello
called "la voz múltiple de la masa" ["the multiple voice of the
people"] ("Hazaña y triunfo americanos de Nicolás Guillén,"
p. 76). For this reason Guillén's poetry capitalizes less on knowing
glances than on penetrating sounds (like that of the *bongó*), and it is
appropriate and meaningful that the first poem in *Motivos de son*
should present someone who has a "boca santa" ["wonderful
mouth"]. Guillén composes by ear, insisting upon the voiced or oral
aspects of language. For the author of "Negro bembón," poetry is a

matter of word-of-mouth. There exists an important conceptual link, I believe, between onomastics and orality, between *voz* as word and *voz* as voice: a preference for the former harmonizes with, and perhaps originates in, a privileging of the latter. As in "Acana," an attachment to local words betrays an attachment to voice, in its diverse musical and non-musical manifestations.

By contrast, Florit's double accent is visual rather than voiced, seen but not heard. This is not to say that Florit's countryside is completely silent; even in the highly visual description of the *cocuyos* there is a passing reference to "the sonorous breezes." The point is rather that in *Trópico* one finds no particular cultivation of the phonic qualities of language, and that this indifference toward phonic or onomatopoetic effects is conceptually linked to his avoidance of *cubanismos*. Hence, when he names his work in "Inicial," he calls it a *canto*, a word that lacks tropical flavor and that in poetry has only vestigial musical connotations. Guillén, in similar circumstances, opted for the musical and picturesque rubric, *son*. The distance between Guillén's and Florit's criollism can be expressed as the difference between a *son* and a *canto*.

Clearly, Florit's emphasis on the visual blends in with his perceptual distancing. Perched atop *un pico de sierra*, one can see a great deal, but one probably does not hear much. Indeed, from such a vantage point one does not simply see; more precisely, one *contemplates*. Visual distance goes along with analytical detachment. The cliff is also the philosopher's promontory. As Richard Rorty and others have reminded us, when we think of thinking we think of it in visual terms, a kinship born out in the etymologies of such words as theory, speculation, and contemplation.[21] Florit's poems, therefore, are visual *and* abstract: contemplative in both senses. Witness his rendering of the royal palm:

> Flecha en un éxtasis verde
> ilusionada en su altura,
> contempla la tierra dura
> y en un suspiro se pierde.
>
> [A green ecstatic arrow
> exhilarated by its height,
> contemplates the hard earth
> and disappears in a sigh.]   (p. 21)

All of the main characteristics of Florit's descriptive technique appear here: the distance from "the hard earth"; the consequent emphasis on "contemplation"; and the resulting reduction of the depicted object to what the poet regards (again in both senses) as its defining traits, its green color and erect shape. Dámaso Alonso's analysis of the purpose of Góngora's periphrases describes the consequences of this procedure exactly: "Abstraen del objeto sus propiedades físicas y sus accidentes, para presentarle sólo por aquella cualidad, o cualidades, que para el poeta, en un momento dado, son las únicas que tienen estético interés" ["They abstract from the object its physical properties and characteristics in order to present it only through the quality or qualities that, according to the poet, are the ones that in a given moment have aesthetic interest"].[22] Florit does not say "palma" but "flecha en un éxtasis verde"; he does not say "cocuyo" but "átomo de diamante." Whereas Nicolás Guillén has a knack for the telling detail or the palpable peculiarity – Bito Manuel's macarronic English or the fat lip of the *negro bembón* – Florit is interested in something less particular, less precise. What catches his eye is the almost ineffable essence of the tropics, what in another poem he calls its "quintaesenciado matiz" ["quintessential color"] (p. 101). And in this expression, once again, Florit typically combines the visual ("matiz") with the abstract ("quintaesenciado").

Like the few examples I have discussed, most of the *décimas* in *Trópico* deal with the commonplace scenes and incidents of nineteenth-century nativist poetry – the light of the firefly, the palm tree, the view of dawn in the tropics, the stream hidden in the mountain, the creaking of the *carreta*. In his choice of subjects, as in his choice of epigraphs, Florit repeatedly quotes the *siboneísta* tradition. What is different is the generic or abstract rendering of these subjects, which elides the picturesque name in favor of the luminous reality. Like Góngora, and like some of the members of the Generation of 1927, Florit abstracts from his objects one or two poetically significant components. As Alfonso Reyes saw in a perceptive early review, the collection's aim was to "purify" the tropics, to reduce them to their essential elements.[23] By taking this approach, therefore, Florit performs on criollism the kind of reduction or purification that the advocates of "pure poetry" advocated for poetry itself. Just as, according to Jorge Guillén's famous statement, pure poetry removes from the poem everything that is not poetic,[24] Florit's *Trópico* cleanses criollism of the dross of detail and the excrescence of the particular, leaving only the "quintessential" Cuban countryside, the miraculous essence of the tropics:

> Hoy, en voces de la ausencia,
> lejos de ti, por mirarte
> cerca llega de tu parte
> milagro fiel de tu esencia.
>
> [Today, in voices of absence,
> far away from you, so that I
> can see you the faithful miracle
> of your essence arrives.]   (p. 105)

Unsympathetic readers might say, of course, that the end result of this procedure is the disappearance of the object, and they might quote in support of their criticism the poem about the royal palm, where the green arrow finally "se pierde" ["disappears"]. Somewhat along the same lines, Juan Marinello, in an important early discussion of *Trópico*, criticized what he perceived as Florit's retreat from life, a flight that Marinello attributed to the poet's "imprisonment" in the Gongorine manner of his Spanish contemporaries.[25] And yet, not many years after the book's original publication, Florit referred to *Trópico* as "mi libro de décimas cubanas" ["my book of Cuban *décimas*"] ("Una hora conmigo," p. 163). Certainly Florit's writing is not "Cuban" in the same sense as Guillén's or Ortiz's; and *Trópico*'s cold, cerebral landscapes are a far cry from the hot tropics of Guillén's "Palabras en el trópico":

> Te veo venir por los caminos ardorosos,
> Trópico,
> con tu cesta de mangos
> tus cañas limosneras
> y tus caimitos, morados como el sexo de las negras.
>
> [I see you coming down the steaming roads,
> Tropics,
> with your basket of mangos
> your impoverished sugar cane
> and your *caimitos*, purple like the sex of black women.][26]

This does not mean, though, that Florit's work does not share the desire to describe the specificity of life and nature in the New World.

Especially when considered in the light of such works as Agustín Acosta's *La zafra* (1926) or Luis Felipe Rodríguez's *Relatos de Marcos Antilla* (1932), Florit's contemplative landscapes provide a refreshing critical counterpoint to the more intimate and unmediated descriptions of the Cuban countryside found in criollist literature. Like the "titillating spark" of the *cocuyo*, Florit's short poems are brief illuminations, flashes of insight that give the reader a new, if somewhat removed, view of the Cuban countryside.

7

The creation of *Juan Criollo*

Although Carlos Loveira is widely recognized as the most important modern Cuban novelist before Alejo Carpentier, Loveira's commentators – and they are not legion – have usually stressed the documentary rather than artistic value of his novels. The consensus is that Loveira's novels, as novels, are not particularly interesting or well-crafted; they merit attention, rather, as faithful chronicles of private and public life in Cuba during the first two or three decades of the Republican period. Typical is the following statement by Enrique Anderson Imbert, which stresses equally Loveira's powers of observation and his shortcomings as an artist: "Documentó los últimos años de la colonia y los primeros de la república, pero su capacidad de observación fue contrarrestada por su incapacidad para componer relatos bien estructurados con personajes bien vistos" ["He documented the last years of the colonial epoch and the first years of the Republic, but his powers of observation were counterbalanced by his inability to compose well-structured narrations with well-defined characters"] (*Historia de la literatura hispanoamericana*, vol. 2, p. 447).

Anderson Imbert's statement closely parallels the opinions that are usually expressed about criollist literature in general: like Loveira's fictions, such works are impressive for their documentary content, for the wealth and accuracy of their historical detail – but they are not particularly noteworthy or interesting as literature. It seems to me, however, that at least one of Loveira's novels, *Juan Criollo*, repays the kind of attention usually not accorded to criollist fiction. And it does so for precisely the reasons singled out by Anderson Imbert, that is, Loveira's handling of structure and perspective. Although *Juan Criollo* certainly paints an impressive historical canvas, its structure and narrative technique also raise issues of a different nature, issues that speak to the ongoing concern of this book, that is, the relation between the cultural products of the New World and its foreign antecedents.[1] If we recall that a *criollo* was originally someone born in the New World of Spanish parents,[2] already in the title this novel draws our attention to its transatlantic relations. If Juan Criollo, the character, is the son of a Spanish immigrant, *Juan Criollo*, the novel, also has roots that go back to the Spanish mainland.

In the preceding chapters I have alluded several times to the Cuban *pícaro*, the *vivo*. Loveira's novel provides further evidence of the significance of the picaresque tradition for Cuban criollist literature. The novel's relations to the picaresque genre are varied and profound. Nearly all of the conventions of picaresque narrative, structural as well as thematic, appear in this novel: it has an episodic plot; it draws a vivid portrait of the lower strata of Cuban society with its misfits, beggars, prostitutes, and thieves; and this portrait is the vehicle for trenchant social commentary. In addition, Loveira's protagonist exhibits the typical features of the picaresque antihero. Of lowly origins, Juan Cabrera becomes an orphan early in life; for many years after that, he knocks about from place to place and from occupation to occupation, serving a number of masters. Finally, after suffering many tribulations and hardships, he learns to survive – and thrive – by capitalizing on his *viveza* or *picardía*. Putting aside moral scruples, he eventually rises in the world, and by the end of the novel he has become a wealthy, influential, and utterly corrupt journalist and politician. Like other picaresque narrations, Loveira's novel traces the protagonist's development from *bobo* to *vivo*, from youthful innocent to adult rogue. The last words of the novel, where Juan scoffs at the prospect of national regeneration, catch him at his venal best: "¡Que vengan regeneraciones! Ahí nos las den todas" ["On with regenerations! The more the better"] (p. 486).[3]

These general affinities between *Juan Criollo* and the picaresque tradition suggest further links with specific picaresque novels, and particularly with *Lazarillo de Tormes*. Like the protagonist of the Spanish novel, Juan loses his father when he is very young and has to eke out a meager existence with his mother who, like Lazarillo's own mother, makes a living by washing clothes. When Juan's mother, like Lázaro's, is no longer able to support him, he has to leave her side and fend for himself. For both protagonists this separation marks the beginning of a period of worldly apprentice-ship that culminates in the achievement of a very dubious social respectability – dubious because, in both cases, it entails acquiescing in the infidelity of their respective wives. If Lázaro agrees to marry a cleric's concubine, Juan, motivated by "philosophical indifference," ignores Julita's many affairs (p. 461). Furthermore, in their final occupations the two protagonists also resemble each other, since Lazarillo's *pregonar* has a modern equivalent in Juan's muckraking. And even *Juan Criollo*'s precipitous conclusion, which has been criticized by some commentators,[4] finds a precedent in the Spanish novel, whose hasty final chapters have also elicited much comment. Lastly, the crucial distinction between the young and the mature protagonist, between *bobo* and *vivo*, is rendered in both novels by means of an onomastic discrimination – Lázaro vs. Lazarillo in the Spanish novel, Juan Criollo vs. Juan Cabrera in the Cuban work.

Loveira's novel also includes several echoes of *Guzmán de Alfa-rache*, the other founding work of the picaresque genre. If Juan's mother has the same occupation as Lazarillo's, Juan's father, a barber, has the same occupation as Guzmán's. Juan's parents link the Cuban novel with its own Spanish forebears: his father's occu-pation sends us back to *Guzmán de Alfarache*; his mother's sends us back to *Lazarillo*. In his choice of profession, also, Juan's lineage is similarly mixed. If his journalism can be considered a "free American version" of Lazarillo's job as town crier, the circum-stances in which Juan becomes a writer are reminiscent of Alemán's novel, for Juan, like Guzmán, begins to write his memoirs while in prison (p. 380).

This last connection is particularly significant, for it brings up an additional aspect of *Juan Criollo*'s filiation with the picaresque tradi-tion, namely, Loveira's employment of point of view. During his stay in Mexico, Juan is put in prison after a scuffle with El Coronel, a local kingpin. While in jail, he starts writing his memoirs and reads them to a fellow prisoner, who praises his narration for its "soltura y viveza" ["agility and liveliness"] (p. 380). After this episode Juan's literary vocation becomes one of the central motifs in the story. Back in Havana, he begins to make a reputation for himself as a novelist, publishing not only a successful historical novel modeled on Pérez Galdós's *Episodios nacionales* (shades of Ortiz!) but also his prison diary "en forma de novelesco relato" ["in the form of a novelistic narration"] (pp. 442–443). As the novel nears its conclusion, references to Juan's writing proliferate, and the last scene reproduces the text of a political tirade, "A tiro limpio," that turns Juan into a celebrity.

How is one to construe this rather abrupt emphasis on Juan's literary vocation? In light of the novel's other links to the picaresque tradition, the simplest answer is that Loveira, by drawing attention to Juan's writing skills, is trying to establish his protagonist's credibility as the author of the account that we read. If the novel, as it approaches its conclusion, belabors Juan's vocation, the likely reason is to justify his autobiographical narration. Thus, the text even incorporates "tres o cuatro pensamientos ... que acaso algún día sirvieran a Juan, como tesis de primera página, en el libro de sus memorias" ["three or four thoughts ... that perhaps someday Juan will use, as the opening thesis, in the book of his memoirs"] (p. 474). If Juan is a writer, then the "book of his memoirs" might be simply *Juan Criollo*. What happens, though, is that, in spite of these seemingly self-referential statements, *Juan Criollo* is narrated by an anonymous, undramatized narrator. This constitutes an important deviation from the picaresque tradition. In Alemán's novel Guzmán, while in jail, recounts his life in order to exculpate himself and instruct his readers. The text that we read is the text he writes. Guzmán may be an *homo duplex* – penitent and sinner, author and actor – but throughout the novel that doubleness is glued together by Guzman's narrative voice. In *Juan Criollo*, however, even if the circumstances of Juan's putting pen to paper hark back to *Guzmán de Alfarache*, Loveira ignores the most basic feature of picaresque narrative, its autobiographical format.[5] Unlike Guzmán, Lázaro, and other *pícaros*, Juan does not speak for himself, and *Juan Criollo* is therefore not that "book of memoirs" evoked in the novel.

I believe that the impression of incoherence produced by the novel stems from this tacit tension between the work's genre and its narrative perspective. This impression has surfaced especially in

critics' remarks about the inadequacy of the hasty conclusion; but
what is really discomfiting in the conclusion is less its abruptness
than its content, the fact that it is given over almost completely to
documenting Juan's growth as a writer. From the standpoint of the
reader of *Juan Criollo*, if Juan does not write in the most palpable and
immediate sense, that is, if he is not the "author" of his life's story,
this emphasis is unwarranted. Loveira's insistence upon Juan's
vocation only makes sense as justification for the disclosure or the
realization that the account we have just read comes from Juan's
pen. All of the novel, in fact, seems to lead up to Juan's peremptory
command to his wife, "¡Dame papel!" ["Give me paper!"] (p. 482),
an order with which Juan seals his writerly fate. But without
something to fulfill or instantiate his ambition – "poder escribir,
escribir, escribir" ["to be able to write, write, write"] (p. 453) – all
of this huffing and puffing becomes a meaningless and incoherent
gesture.

The way to solve this puzzle, I think, is to assume that *Juan Criollo*
is a third-person autobiography. Juan *does* tell his story, but in the
third person, in other's words. According to Claudio Guillén, the
picaresque novel is fundamentally a "pseudoautobiography"
(*Literature as System*, p. 81); in order to describe the narrative situation in *Juan Criollo*, one needs instead a term like "pseudo*hetero*biography," where the first prefix – *pseudo* – designates not only the
fictional status of the text as a whole but also the fictionality or
spuriousness of the impersonal perspective, designated by the
second prefix – *hetero*. For reasons that we shall examine, Juan
chooses to speak of himself as a "he" rather than an "I," a not
unprecedented phenomenon in autobiographical literature,[6] but
one that nonetheless sets this novel apart from its picaresque forebears. Herein lies the novel's technical interest and Loveira's
originality. When Juan looks back on his life, he sees himself as
other, feigning a detachment and distance belied by a close reading
of the text. As always happens in autobiographical accounts, the
protagonist here is both author and actor, but Loveira accentuates
this necessary dichotomy by having his narrator–protagonist treat
his past as if it had happened to someone else. Like other *pícaros*,
Juan is also an *homo duplex*, but his doubleness includes a division of
grammatical persons.[7]

In his perceptive discussion of third-person autobiography, Philippe Lejeune has pointed out that structurally this form is not very different from the more common first-person accounts, since the latter also supposes the split of the protagonist into two distinct personae. The difference is that, whereas the employment of the first person tends to dissemble this split, the third person brings it to the fore. Thus this mechanism – which Lejeune labels a "figure d'énonciation" –

ne doit pas être conçue comme une manière indirecte de parler de soi, qui serait à opposer au caractère "direct" de la première personne. Elle est une autre manière de réaliser, sous la forme d'un *dédoublement*, ce que la première personne réalise sous la forme d'une *confusion*: l'inéluctable dualité de la "personne" grammaticale.

[should not be looked upon as an indirect way of speaking of oneself, which would be in opposition to the "direct" character of the first person. It is rather another way of achieving, in the form of an *undoubling*, what the first person achieves in the form of a *confusion*: the ineluctable duality of the grammatical "person."]

("L'Autobiographie à la troisième personne", p. 34)

This clear, unambiguous separation of the narrator's two identities is precisely the effect – and perhaps the intention – of the narrative protocol of *Juan Criollo*. By seeing his younger self as an other, by "altering" himself, Juan underscores the discontinuity between his two selves, the adult *vivo* and the young *bobo*, a discontinuity that merges with that between the narrating "I" and the narrated "he." It is no accident, therefore, that Juan's cellmate praises his memoirs for their "viveza" (p. 380), a word that in retrospect acquires a richer meaning. As a writer, Juan is nothing short of *vivo*, and his authorly wiles are nowhere more evident than in his choice of a point of view.

Juan's concluding conversation with his friend Julián is instructive on this point. Julián, into whose safekeeping Juan had entrusted the love letters and other memorabilia given to him by Nena, his childhood sweetheart, asks what should be done with "aquel famoso paquete de papeles amorosos" ["that famous packet of love letters"]. Juan answers: "Rómpelos" ["Tear them up"] (p. 485).[8] This *romper*, this act of rupture, separates Juan's successive roles as actor and as author. In the letters Juan appears as a character, as one of the protagonists in an adolescent romance. Nena's words not only link him to his past, they "write" him, they provide another's version of important episodes from his youth. By shredding Nena's letters, Juan opens the way for his own reconstruction of the events of his life. Appearing within a few paragraphs of each other, Juan's two imperatives, "Rómpelos" and "¡Dame papel!," signify in complementary ways his writerly vocation. The first embodies a desire not to be the object of another's writing; the second embodies the desire to speak or write for one's self. This is the same ambition embodied in his abandonment of his "first" last name, Cabrera, and his assumption of his "last" last name, Criollo. As Juan's patronymic, as the name of his Spanish father, Cabrera is an onomastic link to his past and his parentage. Criollo, on the other hand, is not only a mark of New World discontinuity, but in its etymological relation to *creare*, create, also suggests Juan's enterprise of fictional self-creation.

These two names, therefore, identify the protagonist's separate identities as author and actor: as actor, he is Juan Cabrera; as author, as narrator, he is Juan Criollo. Furthermore, since "Juan Criollo" is his *nom de plume*, the name he uses when he writes for the newspapers, it fits his narratorial stance precisely. Significantly, the protagonist is never called "Juan Criollo" by any of the other characters. The name appears only twice: first in Juan's thoughts, and then at the foot of the newspaper column reproduced in the last scene. Juan Criollo is as much a signature as a title, and the novel as a whole may be considered the process whereby a title becomes a signature, whereby Juan evolves a writerly self.

Like *Lazarillo de Tormes*, *Juan Criollo* tells the story of the birth of an author, and Juan's onomastic mitosis closely parallels the Spanish pícaro's schism into the adult "Lázaro," who writes, and the young "Lazarillo," who is written about. Right after asking his wife to bring him paper, Juan reflects: "Mientras se lo traen, decide acerca del pseudónimo que va a escoger. El mejor es uno en que viene pensando desde hace días: *Juan Criollo*" ["While they bring it to him, he makes up his mind about the pseudonym he will use. The best is one he has been thinking about for days: *Juan Criollo*"] (p. 482). This is the moment of Juan's birth and baptism as a writer, and thus the moment that generates the entire novel. The novel's precipitous conclusion after this scene is understandable when one realizes that by becoming a writer Juan has reached a terminus, something like the "height of all good fortune" mentioned at the conclusion of *Lazarillo de Tormes*. But the novel does not "end" here; indeed here is where it may be said to begin, for one crucial thing happens afterward – the autobiographical act itself, Juan's reconstruction of his past. The birth of Juan Criollo, the writer, is followed by the creation of *Juan Criollo*, the novel.

In fact internal evidence suggests that the account's composition follows closely after the events of the last pages, as if to reinforce the connection between Juan's vocation and its fulfillment. The narration takes Juan up to about age forty-six; but this is also his age when he sits down to recall the events of his life. The first words of the novel are: "Los primeros recuerdos, con imágenes claras y firmes, que conserva él de su extraordinaria vida, son de hace cuarenta años, de cuando tenía seis años de edad" ["His earliest memories, etched in clear and firm images, of his extraordinary life, go back forty years, to when he was six years old"] (p. 5). Two time-frames appear in this passage. There is, first, the frame that corresponds to the time when Juan was six years old, which is when the story begins. This is the plane of the *énoncé*, the narrated past, which will cover about forty years of Juan's life, approximately between 1885 and 1925. The second temporal frame corresponds to the time when Juan is forty-six, that is, to the moment from which the past is recalled; in linguistic terms, this is the plane of *énonciation*, the time of narration or utterance, which in this instance (though not necessarily) follows closely in the wake of the *énoncé*.[9] Juan's "last words," therefore, are not the cynical exclamation of the novel's final page ("¡Que vengan regeneraciones! Ahí nos las den todas"); rather, his last words are the novel itself, which means that Juan does "regenerate" himself, but in a textual or literary sense. By turning back to his past, he recreates himself as the protagonist of his life's story; and this literary regeneration "arrives" shortly after Juan's forecast of national regeneration.

The curious thing about the opening of *Juan Criollo*, however, is that the act of *énonciation* is identified not as a narrative occasion but only as a moment of recall, as a kind of relay or middle step between the story and its telling. Rather than writing or narrating, Juan is seen remembering; said differently, the moment of *énonciation* is presented not as *record* but as *recuerdo*. And a *recuerdo*, moreover, mediated by the intervention of a narrator, or a narrating function, that transposes first-person recollections into a third-person account. This means that the *énonciation* is itself doubly layered, for we have to posit an additional narrative level, implicit in the passage from an "I" to the "he," that would correspond to the real *énonciation*, to the actual production or generation of the story. If the second level is that of the modalizing *recuerdo*, the third is that of the actual narrative record. Three narrative levels materialize: the story of Juan's "extraordinary life"; Juan's recreation of his life, the "memories" mentioned at the outset; and some sort of redaction, by an invisible scribe or editor, of Juan's memories.

The presence of these three levels is not entirely without precedent. In many first-person accounts, including some picaresque novels like *Guzmán*, an editor intervenes to arrange the manuscripts left behind by the story's protagonist, and there is often (as in *Guzmán*) an editor's prologue explaining these interventions. What is unusual is that Loveira has fused the roles of narrator and editor; that is to say, although it is clear from the opening sentence that the tale is woven from Juan's recollections, the responsibility for the actual *énonciation* is given over to someone other than Juan Criollo (or, at least, to someone who speaks of Juan Cabrera in the third person). The impersonal *record* then emerges from the transposition of the personal *recuerdo*.

Throughout the novel that moment beyond the depicted events from which these events are recollected is persistently evoked. Although these references are too numerous to enumerate, it will be helpful to examine a couple of them. Toward the end of the book, we find the following two passages:

Por muchos años su vida no pasó de ser la de un verdadero burócrata: existencia resignada, monótona, anquilosante, que no ha querido recordar él más que a grandes rasgos, por épocas de años enteros; todo lo contrario de los capítulos de su pasado, siempre reproducidos con verbo fácil, cálido, evocador.

[For many years his life did not go beyond that of a true bureaucrat: a resigned, monotonous, stultifying existence, that he has not wanted to remember except in broad strokes, in periods of whole years; just the opposite from the chapters of his past, always reproduced with fluid, warm, evocative words.]   (p. 436)

[Pasó años] en la inalterable monotonía de la vida del burócrata, que es la gran masa de criollos no ricos; de la inmensa mayoría del cubano de las ciudades. Vida rutinaria, sin salientes emotivos, sin notas inusitadas, sin materia prima para el recuerdo, mental o escrito, de hombre hasta entonces tan extraordinario como Juan Cabrera.

[(He spent years) in the unchanging monotony of the life of the bureaucrat, which is the lot of the great mass of Cubans who are not rich; the vast majority of Cubans who live in the cites. The routine-bound life, with no emotional high points, no unusual events, no raw material for memories, mental or written, of a man like Juan Cabrera, who, up to that point, had been so extraordinary.]   (p. 457)

Again three different levels are embedded in these two excerpts. The first level is that of the "materia prima del recuerdo," the raw material of Juan's remembrances; the second level is the "recuerdo" itself; and the third is that of the narrative record, distanced from the second by the present perfect that renders Juan's recollections: "existencia ... anquilosante, que no ha querido recordar él" ["a stultifying existence that he has not wanted to remember"], etc. The labeling of that first level as "raw material" is a bit misleading, however, for the term tends to disguise the obvious process of selection that is already operative here, since Juan Criollo (the narrator) only has access to experiences or events of which Juan Cabrera (the actor) was aware. In another indication that the actual narrative voice is Juan's, throughout most of the novel the narrative limits itself to what Juan Cabrera witnessed or felt with almost Jamesian scrupulousness. There is a double "focalization" in the text: events are filtered first through the consciousness of Juan Cabrera; and then this "raw material" is "regenerated" by the consciousness of Juan Criollo.[10] The result is an account that, contrary to appearances, bears the traces of multiple mediations. From a narrative standpoint, *Juan Criollo* is far from being the textually unproblematic "document" that its commentators have assumed.

One important function of these passages, therefore, is to justify the material actually recorded in the book. Explaining why Juan remembers some things and why he forgets others, they motivate the novel's ellipses as well as its indulgences. The counterpoint to the selective recall of these excerpts would be a passage like the following, which registers Juan's reaction to Doña Juanita's harsh indictment of his mother: "Frase de dura intención, reforzada por el más despreciativo gesto. Frase que Juan ha recordado siempre, íntegra, textualmente" ["A phrase with a harsh intention, reinforced by the most contemptful gesture. A phrase that Juan has always remembered, all of it, word for word"] (p. 11). Broadly speaking, passages like these provide the rationale for the precise shape and content of Juan's "heterobiography." Critics who have remarked on the novel's abrupt transitions, on its hurried conclusion, its gaps and its *longueurs*, have not paid enough attention to the fact that these narrative quirks are recognized and rationalized by asides like the ones I have quoted. Whether Juan Criollo (and I use the name again to designate Juan's narratorial persona) shows good judgment in what episodes of his life he scants or dilates upon is a separate (and moot) question; what is important is that the syncopated narrative rhythms of the novel harmonize with its narrative orchestration. The question to ask, then, is not whether the novel is well-told, but what are the criteria on the basis of which Juan Criollo exercises his editorial privileges. If one asks the latter question, one realizes, for example, that the detail with which the narrator describes the squalid circumstances of Juan Cabrera's upbringing justifies Juan's conduct as an adult, and that the speed with which the narrator glosses over his participation in Cuba's political corruption stems from the same desire to portray Juan in a favorable light.[11] Discussing the shortcomings of the novel, Arturo Torres Rioseco remarks that "El estilo de *Juan Criollo* es más de periodista que de novelista; su modo de desarrollar sus ideas y sus teorías, más de sociólogo que de esteta" ["*Juan Criollo*'s style is more that of a journalist than that of a novelist; its way of developing its ideas and theories is more that of a sociologist than that of an aesthete"] (*La novela en la América Hispana*, p. 209). But if one supposes that the account, in fictional terms, does indeed come from the pen of Juan Criollo, a journalist, one needs to revise this judgment; if the narrator is Juan Criollo, the pertinent issue is how well Loveira has reproduced journalistic style. What Torres Rioseco sees as a defect is actually a virtue.

In their references to Juan's memories, the two passages quoted above evince a significant ambivalence: "recuerdo, mental o escrito" ["memories, mental or written"], says one passage. From a literary standpoint, the difference is crucial. Were they to be "written," the memories would turn into memoirs; and it is precisely this passage from memory to memoir that the third-person reconstruction of Juan's life tends to dissemble. Since in Spanish one word, *memorias*, designates the mental event as well as the textual one, *Juan Criollo* as a whole may be said to oscillate between the two senses of *memorias*. When the narration refers to Juan's projected "libro de memorias" (p. 474), it is capitalizing on this ambiguity, leaving open the question of whether these *memorias* are written or mental. Similarly, in the other passage quoted above the narrator begins by referring only to Juan's presumably unspoken and private memories, but by the end of the sentence the ontological register has been subtly altered, and he concludes by referring to the "words" (*verbo*), which "reproduce" the "chapters" from Juan's past. Juan modulates from remembrance to verbalization. At some point, it seems, Juan verbalizes his memories, casts them in the form of memoirs, spoken or written. The novel does not make clear, however, under what circumstances this verbalization occurs, nor who is the listener or reader who passes judgment on Juan's life and language ("existencia resignada, monótona, anquilosante" ["a resigned, monotonous, stultifying existence"]; "verbo fácil, cálido, evocador" ["fluid, warm, evocative words"]). My supposition is that the simplest explanation is the most useful: that implied listener or transcriber is a mirage created by the transposition of pronouns. The narrator of the novel is Juan himself, who not only reconstructs his past, but takes cover in the anonymity of the impersonal narration in order to pass judgment on it.

In support of this explanation, let me offer some contextual evidence from Loveira's other novels. Because of its marked autobiographical content, all of Loveira's fiction tends toward the genre of the memoir, a genre that Loveira cultivated in one of his earliest works, *De los 26 a los 35: Lecciones de la experiencia en la lucha obrera* (1917). This inclination toward the memoir is especially evident in *Generales y doctores* (1920), which is narrated in the first person by its protagonist, Ignacio García; but it surfaces even in those novels that adopt a third-person omniscient point of view. In *Los ciegos* (1922), for example, the following statement occurs: "Del resto de aquel día de violentas emociones, de aquellas últimas horas de locura, sólo le queda un recuerdo turbio e ingrato" ["Of the rest of that day of violent emotions, of those last hours of madness, he has only a troubled and unpleasant recollection"] (*Los ciegos*, p. 154). Since this statement also supposes that the "raw material" of the narration has been filtered through the consciousness of the protagonist, it closely resembles the passages from *Juan Criollo* that I have discussed. In *Los ciegos*, however, the hypothesis of a disguised autobiography is not viable because entire sections of the novel deal with events about which the protagonist had no knowledge. What happened, surely, is that Loveira, under the weight the novel's autobiographical cargo,[12] inadvertently let the narrative register slide toward a personalized account, even though this was inconsistent with the point of view adopted in the rest of the novel.

This autobiographical bias continues into *Juan Criollo*, a novel that closely parallels the circumstances of Loveira's own upbringing.[13] The difference is that, whether by chance or by design, here Loveira's inclination toward autobiography finds a felicitous vehicle, since it blends in with other parts of the narration. The implied autobiographical format is consistent both with the double identity of the protagonist – Cabrera and Criollo – and with the pace and focus of the novel's last pages, which deal with Juan's vocation as a writer. Moreover, the use of a disguised or displaced memoir as the skeleton for the account heightens the novel's interest as a "creole" descendant of the Spanish picaresque.

In the opening passage of the novel, after the narrator has indicated that Juan's "firm and clear" memories go back to when he was six years old, there follows a description of Juan's childhood pastimes:

En el colgadizo se entretenía él viendo chisporrotear un anafe lleno de planchas o coronado por una humeante cazuela de barro, cuando no estaba en su predilecto juego de imitar, en la batea de la madre, con trocitos de madera y velitas de papel, las embarcaciones que blanqueaban allá abajo, en la azul llanura del Golfo.

[He entertained himself in the shed watching the flames in a stove full of irons or crowned by a smoking earthen pot, when he was not busy with his favorite game of imitating, in his mother's wash-basin, with little pieces of wood and little sails of paper, the ships that stood out, white, down there in the blue plain of the Gulf.]   (p. 5)

Making toy sailboats out of wood and paper is the first of Juan's many occupations, and in some ways it is the most suggestive. To begin with, it has a proleptic function, for his fascination with the boats in the harbor anticipates his nomadic life; more importantly, this game of "imitation" also anticipates Juan Criollo's fictional recreation of himself. There is a frail but crucial link between those paper sails and the "¡Dame papel!" ["Give me paper!"] of the novel's climax. Our first glimpse of Juan shows him as the creator of simulacra, as a player in the game of pretend. Our last glimpse of Juan, as the author of his life's story, will show him also engaged in a game of imitation played with paper. In his childhood game Juan behaves much like the god-like narrator of the classical novel. Transmuting his mother's wash-basin into an ocean, he creates and sustains a fictional microcosm that is surveyed from a point outside and above. When Juan embarks on the reconstruction of his life, he will adopt a similarly detached perspective. But we know, however, that his detachment is only a pose, since he is, in effect, both navigator and observer. The omniscient narrator of the novel is a doubly fictional entity, a "fictive fiction," to borrow Lejeune's term, for "he" is Juan's creation: a paper-voice confected in order to shift the novel away from the autobiographical register.

Earlier in this book I discussed the paraleptic structure of some of Fernando Ortiz's texts, a notion that I would now like to apply to Loveira's novel. *Juan Criollo* is a paraleptic memoir, that is, an autobiographical account that, by the transposition of grammatical persons, gives the appearance of objective narration. Like Ortiz, Loveira knows how to have his words and eat them too. Even as he takes his distance from his "literary precedent," he maintains it within his sights. The choice of a "point of view," after all, is also a matter of distance, and just as Juan Criollo distances himself from his younger self by the transposition of pronouns, *Juan Criollo* distances itself from its generic past in the same way, since this grammatical transposition violates one of the fundamental conventions of the picaresque genre. Loveira's transculturation of picaresque conventions involves a faithful adherence to some norms as well as an innovative revision of others. Like Nicolás Guillén's sonnets and madrigals, Loveira's novel is "faithful and transforming."[14] It assumes and transumes tradition. For this reason, if for no other, *Juan Criollo* deserves a better press than it has received. To my mind, it is one of the most interesting experiments in picaresque fiction in Spanish-American literature, a field where there have been more than a few instances of the genre.[15] *Juan Criollo* is a truly "creole" creation. By balancing, or counterpointing, inherited traits and acquired inclinations, Loveira has written a novel worthy of its name.

8

Shifting grounds

La cubanidad es la pertenencia a la cultura de Cuba. Pero ¿cuál es la cultura característica de Cuba? Para saberlo habría que estudiar un intrincadísimo complejo de elementos emocionales, intelectuales y volitivos. No sólo en las manifestaciones de las individualidades destacadas en la vida cubana por la culminación de sus personalidades, sino también en todas las sedimentaciones, en las cumbres, en las laderas, en los valles, en las sabanas y hasta en las ciénagas.

[*Cubanidad* is belonging to the culture of Cuba. But what is Cuba's characteristic culture? In order to find out one would have to study an intricate complex of emotional, intellectual, and volitive elements, which are manifested not only in the personalities of certain outstanding individuals, but also in all the sedimentations of Cuban life, on the peaks, in the slopes, in the valleys, in the plains, and even in the swamps.]   Fernando Ortiz

As nativist poetry, Eugenio Florit's *Trópico* finds its counterpoint in *Motivos de son*. But as a description of the Cuban countryside, the appropriate counterpoint might well be a work like Luis Felipe Rodríguez's *Ciénaga*, originally published in 1923 and republished in expanded form in 1937. Rodríguez's novel contains all of those nativist elements that are missing from *Trópico*. Combining social commentary with a detailed description of customs, types, and landscapes, Rodríguez paints a vivid portrait of the squalid life of the Cuban farmer, victimized by local *caciques* and foreign intruders. If *Trópico* centers on an abstract "campo," *Ciénaga* will focus on the concrete "campiña." If *Trópico* perpetuates some of the idealizations typical of *siboneísmo*, *Ciénaga* aspires to the historical and representational accuracy of what Angel Augier termed *guajirismo* ("*Ciénaga*, novela cubana," p. 215).

Moreover, although this novel is little read today, *Ciénaga* is

Cuba's principal contribution to the paradigmatic genre of criollist literature, the so-called *novela de la tierra*, with all of the excellences and limitations that the label implies; in fact Rodríguez's novel enjoys a certain priority in the genre, since *Ciénaga*, in its original version, antedates the earthly trinity of criollist fiction, José Eustasio Rivera's *La vorágine* (1924), Ricardo Güiraldes's *Don Segundo Sombra* (1926), and Rómulo Gallegos's *Doña Bárbara* (1929). And although it would be foolish to claim for Rodríguez's tale, especially in its sketchy original version, the ideological and artistic density of these classic novels, *Ciénaga* possesses considerable interest for two reasons: first, because it is a serious fictional attempt to grasp "the hidden and untransferable essences"[1] of the Cuban people; and second, because it engages the problematic of the "novel of the earth" in a way that calls into question the founding premise of this kind of literature. Thus, even though *Ciénaga* is not a work that withstands the kind of scrutiny to which I have subjected texts by Guillén, Florit, and Loveira, it does merit a closer look than it has received thus far.[2]

That Rodríguez intended his novel to be compared with the "exemplary novels" of Spanish America, as Juan Marinello once called the canonic criollist novels,[3] is evident from the introduction to the revised edition, where the author confesses that his perhaps excessive ambition is "to be on a par with the great novelists of America" (p. 8). In 1937, when Rodríguez wrote this, the great Spanish-American novelists, as Marinello pointed out, were writers like Gallegos, Güiraldes, and Rivera, and it is to their works that *Ciénaga* must in the first instance be compared. The basic similarity between *Ciénaga* and the novel of the earth lies in Rodríguez's emphasis on the conflict between man and nature, or, more generally, between civilization and barbarism. His protagonist is Santiago Hermida, a budding novelist who, planning to write a "nationalistic and patriotic novel" entitled *Ciénaga* (p. 188), moves to the countryside in search of peace and quiet. There he has a liaison with Conchita Fundora, the daughter of one of the town's patriarchs, and this provokes the rage of Mongo Paneque, the girl's spurned suitor. Paneque avenges himself by throwing Hermida into the swamp. In an ironic twist of fate, Hermida – a novelist swallowed by his novel – eventually falls victim to that very quagmire that he intended to write about. As his friend Vicente Aldana points out, Hermida went to the country to write a novel and ended up living one (p. 188).

In *Ciénaga* Santiago Hermida has the role that in *Doña Bárbara* and *La vorágine* falls to Santos Luzardo and Arturo Cova, respectively. Like Arturo Cova, Hermida is an artist; like Santos Luzardo, he is the emissary of civilization, an educated, idealistic young man from the city who comes face to face with the barbarism of the Cuban countryside, a force represented by the central, engulfing symbol of the swamp. Unlike Santos Luzardo, however, Hermida does not survive his ordeal, and Rodríguez's novel lacks the hopeful conclusion of the Venezuelan work. The character who does survive is Vicente Aldana, Hermida's friend and companion, and the author of "a kind of novel" ("una especie de novela," p. 13) that relates Hermida's catastrophe. This is already significant. Although Hermida is the novelist, the story is not narrated by him but by Aldana, a census taker or *numerador*. While Hermida spends his time romancing Conchita Fundora, Aldana canvases the countryside, "enumerating" the inhabitants and putting together a register or *padrón*. In *Ciénaga*, the avowed novelist is a helpless and pathetic figure who disappears into the swamp before he can write more than a few paragraphs; the one who lives to tell the story, the accomplished writer, is Aldana, who lacks Hermida's imaginative gifts but has a firm grasp on facts and figures. If there is an author-figure in *Ciénaga*, it is not the novelist but the enumerator. As a work of criollist fiction, the novel pays less attention to fabulation than to documentation, and Hermida's downfall is precisely having gotten caught up in a novel of his own making. Behind Aldana's profession lies the *mundonovista* bias toward the individual or the particular, criollism's espousal of an aesthetics of singularity, in both the generic and numeric senses of the word. Here again one thinks of Santos Luzardo, the protagonist of *Doña Bárbara*, a lawyer who spends much of his time surveying his lands. And one thinks also of Ortiz and his dictionaries: if the lexicographer enumerates *cubanismos*, the census taker enumerates *cubanos*. By making Aldana the author and narrator of the framed narrative, "La conjura de la ciénaga" (not coincidentally the original title of the novel), Rodríguez models his work on the statistical and quantitative activity of the enumerator. Mario Vargas Llosa's caricature of criollist fiction fits *Ciénaga* precisely: "The novel became a census, a matter of geographical data, a description of customs and usages, an ethnological document, a regional fair, a sample case of folklore" ("Primitives and creators," p. 1287). As novelist, Rodríguez is interested in identifying and cataloguing, in imposing an order and a name on the places and inhabitants of his fictional domain.

In addition to the human protagonists, the most important character in the novel is of course the eponymous swamp. In fact the swamp is eponymous on several levels, for it not only gives a title to the novel we read and to the novel Hermida intended to write, but also names the town where Hermida and Aldana take up residence. The reason for the synonymity of town and terrain is obvious: the former emanates from the latter; all of the town's inhabitants are children of the mire, "hijos de la ciénaga" (p. 225). Thus, Fengue Camacho and Mongo Paneque, two of the local luminaries, are "mosquitos incubados por la ciénaga" ["mosquitoes incubated by the swamp"] (p. 226); Camacho, the mayor of the town, is likened to an alligator that has crawled out of the swamp (p. 226); Conchita Fundora is repeatedly called "la flor de la Ciénaga" ["the flower of the Ciénaga"] (pp. 19, 65, 232); and when Hermida makes love to her, it is almost as if he were already sinking into the quagmire: "Santiago penetró otra vez en el reino sin forma y sin nombre, donde se muere momentáneamente para resucitar más tarde con una indefinible angustia en el espíritu y un poco de sopor en el cuerpo" ["Santiago penetrated once again into the kingdom without form and without name, where one dies momentarily to be resurrected later feeling an indefinable anguish in one's spirit and a slight drowsiness in one's body"] (p. 189). On a symbolic plane, Conchita's "kingdom without form and without name" is the swamp itself, into whose "bosom" (p. 43) Hermida finally disappears; Hermida's sinking feeling will soon become a literal descent.

But if the characters are extensions of the swamp, the swamp itself is a symbol of the Cuban condition, "una imagen objetiva de las fuerzas enemigas que nos acechan constantemente" ["an objective image of the enemy forces that constantly lurk around us"] (p. 198). When Hermida leaves Havana, he wants to get away from "las emanaciones de la gran ciénaga política y capitaleña" ["the emanations of the great political quagmire of the capital"] (p. 21); in his novel, therefore, the swamp was to be the metaphor of Cuba's social ills: "Mi novela será la visión humana e integral de nuestros hombres y nuestro medio. Pienso descender a lo más profundo de la ciénaga que contamina entre nosotros lo más puro y lo más grande" ["My novel will be the integral human vision of our people and our environment. I intend to descend to the deepest part of the quagmire that contaminates what is most pure and most great among us"] (p. 24). The irony of Hermida's declaration, anticipated in Aldana's comment on the proposed title, "No está mal el nombre, chico; ahora hay que tener cuidado con lo que se hace, porque casi siempre en toda clase de ciénaga, por lo regular hay tembladeras" ["That's not a bad name, buddy; but you have to be careful, because almost always in any kind of quagmire there are quicksands"] (p. 25), comes cruelly to the surface in the description of his death: "Santiago Hermida, abandonado de todos, en medio de la gran impasibilidad natural, descendió hasta el fondo de la charca" ["Santiago Hermida, abandoned by everyone, in the midst of the great impassiveness of nature, descended to the bottom of the swamp"] (p. 203). In their mocking echo of Hermida's noble artistic intentions, these words suggest the allusive richness of the novel's central image. The swamp is both setting and symbol. As in *Doña Bárbara* and *La vorágine*, realistic description and allegorical significance are glued together with a stickiness whose most accurate representation is perhaps the swamp itself.

This opposition between Hermida and Aldana, on the one hand, and the swamp, on the other, forms the core of the novel. Much as Gallegos used the Venezuelan plain as his image of barbarism, Rodríguez uses this feature of Cuban topography as his "objective image" of Cuban corruption. As the enemy of the forces of civilization, the swamp is appropriately recalcitrant to Aldana's enumerative activities. Not only is it a physical obstacle to Aldana's excursions; by its very nature it resists accounting, quantification: its beauties are "bellezas innumerables" (p. 23); its sounds are "rumores innumerables" (pp. 109, 112); its furtive eyes are "ojos innumerables" (pp. 75, 125). When Aldana goes into the wilderness, the *numerador* comes up against the *innumerable*. He tries to bring measure, in both the arithmetical and ethical senses, to the countryside; but he fails: "Aquella ciénaga iba ensanchándose hasta tomar las dimensiones de toda la tierra de Hispanoamérica, y me parecía que en ella, desde el tiempo de la Conquista, habían venido hundiéndose, como Santiago Hermida, las más puras aspiraciones de sus mejores hijos" ["That swamp kept widening until it had the dimensions of the whole of Spanish America, and it seemed to me that, from the days of the Conquest, the purest aspirations of our best sons had been sinking into it, like Santiago Hermida"] (p. 224). The swamp is incommensurable, it cannot be counted or reduced to a *padrón*, a word that derives from the same root as *patrón*, pattern.

The expansive swamp also engulfs the novel's imagery and structure. Throughout the text there are numerous verbal echoes that remind us of the swamp. At the beginning the narrator remarks that Aldana's account is probably "un cuento bonito, quizá trágico en el fondo" ["a pretty story, perhaps tragic at bottom"] (p. 14). But the tragedy does indeed lie "en el fondo" – in the bottom of the quagmire. A few pages later Aldana asks Hermida whether he is "metido de lleno" ["completely immersed"] in his novel, "Ciénaga" (p. 21). Although Aldana doesn't know it, Hermida will indeed be immersed in the *ciénaga* before very long. In addition, Conchita and Hermida's affair is called a "pasión desbordante" ["overflowing passion"] (p. 124), words that recall the reference to the marsh's spilling over during the rainy season (p. 53); and Conchita herself is constantly under the semantic influence of the swamp: her glance is "provocativo y hondo" ["provocative and deep"] (p. 41), her embrace is "absorbente y profundo" ["absorbing and deep"] (p. 225), and she is herself a "profunda y complicada enredadera carnal" ["deep and complicated carnal vine"] (p. 186). Even her last name, "Fundora," with its echo of *fondo* and *profundo*, conveys her treacherous association with the swamp.[4]

Something similar can be observed in the novel's construction. If one compares the first and second versions of the book, there are only two significant changes. One is that Rodríguez has added a few *costumbrista* episodes, like the one describing the preparations for Don Venancio's party; the other is that he has enclosed Aldana's account in an outside frame. In *La conjura de la ciénaga*, Vicente Aldana's narration was offered directly to the reader; *Ciénaga* adds an introductory chapter, "La casa de los Aldanas," in which an unnamed narrator tells of going to Vicente's house and being given the manuscript of a "narración vernácula" ["vernacular story"] entitled "La conjura de la Ciénaga." The original version has been absorbed by the revision; reading the novel, the reader proceeds from *Ciénaga*, the tale narrated by the anonymous narrator, to "La conjura de la ciénaga," Aldana's story, to "Ciénaga," Santiago Hermida's unfinished work, which, because of the synonymity of titles, circles back to the framing narration. This construction *en abyme*, which might be viewed as a kind of writerly *conjura*, makes the reader "descend" through different narrative strata until, like Hermida, he touches bottom. The swamp is everywhere. Regardless of the point at which one steps into the novel, one finds oneself in a *ciénaga* of one kind or another.

The quagmire is the ground, the *fondo*, the foundation of the novel. As title, setting, symbol, and protagonist, it organizes the narration's plot, structure, and language. Everything in *Ciénaga* gravitates toward the swamp, which possesses a mysterious infernal allure:

El monstruo era insaciable y pérfido. Todo lo que llegaba a su vientre no volvía a salir vivo más nunca. Se cuenta que había tragado hombres, animales y cosas. ¡Ay del ignorante que pusiera la planta confiada sobre aquel cristal turbio y tranquilo de agua estancada! La ciénaga, obedeciendo al sortilegio de su infernal atracción, lo iría enguyendo lentamente, muy lentamente, con una precisión irresistible e inevitable, hasta hacerlo desaparecer de la luz del sol.

[The monster was insatiable and perfidious. Nothing that entered its belly came out alive. It is said that it had swallowed men, animals, things. God take pity on someone who, unknowing, sets foot on that turbid and tranquil surface of still water! The swamp, obeying the spell of its infernal attraction, would devour him slowly, slowly, with irresistible and inevitable precision, until he disappeared from the light of the sun.] (p. 43)

The problem, though, is that the swamp's appetites conflict with its novelistic function. The swamp is an earth into which one cannot sink foundations. One cannot build upon it; one cannot even despoil it, as happens with the jungle in *La vorágine*. The conceptual base of *Ciénaga* is shifting ground: not earth but quicksand, not *tierra firme* but *tierra movediza*. For this reason, *Ciénaga* is a novel poised on the shakiest of foundations, a verbal edifice built up from the ground down, as it were; and this means, in turn, that Rodríguez has written a "novel of the earth" that explicitly undermines the founding myth of such novels, namely, that the earth, the ground, is the ultimate, stable source and support of human endeavors.

In a provocative recent essay ("Doña Bárbara writes the plain"), Roberto González Echevarría has pointed out some of the subtle ways in which *Doña Bárbara* subverts this myth. Something similar happens in *Ciénaga*, except that there is nothing subtle about the process. Here the self-subversion is scandalously explicit, which perhaps helps to explain why Rodríguez's novel never entered the ranks of "exemplary" criollist fiction. As a groundless *novela de la tierra*, as a *novela de la tierra movediza*, Rodríguez's text makes problematic its insertion in a generic *padrón*. It is often said that works like *Don Segundo Sombra* and *Doña Bárbara* constitute the foundation of the modern Spanish-American novel. But *Ciénaga*, a work of shifting ground, calls into question the notion of a ground, a foundation. If *Doña Bárbara* is "uno de los libros fundacionales de nuestras letras: un libro-nación" ["one of the founding books of our literature: a nation-book"],[5] the question is: on what *grounds* could one make such a statement apropos of *Ciénaga*? And what would such an assertion imply about the "nation" depicted in the Cuban novel?

The idea and image of a treacherous, engulfing nature, of course, are not unique to Rodríguez's novel. In *La vorágine*, also, the protagonist is "devoured" by the jungle; the Venezuelan plains of *Doña Bárbara* include a treacherous swamp, the *tremedal* into which Doña Bárbara disappears at the end; and several decades before the appearance of any of these works, the Puerto Rican novelist Manuel Zeno Gandía published *La Charca* (1894), a novel whose central image is also a kind of quagmire. In addition, Rodríguez's symbolic use of the *ciénaga* has an important Cuban precedent in José Antonio Ramos's play, *Tembladera* (1916).[6] Nonetheless, *Ciénaga* stands out because of its single-minded insistence on this central image. Here the quagmire is not simply one element among others, as it is in *Doña Bárbara*. On the descriptive level, it is the dominant feature of the Cuban landscape; on the figurative level, it is the governing metaphor of the Cuban condition.

Although Rodríguez's novel is not a translational work in the same sense as Ortiz's *Contrapunteo cubano* or Loveira's *Juan Criollo*, it is no less an example of "critical criollism" than the other texts I have analyzed. Indeed, one might say that by exploding the myth of the earth as ground, by undertaking a critique of primitive criollism on its own grounds, *Ciénaga* provides the justification for the translational performances of an Ortiz or a Guillén. In a stark and striking way, Rodríguez's novel expresses the "groundlessness" of Cuban criollism.

When Hermida sinks into Conchita's embrace, he experiences an "indefinible angustia" ["indefinable anguish"] (p. 189), a phrase that echoes Mañach's diagnosis of the failings of the Cuban nativist movement – "las angustias a que todo nativismo se había de sentir vocado en nuestra isla" ["the anxieties that befall every kind of nativism in our island"] (*Historia y estilo*, p. 116). The root of this anguish is rootlessness, the sinking feeling that one cannot find a firm place on which to stand. In anthropological terms, *Ciénaga* can be read as another absorbing assertion of the uprootedness of Cuban culture, of its lack of an indigenous substratum. In Rodríguez's own words, the swamp is "a synthesis of the history of our island" that bears out "the provisional, inconsistent, piratically usurping character" of Cuban culture (p. 53). Mañach and Ortiz, we should recall, had described Cuban culture in similar terms: for Mañach Cuba was a "subordinate and provisional land" (*Historia y estilo*, p. 113); and for Ortiz everything in Cuba was "foreign, provisional, changeable" (*Contrapunteo cubano*, p. 133).

The crucial difference, especially between Ortiz and Rodríguez, is that in Ortiz's view the unstable, shifting soil of Cuban culture was not something to be despised or disdained. Mr. Cuba's writings, both in content and form, celebrate inconsistency. His terrain is precisely that "tierra inconsistente" ["inconsistent earth"] (p. 53) denounced in Rodríguez's novel. As Ortiz said in the *Glosario de afronegrismos*, his research took him into shaky grounds, into a *monte* "lleno de temblores" (p. xv), but he was not fazed by the prospect. Rodríguez's choice of imagery indicates that he does not share Ortiz's sanguine outlook. One night, after nearly falling into the swamp, Aldana has the following nightmare:

Era un caldero enorme, inmenso, en cuyo seno fermentaba una mixtura incalificable. Con un pavor invencible yo vi surgir de este caldero diabólico una como humareda densa, que envolvía el espacio y la campiña. Luego, esta humareda se fragmentó, tomando cuerpo en innumerables tubos vegetales que se agitaban vertiginosamente de aquí para allá, cual un torbellino de burbujas de agua en una paila hirviendo. Después a cada tubo le surgió una cabeza humana.

[There was an enormous, immense cauldron in whose bosom an unnameable mixture was fermenting. With an invincible dread I saw a thick cloud of smoke emerge from this diabolical cauldron, filling the air and enveloping the countryside. Then, the cloud broke up, taking the shape of innumerable vegetable tubers that shook vertiginously from side to side, like a whirlpool of boiling bubbles in a pan. Afterwards each tuber grew a human head.]   (p. 137)

In Aldana's grotesque vision, the swamp is transformed into nothing less than a devilish hodgepodge or *ajiaco*, for Ortiz's tasty dish reappears here as a "mixtura incalificable" ["unnameable mixture"]. Aldana's inability to name this concoction is especially significant in view of the fact that names are his game; even in his dreams, the numerator cannot avoid the unnameable. Not surprisingly, he reacts with disgust, labeling the swamp a "nauseabundo elemento" ["nauseating element"] (p. 136). Confronted by the same element, Ortiz would not feel nausea but appetite; he would call this cultural stew an *ajiaco*, and rejoice in the name and the flavor. For Ortiz, the boiling cauldron is an image of receptivity, of enriching absorbency, of what I have termed Cuba's "translation sensibility." But for Rodríguez the mixture only breeds monsters, as is evident in the grotesque creatures that emerge from the cauldron. From Rodríguez's dystopic perspective, *ciénaga* is the name for that which cannot be named, for the ineffable rottenness of Cuban society, that "kingdom without form and without name" to which Conchita is likened.

The final lesson of *Ciénaga* seems to be that Cuba is an island without a ground, a "patria sin nación" ["nation without nationhood"], in Mañach's formula. The "hidden essence" of Cuban society is the fetid pit of the quagmire, which not only swallows everything that treads on it, but keeps expanding, like an open wound that continually grows larger. This is a rather depressing lesson. What the criollist seeks are foundations – literary, ethnic, political; he seeks a common ground, a base for the nation's or continent's identity and endeavors. But if that common ground is the shifting earth of a quagmire, his foundations sink from sight.

Nonetheless, it is well to keep this lesson in mind as we proceed to the next chapter, where I will discuss another novel that also treads on shaky ground, Alejo Carpentier's *Los pasos perdidos* (1953). Published some years after the heyday of criollist fiction, Carpentier's novel not only follows in the steps of the novel of the earth; more importantly, it constitutes itself as a commentary on the criollist project, and particularly its language. In this respect Carpentier's novel works out the ultimate consequences of the critique initiated in *Ciénaga*. Aldana's inability to find a name, his incipient aphasia, reaches a disabling extreme in Carpentier's novel, which renders problematic the very language in which Spanish-American culture seeks to define itself. As we will see, in *Los pasos perdidos*, the narrator's own words become an "unnameable mixture" of nightmarish proportions.

9

Land or language

A language is a place.   Elias Canetti

Toward the end of "La biblioteca de Babel," the speaker interrupts
a disquisition on the arbitrariness of signs to ask the reader an
embarrassingly direct question: "Tú, que me lees, ¿estás seguro de
entender mi lenguaje?" ["You, who read me, are you sure that you
understand my language?"] (*Ficciones*, p. 99). The question is
intended in the most literal sense possible: Do we really know what
language the speaker is using? Could we name it? Can we be sure
that when he writes, and we read, "biblioteca" ["library"], we both
mean the same thing? Indeed, can we even be sure that we have
understood the *question*? As sometimes happens in Borges, the
remark is teasingly circular, for his apostrophe is an antinomy, a
formally undecidable proposition. Since the question necessarily
involves a questioning of its own language, if we understand the
question, we cannot possibly be sure that we have understood the
question. Conversely, if we do *not* understand the question, then
perhaps we really have understood the question. Either way, the
result is self-contradiction.

I should like to borrow Borges's deceptively simple apostrophe –
deceptive like the placid, glistening water of the swamp – and
address it to Carpentier's *Los pasos perdidos*, a novel that has been
termed "a synthesis of the Spanish-American literary tradition."[1] I
want to ask whether we can be sure that we have understood the
language of Carpentier's novel. *Los pasos perdidos* is one of the few
works by Carpentier where one of the characters has responsibility
for the narration; in this case, the narrator is a nameless Cuban
musicologist who goes into the South American jungle in search of

138

some primitive musical instruments and who, on his return, recounts his adventures. My question, like Borges's, refers not to the text's actual language, which is obviously Spanish, but its virtual language, that is, to the speech of its narrator. Just as we ask someone whose accent we can't place about his or her "first" language, I am interested in placing the "first" language of *Los pasos perdidos*, that in which the narrator gives his account. As we will see, this is not at all a simple task.

Because the narrator knows, and quotes from, any number of languages – Spanish, French, German, English – polyglossia is an integral part of his identity. Nonetheless, among his many languages, two stand out: Spanish, his "mother" tongue (in fact the language of his mother); and English, his adopted tongue, the language of daily life in the North American city where he lives. It is not clear, however, in which of these languages he tells his story, since it is just as improbable to suppose that he speaks in Spanish as it is to suppose that he speaks in English. Evidently the narrator's Spanish has little in common with the halting, uncertain speech of someone who has not used his native language since childhood. As he confesses upon his arrival in South America, he had all but forgotten his mother tongue (p. 108). Given these many years of disuse, several weeks in the jungle do not seem adequate preparation for the linguistic virtuosity of his account. And yet, the other possibility is equally implausible, for a different set of reasons: a recounting in English contradicts the goal of his narration, which is to recreate a world that exists in Spanish. If the voyage of cultural recovery has to be undertaken in English, the loss is irreparable. It is difficult to imagine that Carpentier's narrator, so self-conscious about other things, would not recognize the vitiating irony of this situation, especially in light of his claim that the Latin American writer, like Adam, is primarily someone who names (p. 64).[2] If the story was written "originally" in English, if before reaching our hands it has undergone an invisible translation (somewhat in the manner of *Don Quijote*, parts of which were supposedly "translated" from Arabic), Carpentier's protagonist would be in the paradoxical situation of giving foreign names to Spanish-American realities, of naming the autochthonous in other words.

We cannot avoid this dilemma by appealing to the "literary

precedent" (to return to Ortiz's phraseology) of other novels where every character speaks a kind of *lingua franca*, regardless of nationality. Even if this is a long-standing convention of historical romances (a genre with which Carpentier's novel has much in common), here it cannot be assumed innocently. Since the retrieval of his mother tongue is a crucial episode in the narrator's adventures, and since he is very much aware of the existential consequences of his polyglossia, the story's language is a key to its overall meaning: the linguistic medium is the thematic message. I would go further: it is impossible to understand the novel, to inquire into its meaning, unless we first place its language. Before interpreting *Los pasos perdidos*, we need to answer the narrator's own version of Borges's problematic question: "¿Cuál era mi idioma verdadero?" ["What was my true language?"] (p. 277).

From the beginning, the protagonist's predicament is couched in linguistic terms. In the initial subchapter, he stops before a store window that displays Lope de Vega's *Comedias americanas* and Shelley's *Prometheus Unbound*; unable to decide which book to buy, he finally purchases neither. The incident is significant, first, because of its anticipatory character. Shelley's poem will have an important function later on, since the narrator plans to use it as the basis for a musical composition; and Lope's title foreshadows the narrator's imminent return to Spanish America. Beyond this, his indecision, which consists not only in having to choose between two different books, but also in having to choose between two different languages and cultures, summarizes the linguistic indecision of his own account, which also seems to waver between Spanish and English.

On contemplating the copy of the *Comedias americanas*, the narrator realizes that Lope's work affords him the opportunity of a reacquaintance with the language of his childhood, which he no longer used ("el idioma que nunca usaba, aunque sólo podía multiplicar en español y sumar con el 'llevo tanto'") ["the language that I never used, although I could only multiply in Spanish and add by the 'carrying' method"] (p. 77). Deferred for the moment, this reunion will take place a few days later in the plane that takes him to Caracas, the South American city from where he will launch his foray into the jungle. In his journey back to the source, the first threshold will be linguistic:

Me sentía preso, secuestrado, cómplice de algo execrable, en este encierro del avión, con el ritmo de tres tiempos, oscilante, de la envergadura empeñada en lucha con un viento adverso que arrojaba, a veces, una tenue lluvia sobre el aluminio de las alas. Pero ahora, una rara voluptuosidad adormece mis escrúpulos. Y una fuerza me penetra lentamente por los oídos, por los poros: el idioma. He aquí, pues, el idioma que hablé en mi infancia; el idioma en que aprendí a leer y solfear; el idioma enmohecido en mi mente por el poco uso, dejado de lado como herramienta inútil, en país donde de poco pudiera servirme.

[I felt imprisoned, kidnapped, an accomplice in something execrable, locked up in the plane, with the oscillating three-step rhythm of the fuselage battling a head wind that, at times, bathed the aluminum wings with a light rain. But now, a strange voluptuousness lulls my scruples. And a force penetrates me slowly through my ears, my pores: language. Here it is, then, the language that I spoke as a child; the language in which I learned to read and to sol-fa; the language grown mouldy in my mind, cast aside like a useless tool in a country where it could not help me.]

(p. 108)

These sentiments echo Marinello's meditation on linguistic determinism: Carpentier's protagonist, like Marinello's writer, is a "prisoner" who is "penetrated" by language. But the crucial phrase is the deictic, "He aquí" ["Here it is"]. This indication of position is extraordinarily ambiguous, for the crux is precisely location: in the narrator's words, *where* is Spanish? Where is the "here" that he so ingenuously designates – "He aquí, pues, el idioma que hablé en mi infancia" ["Here it is, then, the language that I spoke as a child"]? From the reader's standpoint, this affirmation refers both to the words heard through the microphone and to those inscribed on the page. When reading the novel, *we* also seem caught by Spanish, penetrated by the narrator's language. But is it certain that we have heard correctly? Does the deictic situate both the pilot's and the protagonist's words? Can we be sure that we have understood his language?

On his return from South America, the protagonist's separation from the maternal world of his childhood will be punctuated by another linguistic anagnorisis, this time in the opposite direction. Reinstating the *status ante*, English now displaces the mother tongue. The irruption into the Spanish text of a line, in English, from *Prometheus Unbound* marks the exact moment when the switch into English takes place:

De espaldas a mí habla nuevamente el piloto. Y lo que dice, que siempre es lo mismo, despierta en mí el recuerdo de otros versos del poema: *I heard a sound of voices; not the voice which I gave forth*. El idioma de los hombres del aire, que fue mi idioma durante años, desplaza en mi mente, esta mañana, el idioma matriz – el de mi madre, el de Rosario. Apenas si puedo pensar en español, como había vuelto a hacerlo, ante la sonoridad de vocablos que ponen la confusión en mi ánimo.

[With his back to me the pilot speaks once again. And what he is saying, which is always the same thing, awakens in me the memory of other verses from the poem: *I heard a sound of voices; not the voice which I gave forth*. The language of the men of the air, which was my language for years, displaces in my mind, this morning, the maternal language – my mother's, Rosario's. Confronted by the sonority of words that confuse me, I can barely think in Spanish, as I had done again.]   (p. 292)

In the two passages I have quoted, the novel circumscribes the domain of Spanish. As he travels between North and South America, the narrator crosses a linguistic border, a barrier of sound and sense that delimits the territory of each language. Once outside the Spanish domain, the narrator is incapable even of thinking in Spanish: "Apenas si puedo pensar en español" ["I can barely think in Spanish"]. Even as the novel denies the possibility of translation in the topographical sense, it affirms the necessity of translation in the linguistic sense. A language is immovable; it is anchored in a bounded space and cannot be displaced or transplanted. Outside of Spanish America, Spanish-American experience needs to be spoken in other words. The novel thus establishes an equation between language and place. Language is place, and place is language. One cannot lose one's place and keep its language; one cannot keep a language without staying in place. In Spanish, a person who speaks a language well is said to "dominate" the language. *Los pasos perdidos* suggests that conventional wisdom has it all wrong, for it is the language, and not the speaker, that "dominates." A language determines its domain, its dominion, and we as speakers cannot but submit to language's territorial imperatives.

Consequently, foremost among the protagonist's many losses when he returns to North America is the loss of his mother tongue, which will not be moved. And yet the paradox is that the story reads in Spanish, the very language that the narrator loses once he crosses the language barrier. Another paradox: when the narrator, in the passage quoted above, confesses that he can no longer think in

Spanish, what is the language of his confession? How can he declare in Spanish, and particularly in an elegant, cultivated Spanish, his linguistic ineptness? Who is in command here, language or its speaker? In a well-known passage from *S/Z*, Roland Barthes has remarked that one defining characteristic of modern literature is the reader's inability to answer the question, who speaks? (p. 140). This is precisely the conundrum of *Juan Criollo*, a novel where the protagonist's grammatical person clashes with his authorial persona. But in *Los pasos perdidos* the question is perhaps more disquieting: not, *who* speaks?, but rather, *what* is spoken? It is not the status of the subject that is put into doubt, but that of his language, which antecedes and constitutes him.

I do not pose these questions in order to highlight an inconsistency in the novel, a kind of *olvido carpenteriano* reminiscent of Cervantes's famous slips. I believe, on the contrary, that the linguistic inconsistency of the narration is perfectly consistent with other aspects of the novel, and that it can be assimilated into a coherent reading. The task of interpreting *Los pasos perdidos*, a work so full of transparent symbols, so susceptible to broad and easy allegories, is not unlike the mission undertaken by the protagonist, who insists on "reading" the jungle by casting his experience in scriptive and literary terms. If the protagonist is the reader's stand-in, however, the reader should perhaps beware of losing himself in a forest of symbols, in Carpentier's wild and wily *selva de varia lección*. Before imposing an allegorizing grid (of whatever persuasion: Jungian, Freudian, Marxist) on the events in the text, one needs to place the protagonist's language. What the novel requires, in the first instance, is not allegory but literalism. As a first step toward interpreting the protagonist's journey, one must understand his language. The question that *Los pasos perdidos* addresses to its readers is also embarrassingly direct, and it can be phrased quite simply: do you read me?

This question can be approached, if not answered, by inquiring into the protagonist's stance as narrator. As we saw when discussing *Juan Criollo*, the prominent structural feature of first-person accounts is the protagonist's division into a narrating self and an experiencing self, an "I" who narrates and another "I" who plays a part in the events narrated.[3] Even if autobiography is technically defined by the "identity" of narrator and protagonist, for the narration to take place this identity must be fractured. As Jean Starobinski has explained, the narrating-I is never "identical" with the acting-I (*La Relation critique*, p. 83). The autobiographical subject necessarily looks upon his past as another, as a being whose similarity to the narrating-I may be tenuous indeed. For this reason, it may be more apt to speak of "continuity" rather than "identity" when discussing the doubleness of the autobiographical subject. What an autobiography supposes is not the identity of author and actor but their continuity; it supposes that, with the passage of time and the unfolding of the narrative, the latter will merge into the former; and in effect one of the essential plotlines of an auto-biographical narrative is to retrace the steps that have led the protagonist from character to narrator.

Because of this structural schism, the plot of an autobiography is always double, since the reader's attention can focus on the act of narration or on the events in the plot. In an autobiography there is always another story: the story of how the story gets told. In *Tristram Shandy*, to give an obvious example, the behind-the-scenes story is at least as important as the episodes from Tristram's past; the novel's temporal frame continuously oscillates between the time of writing, the world of Tristram as author, and the time of the plot, the world of Tristram as actor. But what happens in *Los pasos perdidos* is that the story of the story's composition is systematically suppressed. The scene of writing is hidden behind the plot scenery, for the protagonist tends to cover up the structural schism that makes possible the autobiographical act. Using resources that we will discuss shortly, Carpentier's narrator tries to make us forget – and perhaps tries to make himself forget – his authorial role. As actor, he is everywhere; as author, even though he must also be ubiquitous, he refuses to show his face. Except for a couple of passages that I will mention later, the act of narration remains invisible throughout the novel. To put it in the Sartrean terminology of which Carpentier was so fond: the one thing in *Los pasos perdidos* that lacks a context is the act of narration, the originating event that makes everything else possible.[4] In this sense Carpentier's novel, like Rodríguez's *Ciénaga*, is a groundless verbal edifice, a *civitas verbi* without foundations.

This dissembling creates the impression that the novel goes

without saying, that by the time of writing it has already been told or written. It is as if the events of the journey were contemporaneous with their telling, thus obviating the need for retrospective recollection by a temporally and spatially distant narrator. The contrast with other Spanish-language autobiographies is instructive. In *Lazarillo de Tormes* the reader finds out in the prologue that Lázaro writes for "Your Grace," who has demanded an account of his "case."[5] In Cela's *Pascual Duarte* we know that Pascual writes his memoirs in jail as he awaits execution for the murders he has committed. In both instances the protagonist–narrator details the circumstances of the act of narration. (Pascual even provides information on his writing implements, his work habits, and the cell from which he writes.) In these works the double focus of autobiography – on the plot and its telling – is plainly visible. But in *Los pasos perdidos*, since the protagonist refuses to show his authorial face, the reader knows next to nothing about the context of the story's composition. Whatever the protagonist reveals has to do with his experiencing self rather than with his narrating self; the act of narrating gets lost in the jungle of the events narrated. Like the recessed Vs on the tree that mark the way to Santa Mónica de los Venados, the novel's first-person account seems authorless, unsituated, as much a part of nature as the tree itself.

One can say, then, that *Los pasos perdidos* is an elliptical autobiography, a first-person account that elides one of autobiography's twin foci. This elision (or better, effect of elision) is accomplished through various means, two of which are the use of the historical present and the insertion of a "diary" into the account. The constant use of the historical present actualizes past events, presenting them as if they were contemporaneous with their narration. When the narrator states, "El fraile señala con el bastón nudoso: 'Allí viven los únicos indios perversos y sanguinarios que hay en estas regiones,' dice" ["The friar points with his cane: 'The only perverse and blood-thirsty Indians in these regions live there,' he says"] (p. 266), the historical or retrospective present tense places us in the jungle, witnessing the priest's gesture and words as they transpire.[6] There is as little distance between us and Fray Pedro as there is between Fray Pedro and the cannibals. The deictic "Allí" ["There"] describes not only the cannibals' location but ours as well: we are there, in the thick of things, vicariously experiencing the vicissitudes of the characters.

By forging this sense of immediacy, the historical present tends to eliminate the distance between the tale and its telling. Abetting the false impression that action and redaction coincide, this tense actualizes the narrated past at the expense of the narrating present; we are induced to overlook the fact that the story is being told by someone somewhere far away from the jungle. (It is not incidental, thus, that in the sentence quoted above the only *dicendi* verb is attributed to the friar.) And yet, the distance between action and redaction could not be more pronounced, as one can see when the passage is quoted at greater length:

El fraile señala con el bastón nudoso: "Allí viven los únicos indios perversos y sanguinarios que hay en estas regiones," dice. Ningún misionero ha regresado de allá. Creo que, en aquel instante, me permití alguna burlona consideración sobre la inutilidad de aventurarse en tan ingratos parajes. En respuesta, dos ojos grises, inmensamente tristes, se fijaron en mí de manera singular, con una expresión a la vez tan intensa y resignada, que me sentí desconcertado, preguntándome si les había causado algún enojo, aunque sin hallar los motivos de tal enojo. Todavía veo el semblante arrugado del capuchino.

[The friar points with his cane: "The only perverse and blood-thirsty Indians in these regions live there," he says. None of the missionaries who have gone there have returned. I believe that, at that moment, I allowed myself some mocking remark about the uselessness of venturing into such thankless places. In reply, two immensely sad grey eyes fixed on me in a singular manner, with such an intense and resigned look that I felt disconcerted, asking myself whether I had made him angry, although I could not find the reason. I can still see the friar's wrinkled face.]   (p. 266)

Marking the distance that disjoins the narration from the narrating, *énoncé* from *énonciation*, the deictic *aquel* – "en aquel instante" ["at that moment"] – shatters the impression of immediacy created in the preceding sentences. The reader then realizes that the present tense of the verb "creo" refers *not* to the protagonist as actor but to his narratorial persona; the assertion of belief belongs to a time-frame outside the events in the jungle. The same thing happens with the "todavía veo" ["I can still see"] of the last sentence, since the person who still sees the eyes that watch him is not the acting-I but the narrating-I. Significantly, the verbs between "creo" and "todavía veo" are not in the present but in the preterite: "me permití ... se fijaron ... me sentí." By framing the thoughts and actions of the acting-I in the past tense and those of the narrating-I in the present tense, the protagonist here clearly distinguishes between his role as actor and author. At the same time, by prefacing one of the perceptions of his narrating-self with the durative *todavía*, he points to the continuity between his two identities. Observing distinctions that the rest of the narration tends to blur, this passage is one of the rare moments of narrative truth in the story, one of the few occasions when the reader can fix *his* gaze on the narrator. Here the protagonist slips out of character, as it were, for he lets us get a glimpse of his life outside of the narrated events.

The larger context in which these words appear also deserves some comment, since this incident is part of the supposed travel diary of the protagonist. And I say "supposed" because the injection into this paragraph of a time-frame posterior to the trip (the time of writing, the "true" present) shows that the diary cannot be a diary; it cannot be a transcription, *in situ*, of the events of the trip. In a true diary, *énoncé* and *énonciation* are contiguous. As Gerald Prince has shown, the fundamental generic feature of the diary novel is its insistence on the daily routine of fragmentarily jotting down of events as they happen ("The diary novel: notes for the definition of a sub-genre," pp. 477–478). But in Carpentier's novel, in spite of the careful dating of the manuscript, there are no such markers, and the only references to the act of writing point to a single, deferred reconstruction of events. Furthermore, in the narrator's repeated references to the lack of paper and pencil in the jungle, the diary acknowledges its own impossibility. The narrator repeatedly complains that he has no paper on which to write the score of his Threnody; and yet these complaints are recorded in a diary. The only conclusion is that the "diary," like the narration as a whole, is nothing other than a retrospective fiction, a reconstruction undertaken much after the fact. When he labels his text a diary, the narrator makes a category mistake, for his work is not a "diary" but a "memoir."

This conclusion has an important corollary: the dates in the diary, about which so much has been written, must *also* be retrospective.[7] No matter how we may interpret the apparent inconsistencies in the dates, we have to remember that these "mistakes" are committed not by the acting-I but by the narrating-I, that they are produced by someone who, far away from the jungle and unable to return, attempts to transit in words the path that has been physically closed. In the diary, verbal passages have replaced jungle passages, for the diary is nothing more than this: a "passage" that opens the way to Santa Mónica. Like the persistent use of the historical present, the fiction of the diary aims to create a spurious immediacy to American reality. The diary lets the narrator claim that his trip has not been fruitless. Even if he comes away without the instruments he was asked to find, he has returned with an eye-witness account of the trip. As in Guillén's madrigal, he wants his words to be "signos de selva" ["signs of the jungle"]. But this impression of authenticity disappears when the reader pauses to reflect on what he is reading or seeing.

Something similar can be said about the numerous epigraphs that punctuate the narrator's account. In a novel narrated by an undramatized narrator, by someone who is not also a character (the kind of narrative voice most typical of Carpentier's fictions), the attribution of epigraphs is a complicated question, for they could represent the viewpoint of the author, of the narrator, or even of one or several of the characters. In an autobiography or a diary novel, however, the epigraphs are usually attributable to the narrator–protagonist. This is especially so when, as in Carpentier's novel, the body of the narration reprises the quotations. That is to say, Carpentier's narrator is *aware* of his epigraphs, which he exploits in the body of his account for the purposes of thematic iteration or structural parallelism. In fact one could argue that the epigraphs are "windows" through which the narrator becomes visible, since his choice of quotations implies an interpretation of the plot. Those fragments from Deuteronomy or Shelley or Quevedo or the Chilam Balam sketch the narrator's reading of his past, a reading that, even if it is filtered through other texts, captures his voice and his perspective. Since the protagonist has elected to dissemble his participation as author, the epigraphs give him an alternate outlet for his editorializing. And what is significant is that these epigraphic quotations imply a reading of the trip entirely consistent with that proposed by the protagonist-as-actor. In the majority of cases, the epigraphs do nothing more than anticipate or corroborate the protagonist's discoveries as he immerses himself in the jungle, discoveries that have been shown to be, at best, superficial.[8] The epigraphs contain a retrospective assessment that, strangely enough, has not benefited from hindsight or distance. Once again the impression is that there is no distinction, in knowledge or perspective, between the protagonist's two roles. The narrating self does nothing more than confirm the validity of the insights achieved by the experiencing self.

We can contrast this complicity with the situation that obtains in the only other passage where the protagonist lets us catch him in the act of narration:

Al cabo de un tiempo cuya medida escapa, ahora, a mis nociones – por una aparente brevedad de transcurso en un proceso de dilatación y recurrencia que entonces me hubiera sido insospechable –, recuerdo esas gotas cayendo sobre mi piel en deleitosos alfilerazos, como si hubiesen sido la advertencia primera – ininteligible para mí, entonces – del encuentro.

[At the end of a time whose duration now escapes me – because of its apparent brevity in a process of dilation and recurrence that I could not have suspected then –, I remember those drops falling on my skin like pleasant pin-pricks, as if they had been the first signal – unintelligible for me, at that time – of the meeting.]   (p. 78)

Since this statement not only juxtaposes the "now" of writing with the "then" of the narrated past but also shows the epistemological yield of time and distance, it accurately renders the autobiographical situation. The decisive difference between the protagonist's two selves is that the writing-I understands things beyond the grasp of the acting-I. The phrase – "ininteligible para mí, entonces" ["unintelligible for me, at that time"] – captures the essential movement of the autobiographical act. The subject of an autobiography turns toward the past precisely in search of epiphanies like this one. But excepting the two passages I have mentioned, in *Los pasos perdidos* these epiphanies do not take place. The locus of lucidity does not shift, as it should, from actor to narrator. For the protagonist of this novel, the act of narration leads not to the discovery of the unknown but to the corroboration of the already known, a position strikingly at odds with Carpentier's own view of narration as an epistemological instrument ("Problemática de la actual novela latinoamericana," pp. 7–8).

One last resource that contributes to the dissimulation of the act of narration emerges from the nature of the protagonist's discoveries as he goes back to his continent of origin. Frequently these discoveries consist in the recuperation – usually prompted by some visual, auditive, olfactory stimulus – of a forgotten incident or object from his childhood. As a result, in addition to the division into a narrating present and a narrated past, the novel contains another temporal schism, this one entirely contained within the *énoncé*. The acting-I, anticipating the retrospective gesture that will produce the narration, also turns back to his past. Just as the protagonist-as-author relives the trip to the jungle, the protagonist-as-actor relives his childhood (and, at times, the infancy of humanity itself, since his flashbacks often have a collective dimension). The novel contains three distinct time-frames: the present of writing; the past of the narration; and the "pluperfect" of the narration, the past before the past, a kind of anterior past or "antepasado" (which includes the world of the protagonist's forebears). The preponderance of these two pasts and their complex interrelationship, together with the habitual use of the historical present and the fake diary, create the impression that the events in the jungle are being told as they happen, that there is no time or distance between the tale and its telling.

This relativizing process is evident already in the novel's first sentence: "Hacía cuatro años y siete meses que no había vuelto a ver la casa de columnas blancas, con su frontón de ceñudas molduras que le daban una severidad de palacio de justicia, y ahora, ante muebles y trastos colocados en su lugar invariable, tenía la penosa sensación de que el tiempo se hubiera revertido" ["For four years and seven months I had not seen the house with the white columns, with the grim mouldings that gave it the severity of a courthouse, and now, confronted by furniture and trinkets placed in their usual place, I had the painful sensation that time had turned back"] (p. 67). Two different pasts appear in this sentence: the more remote one is rendered by verbs in the pluperfect tense – "no había vuelto a ver" – the other one is rendered by verbs in the imperfect – "tenía." What is significant is that the moment corresponding to the imperfect is assimilated to the present – "y ahora, ante muebles y trastos ... tenía la penosa sensación" ["and now, confronted by furniture and trinkets ... I had the painful sensation"], etc. The "now" in this sentence designates a spurious present, since the true present is that implicit in the use of the imperfect tense. All throughout the novel these deceptive "nows" proliferate.[9] The true present, of course, is the *hic et nunc* of writing, the "now" from which the narrator looks back in order to reconstruct the events of that Sunday. The novel as a whole turns on these two "reversions," one tending to mask the other. The first consists in a retrocession from a less to a more remote past, as in the passage just quoted. The second "reversion," inevitable but invisible, is that implied in the motions of the autobiographical act, motions disguised from the opening sentence, which even creates the momentary impression that the novel is told in the third person.

Once again, the contrast with other autobiographies is striking. *La familia de Pascual Duarte* begins: "Yo, señor, no soy malo, aunque no me faltarían motivos para serlo" ["I, sir, am not evil, though not for lack of motives"]; *Lazarillo de Tormes* begins: "Pues, sepa vuestra merced ante todas cosas que a mí me llaman Lázaro de Tormes, hijo de Tomé González y de Antoña Pérez, naturales de Tejares, aldea de Salamanca" ["Well, I want Your Grace to know first of all that I am Lázaro de Tormes, son of Tomé González and Antoña Pérez, natives of Tejares, a town in Salamanca"].[10] In both of these works the protagonist–narrator goes on stage from the first. But in *Los pasos perdidos* Carpentier's protagonist hides in the wings, deferring his *mise en scène*. It is significant, therefore, that the opening sentences describe a stage from which, as the play commences, the narrator withdraws: "A tiempo salí de la luz, pues sonó el disparo del cazador y un pájaro cayó en escena desde el segundo tercio de las bambalinas" ["I left the spotlight just in time, because the hunter's shot rang out and a bird fell on the stage from the second drop"] (p. 68). This reluctance to occupy the spotlight will characterize his narrative stance throughout the rest of the novel. Only in the two passages discussed above does the narrator, like the bird shot in the opening of the play, emerge from the wings.

Eduardo González, who has remarked on the importance of these two passages, calls their temporal frame the "present of composition" (*Alejo Carpentier: El tiempo del hombre*, p. 149). I have preferred to speak of a "present of writing," since González's formulation, because of the musical resonance of "composition," lends itself better to designating the historical present, the time spent in the jungle, which is where the protagonist finds the inspiration to compose the Threnody. As we have seen, this historical present differs sharply from the present of writing, the point from which the narrator looks back to reconstruct his adventures. On the one hand, there is the present of writing, which designates the moment of *énonciation*; on the other, the present of composition, which covers the adventures in the jungle. The narrator's divided stance can be summarized in this opposition between "composition" and "writing," between the immediacy of the Threnody, which is born in the jungle, and the secondariness of writing, which aspires to recover or resurrect a past and a place that are lost forever. For the protagonist the Threnody arises from direct and contemporaneous experience; as a creation in close touch with its sources and inspiration, it embodies the immediacy and efficacy desired for the retrospective account, whose goal is also to call the dead back to life (according to the protagonist's theory, this was originally the purpose of a threnody [p. 276]). But the Threnody is not only composed in the jungle but also stays there, since the protagonist leaves the incomplete score behind. Writing, on the contrary, does not enjoy that privileged intimacy with American nature. The contrast is stark: on the one hand, the immediacy of the musical score; on the other, the alienation of writing. In the jungle, the protagonist does not write, he composes. Outside of it, he writes, wishing he could compose. And the narrator's project is simply this: to claim for his text the status of his composition. All of the narrative maneuvers we have discussed endeavor to disguise the fact that the narrator's account is a deferred and displaced act of recall, and thus not directly in touch with the world it inscribes.

Los pasos perdidos is a Threnody that has lost its composure, a "decomposed" Threnody, as it were, a failed attempt to transform the *libro* into a *libretto*.[11] And the narrator's essential ploy in carrying out of this forgery is the suppression of the structural properties of first-person accounts. When he arrives in Santa Mónica, he states, "Pasaron los tiempos de las estafas" ["Gone are the times of forgeries"] (p. 282). Although this assertion reflects his sanguine mood at the time, it fails to do justice to his attitude as narrator, since his narration is indeed a forgery, an *estafa* whose fundamental ruse lies in the manipulation of time. Strictly speaking, the historical present is indeed the grammatical "tiempo de la estafa." Among the innumerable objects described or mentioned in the novel, there are some that symbolize this textual forgery. I am thinking of those fake instruments that, according to Mouche, a friend could contrive:

unos instrumentos "primitivos" – cabales, científicos, fidedignos – irreprochablemente ejecutados, de acuerdo con mis bocetos y medidas, por el pintor amigo, gran aficionado a las artes primitivas, y tan diabólicamente hábil en trabajos de artesanía, copia y reproducción, que vivía de falsificar estilos maestros.

[some "primitive" instruments – accurate, scientific, faithful – irreproachably made, according to my drawings and specifications, by her friend the painter, a great aficionado of primitive art, and so diabolically talented in the craft of copying and reproducing, that he made his living by falsifying the styles of the masters.] (pp. 98–99)

In spite of the repugnance that the narrator feels toward Mouche's suggestion – "la estafa imaginada por mi amiga" ["the forgery thought up by my friend"] (p. 140) – his story is not unlike one of those instruments that would have borne witness to his presence in the jungle. And his recounting, therefore, is no less phony than the "novel" Mouche makes up about the trip (p. 303) or the one that he himself plans to invent for the newspapers (p. 300).

The linguistic indecision of the novel, with which I began my discussion, can now be understood as part of the protagonist's vexed authorial stance. The clash between Threnody and text, between composition and writing, also encompasses the linguistic antinomy. As we have just seen, the tacit model for the retrospective account is the Threnody. The Threnody, nonetheless, is composed from a Spanish translation of the *Odyssey*. Should one read this as a covert insinuation that the novel itself should be read as a translation? This possibility, which accords with the suggestion that the novel is made up, at least in part, of the protagonist's newspaper articles,[12] finds corroboration of a sort in the novel's title, which is *also* a translation (of Breton's *Les Pas perdus*). If this were so, the novel's "original" would have been written in a language other than Spanish, most probably English, and we would have to posit the intervention of an invisible translator or "second author," as in *Don Quijote*.

As I have already said, this possibility is dubious for thematic reasons. But there is also a detail at the beginning of the thirtieth subchapter that seems to foreclose this option. Trying to decide whether to compose his Threnody using *Prometheus Unbound* as the "book," the protagonist comments:

Ciertos versos que ahora recuerdo, hubieran correspondido admirablemente a mi deseo de trabajar sobre un texto hecho de palabras simples y directas ... Y luego, esos coros de montañas, de manantiales, de tormentas: de elementos que me rodean y siento. Esa voz de la tierra, que es Madre a la vez, arcilla y matriz, como las Madres de Dioses que aún reinan en la selva. Y esas "perras del infierno" – *hounds of hell* – que irrumpen en el drama y aúllan con más acento de ménade que de furia.

[Certain verses that I now remember would have suited admirably my desire to work on a text made of simple and direct words ... And then, those choruses of mountains, of streams, of storms: of elements that surround me and that I can feel. This voice of the earth, which is also a Mother, clay and womb, like the Mothers of the Gods who still reign in the jungle. And those "hounds of hell" that spring into the play and howl with an accent more reminiscent of a maenad than of a fury.]   (p. 276–277)

The first words of this quotation offer still another illustration of the actualization of the past through the use of the historical present and a misleading deictic: "ahora recuerdo" ["now I remember"]. In point of fact, underlying this mnemonic act is another unacknowledged mnemonic act: the narrator's memory of remembering. A more comprehensive and exact phrasing would be: "ahora recuerdo que entonces recordé" ["now I remember that then I remembered"]. But this nuancing, of course, would destroy the impression of immediacy that the narrator tries so hard to sustain.

The phrase that I want to highlight, however, is the English phrase in the last sentence – "hounds of hell." This interpolation is crucial because it shows that the text has been thought, has been written, in Spanish. Otherwise, either the English phrase would not appear (having disappeared in the translation into Spanish of the English "original"), or the Spanish translation – "perras del infierno" – would itself not appear, as actually happens in the English translation of the novel. The insertion of the English original after the Spanish equivalent shows that Spanish is the text's matrix, its language of origin, its "mother tongue." The irruption of the "hounds of hell" betrays the Spanishness of the narrator's language, the unlikely fact that he has given his account in a language that, by his own admission, he does not command. Shelley's hounds do indeed howl with an "accent," one that roots the narrator's idiolect in the maternal "voice of the earth."

And yet, a few sentences later he makes the following observation about the possibility of composing the Threnody from a Spanish text: "Nunca había pensado en componer música para poema alguno escrito en ese idioma que, por sí mismo, constituiría un eterno obstáculo a la ejecución de una obra coral en cualquier gran centro artístico" ["I had never thought of composing music for any poem written in that language that, in and of itself, would constitute an eternal obstacle to the performance of a choral work in any great artistic center"] (p. 277). "*Ese* idioma," he says, "*that* language," as if he were speaking of a language other than that in which his sentence is uttered. At this point, true to his biography, the narrator treats Spanish with the distance imposed by his many years of residence abroad. But this distance is inconsistent with the earlier interpolation, which took Spanish for granted. Even as he weaves his account in Spanish, the narrator thinks of "that language" as if it were a foreign tongue. Spanish is and isn't his language, is and isn't the language of his account.

We are thus led back to the narrator's version of Borges's antinomy: "¿Cuál era mi idioma verdadero?" ["What was my true language?"] (p. 277). In the end both the protagonist and his language remain anonymous. One might say that what happens in the novel *no tiene nombre* – an expression that conveys both the namelessness of the narrator's idiolect and the perplexity this engenders. Although the narrator insists that the task of the Spanish-American writer is to give names, to baptize a virgin reality, the language of his names is itself nameless. He speaks a no-man's language, a hypothetical *interlingua* suspended between Spanish and English. As in the first two epigraphs at the threshold of this book, Carpentier's narrator has neither a mother tongue nor an other tongue, neither a native language nor a foreign one. The narration not only dissembles its point of origin – the here and now of writing; it also dissembles its language, the very stuff from which it is made. Lacking a proper name, the narrator's speech becomes another fiction: the hollow sound of a bogus instrument.

The issue comes back to "phoniness," a word I want to invest with a phony phonic sense, using it to summarize the novel's linguistic predicament. In *Los pasos perdidos*, Carpentier has written a complicated, arresting, and utterly "phony" novel. And since the issue is phoniness, let us not forget the semantic echoes of the Spanish *estafa*, a word that, as we have just seen, has a significant role in the novel. According to Corominas (*Breve diccionario etimológico de la lengua castellana*, p. 253), *estafa* derives from the Germanic word *Staffa*, which means "pisada, paso" (hence the Spanish "estafeta," courier, and the English "step"). The real lost steps, the really lost steps, are those that would have led from the plot to the plotting, from the action to the redaction, from the composition to the text, from a virtual speech to a true language. Because of the narrator's evasiveness, what is finally lost is the novel itself – that copious flood of words that, like that other flood that bars passage to Santa Mónica, hides the place of an inscription.

But where does this leave Cuban criollism? Nowhere and everywhere, like the protagonist's Spanish. I read *Los pasos perdidos* as the closing episode in the Cuban criollist project. For me, the protagonist's search for primitive instruments, which recalls Ortiz's monumental research on the equally primitive instruments of Afro-Cuban music, is a moving emblem of criollism's search for a vernacular culture. The plot of the novel *is* the criollist adventure. Thus, if conceptually and historically Cuban criollism begins with Ortiz going into the black neighborhoods of Guanabacoa in order to collect items for his dictionaries, it concludes with Carpentier's protagonist, holed up in a room somewhere in New York, trying to recapture in uncertain words his experience of *lo criollo*. If Ortiz took the first steps, Carpentier's protagonist takes the last, lost steps.

I do not believe (I choose not to believe) that this reading of criollism is primarily a product of my own cultural embedding. I do not think (I prefer not to think) that mine is an anachronistically modern reading of an anachronistically premodern canon. I have claimed just the opposite, in fact: the historical specificity of these works *demands* the kind of reading I have given them. The seeds of alienation were there from the start, for Cuban criollism was always perceived as a precarious enterprise. This precariousness was expressed by different writers in different ways: Marinello expressed it in the paradox of a native foreign language; Mañach expressed it in the epigram of a nation without nationhood; Ortiz celebrated it in the heterogeneity of the *ajiaco*; Guillén put it to music in Petrarchan *sones* and mulatto madrigals; Florit cerebralized it in Gongorine *décimas*; Rodríguez condemned it in the metaphor of an "inconsistent earth." What these varying formulations share is a problematic, critical assessment of the possibilities of nativism in an island without natives. Knowing that in Cuba transience precedes essence, these writers take their distance from the foundational gestures typical of the criollist program. Cuban criollism is rootless, unearthly, movable – translational rather than foundational. Which engenders another paradox: in Cuba, nativist literature shades into its opposite, the literature of exile. Inconsistent Cuba: an island without a ground.

For Carpentier's protagonist, as for me, the congenital inconsistency of Cuban criollism, indeed the congenital inconsistency of Cuban culture, culminates in a linguistic antinomy, in a painful but productive indecision between the mother tongue and the other tongue. At the risk of mystifying, I want to say that there is something profoundly *criollo* in the fate of Carpentier's protagonist, living in a North American city, forced to express himself in a native language that is not his own. The fate of the Cuban writer, the feat of the Cuban writer, has always been to speak in other words. Cuban *voces*: other voices. In translation, the Cuban writer finds, and keeps, his word.

Notes

All translations from the Spanish are my own. Full bibliographic information for the works cited in the text and notes is provided in the concluding bibliography.

Introduction: In other words

1 Mañach, *Historia y estilo*, p. 113. Other page references are given in the text.
2 Fernando Ortiz's phrasing, in *Contrapunteo cubano del tabaco y el azúcar*, p. 133: "No hubo factores humanos más trascendentes para la cubanidad que esas continuas, radicales y contrastantes transmigraciones geográficas, económicas y sociales de los pobladores; que esa perenne transitoriedad de los propósitos y que esa vida siempre en desarraigo de la tierra habitada, siempre en desajuste con la sociedad sustentadora. Hombres, economías, culturas y anhelos todo aquí se sintió foráneo, provisional, cambiadizo, 'aves de paso' sobre el país, a su costa, a su contra y a su malgrado." This passage will be discussed in chapter 1.
3 It might be well to point out at this juncture that I do not intend to decide on the theoretical soundness of the notion of a "national culture" or a "Cuban character." For me, it is enough that the concept has historical validity. Regardless of what we may think today about the usefulness of these notions, the writers I will be discussing habitually thought in terms of Cuba's "national character" or "national culture."
4 The interest in linguistic research extended to writers whose principal work was done in other fields; thus, for example, Juan Marinello compiled an addendum to Ortiz's list, "Un guacalito de cubanismos" (1926), published in *Archivos del Folklore Cubano*.
5 The term *mundonovismo* was coined by the Chilean writer Francisco Contreras; it appears in his novel, *El pueblo maravilloso* (1927) as well as in his *Le Mundonovisme* (1917). On *criollismo* as a literary term, see, among many others, Rufino Blanco Fombona, "El criollismo"; Félix Lizaso, "Criollismo literario"; and Ricardo A. Latcham, "La querella del criollismo." On the history of the word *criollo* the best guide is José Juan Arrom, "Criollo: Definición y matices de un concepto." For the sake of onomastic convenience, I will anglicize the word and speak of "criollism" and of "criollist" writers. (The cognate English word, "creole," has a range of meaning that exceeds that of *criollismo* as a literary term.) I also prefer to speak of criollism as a "moment" rather than as a "movement," since the latter implies a coordination of effort that belies the variety and dispersion of the

literature. Although these writers espoused similar views, they did not form part of a "movement" in any significant sense of the word.

6 See Vargas Llosa, "Primitives and creators" and "The Latin American novel today." Recently there have been some interesting attempts to revise our understanding of criollism, Carlos Alonso's unpublished dissertation, "The *novela de la tierra*: the discourse of the autochthonous," and Roberto González Echevarría's "Doña Bárbara writes the plain." Although I have learned from both Alonso and González Echevarría, my own argument heads in a different direction.

7 Vargas Llosa, "Primitives and creators," p. 1287.

8 I am quoting from the first edition (1927), p. 137.

1 Mr. Cuba

1 Raimundo Lazo typically remarks: "A lo largo de su prolongada vida Ortiz ha construido una especie de enciclopedia de asuntos culturales, ya generales o especializados, en que Cuba y sus problemas forman el núcleo principal." (*La literatura cubana*, p. 214). According to Julio Le Riverend, "El enciclopedismo fue una característica de su actividad desde el inicio. Fenómeno hispánico, o también cubano, este del hombre universal dentro de ciertos campos afines, como resultado quizás del retardo en seguir las tendencias modernas a la especialización. Pensamos en Ortiz como podemos hacerlo en un Joaquín Costa que él todavía en sus años de superior madurez admiraba sin reservas. Y su biografía revela esta propensión a saberlo todo" (from Le Riverend's prologue to *Orbita de Fernando Ortiz*, p. 19).

2 For the former, see "La 'tragedia' de los ñáñigos" (1950); for the latter, *El huracán. Su mitología y sus símbolos* (1947).

3 Liborio was a folkloric character, popular in the early part of this century, who was used as a symbol of the Cuban people. See Adelaida de Juan, *Caricatura de la República*, pp. 7–86.

4 Juan Marinello, "Don Fernando Ortiz. Notas sobre nuestro tercer descubridor" and Lino Novás Calvo, "Mister Cuba." The Portuguese version of this article appeared under the title "Cuba em pessoa"; the Spanish version was called "Cubano de tres mundos." The notion that Ortiz is Cuba's "third discoverer" has even infiltrated tourist literature; in *Hildebrand's Travel Guide: Cuba*, right after a discussion of "Sunburn and socialism," one finds a section devoted to "The three discoverers of Cuba" (Columbus, Humboldt, and Ortiz), where Ortiz is credited with having made the "process of cultural integration . . . part of the national consciousness" (p. 73).

5 "Ortiz hizo familiar, cotidiana, la noción de mestizaje nacional, y fijó para siempre el carácter de nuestra cultura, partiendo de un punto de vista estrictamente científico" (Guillén, "Ortiz: Misión cumplida," pp. 5–6). Along the same lines, Fernando G. Campoamor remarks, "Tenemos ahora arquitectura, canto sobre canto, porque Ortiz nos encontró piedra y argamasa. Sabemos quiénes somos, porque Ortiz nos identificó . . . Afirmamos, sin asomo de hipérbole, que es la suma de la cultura insular" ("Don Fernando Ortiz, el Maestro fuerte," p. 225).

6 See "Por la integración cubana de blancos y negros." This was originally a speech delivered before the Club Atenas, a black society, on the occasion of Ortiz's induction as an honorary member.

7 Typical of the way Ortiz is generally seen is the following statement by Julio Le

Riverend, "Su mensaje intemporal, que debemos recoger entero, es el de la ciencia como requisito indispensable del progreso verdadero" (from the prologue to *Orbita de Fernando Ortiz*, p. 50). For a useful overview of Ortiz's life and work, see the two essays by Salvador Bueno, "Don Fernando Ortiz: Al servicio de la Ciencia y de Cuba" and "Aproximaciones a la vida y la obra de Fernando Ortiz." Also worth reading is Alberto Gutiérrez de la Solana's, "En torno a Fernando Ortiz, lo afrocubano y otros ensayos." But little of substance has actually been written about Ortiz. The most complete bibliography is Araceli García-Carranza's *Bio-bibliografía de don Fernando Ortiz*.

8 One should also remember Ortiz's influence on such writers as Alejo Carpentier and José Lezama Lima, for which see Roberto González Echevarría, *Alejo Carpentier: The Pilgrim at Home* and "Lo cubano en *Paradiso*." In *La música en Cuba*, Carpentier mentions Ortiz's influence on writers of his generation (pp. 306–307).

9 *Guayaba* in the sense of "lie" or "deceit" is not, however, exclusively a cubanism, since the word is used with this meaning in the rest of the hispanophone Caribbean as well as in some parts of Central and South America. This usage goes back at least to the middle of the last century, as is shown by the following lines from Estanislao del Campo's *Fausto* (1866):

– ¡Bien haiga gaucho embustero!
¿Sabe que no me esperaba
que soltase una guayaba
de ese tamaño, aparcero?

To this Cuban reader, finding this species of *guayaba* in the mouth of a gaucho is a somewhat unsettling experience.

10 My metaphor is not gratuitous; compare the following from *La africanía de la música folklórica de Cuba*: "Ciertos aspectos de este estudio para alumnos estarán algo 'sobretrabajados,'" como se dice ahora, y con páginas demasiado rellenas de datos y opiniones ajenas. De esta manera el lector podrá hallar en nuestra monografía mejores sustancias y sabores que los de nuestra casera elaboración, como pasta de guayaba hecha con azúcar sin refinar pero mechada con finas jaleas" (p. xv).

11 Remarking on the naiveté of the typical criollist writer, Carpentier states, "Cree que con haber asistido a una fiesta típica ha entendido los móviles, las razones remotas, de lo que ha visto. Y la verdad es que no ha entendido, acaso, que tal fase de un baile folklórico es el estado presente de un antiquísimo rito solar o de liturgias tónicas que – como ha sido demostrado muy recientemente al estudiarse prácticas de la 'santería' cubana – habían viajado del Mediterráneo al Nuevo Continente pasando por el Africa" ("Problemática de la actual novela latinoamericana," p. 10). The reference here is to Ortiz's work on Afro-Cuban religious rituals, as is made clear a few pages later when Ortiz is mentioned by name (p. 28).

12 The documentary and even theoretical base of Carpentier's essay, insofar as it discusses Cuban folklore, seems to derive largely from Ortiz, as is suggested by the references to the *ajiaco* (p. 30), the *huracán* (p. 25), and *transculturación* (p. 30).

13 The essay in question is "Del fenómeno social de la 'transculturación' y de su importancia en Cuba," which was originally published in the *Revista Bimestre Cubana* (1940) and subsequently included in *Contrapunteo cubano del tabaco y el azúcar*, whose first edition dates also from 1940, the *annus mirabilis* in Ortiz's career. Here and elsewhere I will be quoting the essay from the Spanish edition

of the *Contrapunteo* (1973); all page references in my text to this book refer to this edition.

14 For the history of the term "acculturation," see Ralph Beals, "Acculturation"; also Gonzalo Aguirre Beltrán, *El proceso de aculturación*.

15 Angel Rama, arguing for the "felicity" of Ortiz's coinage, has recently resurrected the term in *Transculturación narrativa en América Latina* (see esp. pp. 32–33). But in general the word has not found favor with anthropologists.

16 A typical expression of this view: "Si las nacionalidades americanas están en diversos grados de formación – lo que es un hecho cierto – el criollo, que sería su producto representativo, ha de carecer de específica uniformidad como tipo. Pero eso no puede negar su realidad más o menos lograda, y, esencialmente, su realidad potencial" (Félix Lizaso, "Criollismo literario," p. 448).

17 Mañach, *Historia y estilo*, p. 64.

18 "El negro curro es el bastardo de Don Juan Tenorio con su negra esclava. Es la última y olvidada figura de la picaresca hispánica, que el hispalense Mateo Alemán habría llevado a la inmortalidad con sólo pintarla en la tercera parte de su *Guzmán de Alfarache*, si en 1608, al fondear en esta rada habanera la flota de barlovento, sus agobios pecuniarios no le hubieran privado de toda holganza en tierra y de curiosear el *vivío* criollo de los negros curros, hijos quizás de una *morena mondonguera* con aquel gran pícaro, que debió proceder a su narrador en su paso a las Indias" (Ortiz, "Los negros curros," p. 222).

19 See Ortiz's "Cubanidad y cubanía" (1964), which partially reprints the 1940 essay. This might be the appropriate place to mention that Ortiz's penchant for neologisms manifests itself in many other contexts which I cannot discuss here. The following excerpt, for example, is his explanation of the sigmoid designs in certain Indian figurines: "La posición de los brazos de la imagen es siempre rotatoria; pero, salvo en un caso, es hacia la izquierda o sea en sentido contrario a las vueltas de las manillas de un reloj, o sea del signo horario de las XII hacia la izquierda, hacia las VI. Es decir, en sentido *levógiro*, como dirían los físicos; *sinistrorsum*, como decían Plinio y otros clásicos; o *sinistroverso*, como puede ahora escribirse castellanizando el vocablo. Un movimiento opuesto al *dextrógiro*, *dextrorsum* o *dextroverso*" (from *El huracán. Su mitología y sus símbolos* [1947], p. 32).

20 Ortiz's involvement in his research extended to his personal life, as it was rumored that Ortiz himself had become an initiate in some of the Afro-Cuban rituals that he so intently studied. Whether this is true or not, there is no question that one can chart in Ortiz's career an increasing personal and methodological intimacy with his objects of study. Ortiz's earliest book on Afro-Cuban folklore, *Los negros brujos* (1906), shows a marked hostility toward Afro-Cuban culture. Written under the influence of the positivistic criminology of Cesare Lombroso and Enrico Ferri, this book recommends that Afro-Cuban religious practices be made illegal, since they are "repugnant," "nauseous," "savage," and "barbaric." As the years went by, however, his position evolved toward acceptance and even advocacy; the prosecutor had become proselytizer. In this connection, it is striking to contrast Ortiz's early views with the following passage from an article published in 1936: "Será obra de redención y justicia sacar de los templos escondidos esos coros rituales, esas prodigiosas orquestas de tambores clepsídricos de insuperable resonancia, esas mímicas sacras que reviven los cultos de la paganía pretérita aún estremecidas de pasión en la humanidad negra. Cuba tiene todavía un tesoro abandonado, por el blanco que lo ignora, por el negro que lo esconde, por el presuntuoso ignorantón que lo desprecia. Llegará, sin duda, su epifanía . . .

Cuando en el gran teatro de la Habana se canten en público los himnos sacros de Africa a toda orquesta de tambores, por un coro de los buenos cantadores y músicos, hembras y varones, de las capillas santeras y por un solista antifonal con relevante personalidad de mistagogo, aquel día al desarrollarse las teorías procesionales en el escenario quedará definitivamente libertado el espíritu negro todavía escondidizo, y, sólo entonces, ya sin ocultamientos ni recíprocas esquiveces, podrá pensarse en una completa armonización para la gran sinfonía cubana" ("Más acerca de la poesía mulata. Escorzos para su estudio," pp. 226–227).

2 The politics of enchantment

1 See Roberto González Echevarría, "The case of the speaking statue: *Ariel* and the magisterial rhetoric of the Latin American essay."

2 *La literatura cubana*, p. 209. Lazo is discussing the Cuban popular theater of the early decades of this century, in which the *vivo* was a recurring character. Unfortunately most of these plays, many of which were staged at the Teatro Alhambra (a theater for gentlemen only), have never been published. For more information, see José Juan Arrom, *Historia de la literatura dramática cubana*, pp. 89–90; Rine Leal, *Breve historia del teatro cubano*, pp. 108–116; and Eduardo Robreño, *Historia del teatro popular cubano*, pp. 35–39. Robreño, the son of Gustavo Robreño (1853–1957), one of the most popular authors and actors of the Alhambra company, has recently published a collection of plays staged at the Alhambra, *Teatro Alhambra: Antología*.

3 Fernando Ortiz, "No seas bobo," in *Entre cubanos*, pp. 17–20. As a concrete folkloric character, the *bobo* goes back to the nineteenth century, but he achieved greatest notoriety in the caricatures of Eduardo Abela, a political cartoonist who in the 1920s and 1930s used the so-called "bobo de Abela" as a foil for biting attacks against the Machado regime. See Adelaida de Juan, *Caricatura de la República*, pp. 87–236.

4 For the affinities between *El caballero encantado* and the Generation of 1898, see Gustavo Correa, *Realidad, ficción y símbolo en las novelas de Pérez Galdós*, pp. 231–241, and Julio Rodríguez-Puértolas, *Galdós: Burguesía y revolución*, pp. 144–164. Quotations from *El caballero encantado* will refer to Rodríguez-Puértolas's edition.

5 I will be quoting the novel from the book version (Havana, 1910). However, because the book was put together from extracts from the *Revista Bimestre Cubana*, the pagination is irregular and some pages lack numbers altogether.

6 In *La reconquista de América* Ortiz takes aim principally at two advocates of panhispanism, Rafael M. de Labra, the author of *Orientación americana de España* (1910), and Rafael Altamira, a professor of Law at the University of Oviedo and author of *España en América* (1908), among many other works. Curiously, *La reconquista de América* was also the title of Ramón Orbea's defense of panhispanism (1905). Ortiz's collection includes *El caballero encantado y la moza esquiva*, which had earlier been published separately. For much useful information on the panhispanic movement, see Frederick B. Pike, *Hispanismo. 1898–1936*.

7 For his characterization of Cynthia Ortiz seems to be drawing on the prototype of the *mujer esquiva*, a recurring character in Golden Age Spanish comedy (see Melveena McKendrick, "The *mujer esquiva* – a measure of the feminist sympathies of seventeenth-century Spanish dramatists"). The best-known instance of the type, however, is probably Cervantes's Marcela, who appears in *Don Quijote*, Part 1, ch. 14.

8 See Ortiz's *La reconquista de América*, p. 129. The phrase "la inmensa Hispania" was used by the poet Salvador Rueda in a poem entitled "Las nuevas espada," which he recited in a public reading in Havana in 1910.

9 See Rodríguez-Puertolas's introduction to his edition of the novel, p. 70.

10 The phrase is George Steiner's in *After Babel*, p. 26. Given the proliferation of masks and disguises in *El caballero encantado y la moza esquiva*, it might not be inappropriate to invoke here Severo Sarduy's theory and practice of dissimulation as it has been propounded in *La simulación* and other works. One might well wonder whether Ortiz's disappearing act is part of a certain tradition of invisibility or dissimulation in Cuban letters, a tradition whose founding father would be Manuel de Zequeira y Arango, the neo-classical poet who believed that he became invisible when he donned his hat (he would then become a founding father that could not be found: a confounding father), and whose best-known contemporary exponent would be Sarduy. I have discussed this idea in "La palabra invisible: Manuel de Zequeira y Arango en la literatura cubana."

3 Cuban counterpoint

1 The first edition of this book (1940) contains the titular essay and twenty-five "complementary chapters," the first of which explains the function of the complementary chapters. It also contains a "prologue" by Herminio Portell Vilá and an "introduction" by Bronislaw Malinowski. Subsequent editions, while leaving the principal essay essentially intact, either alter the number of additional chapters or include in them material not in the original version. The English translation (1947) contains twelve of the complementary chapters. The 1963 edition published by the Universidad Central de Las Villas contains the twenty-five additional chapters, some of which have been expanded, but not Portell Vilá's prologue (probably because Portell Vilá had by this time left the island); the posthumous edition prepared by Julio Le Riverend (1978) follows the 1963 edition, but adds a prologue and chronology by the editor. The Spanish edition (1973), from which I will be quoting, contains only seven of the complementary chapters. Ortiz's earliest discussion of the contrasts of tobacco and sugar is contained in a brief article published in 1936, "Contraste económico del azúcar y el tabaco."

2 In *El caballero encantado y la moza esquiva*, Ortiz also includes many references to the "poverty" of his language: "Y por ser mísera el habla del que va traduciendo, quede en la castiza forma galdosiana, el notable dicho de la Madre" (p. 45); or, "Muy sabrosas cosas pudiera referir aquí el que traduce, si tuviera ingenio para contarlas" (p. 42). This is obviously another pose, since lack of ingenuity was never one of Ortiz's problems.

3 According to the *Ad Herennium*, paralepsis occurs "when we say that we are passing by, or do not know, or refuse to say that which precisely we are now saying" (p. 321). Some of the other names for this figure are *praeteritio, occupatio*, and *occultatio*.

4 As quoted in Geoffrey Hartman, *Criticism in the Wilderness*, p. 193.

5 Harold Bloom's term, for which see *The Anxiety of Influence*, among many other works.

6 Ortiz is not entirely consistent in linking "darkness" and indigenousness, since on occasion he makes tobacco representative of the African component in Cuban culture, which is no less exogenous than the white. But in Cuban criollist literature of the 1920s and 1930s it is not unusual to regard the black as Cuba's

"Indian." As G. R. Coulthard remarks, "We have also observed an attempt, in Afro-Cubanism, to take the Negro as the basis for a sort of Caribbean indigenism. It is quite obvious that the Negro is no more 'indigenous' in Cuba, Haiti, Jamaica etc. than the white Creole; nevertheless he appears more distinctive, more typical, less European and more of the land, and he undeniably gives Caribbean life its particular tonality" (*Race and Colour in Caribbean Literature*, p. 117). Ortiz himself stated that "nuestro indio ha sido y es el negro" (as quoted in Fernando Romero, "Los *Estudios Afrocubanos* y el negro en la patria de Martí," p. 396). In part this privileging of the black component reflects a desire to correct the long-standing neglect of this aspect of Cuban culture. Nonetheless, there remains in some of Ortiz's work the tacit assumption that the black ingredients in the Cuban *ajiaco* are somehow more authentic, more "native," than the white. I think it is fair to say that Ortiz believed that much of what was most characteristic in Cuban culture was due to the black, rather than the European, influence; thus, for example, with Cuban popular music and with certain defining traits of the national character like *choteo*, which Ortiz regarded as an African inheritance.

7 For a recent discussion of the political and discursive implications of sugar production in Cuba, see Antonio Benítez Rojo, "Power / sugar / literature: toward a reinterpretation of Cubanness." Like Ortiz, Benítez Rojo sets up a binary opposition in which sugar occupies one of the two poles. For Benítez Rojo Cubanness arises from the interaction (Ortiz might have said *contrapunteo*) between the hegemonic discourse of sugar and "discourses of resistance."

8 Martí was referring to the custom of having someone read aloud while the tobacco workers made their cigars. These *lecturas de tabaquería* were responsible for raising the cultural level and political consciousness of tobacco workers. At the time Ortiz was writing, the advent of radio was making this practice obsolete. In *La tribuna* (1882), Emilia Pardo Bazán provides a vivid portrait of this practice in a Galician *tabaquería*.

9 I have discussed the excremental nature of *choteo* in *Literature and Liminality*, ch. 4.

10 All of the *Libro de Buen Amor* is not written in *cuaderna vía*, of course, but the segment that directly concerns us, the debate between Carnival and Lent, does follow this form.

11 On the "Pelea" in the *Libro de Buen Amor*, see Félix Lecoy, *Recherches sur le "Libro de Buen Amor,"* pp. 243–252; Kemlin M. Laurence, "The battle between Don Carnal and Doña Cuaresma in the light of medieval tradition"; Monique De Lope, *Traditions populaires et textualité dans le "Libro de Buen Amor."*

12 "Un romance castizo a lo añejo o unas vernáculas guajiras o acurradas, que tuvieran por personajes contradictores el varonil tabaco y la femenina azúcar, podrían servir de buena enseñanza popular en escuela y canturrias, porque, en el estudio de los fenómenos económicos y sus repercusiones sociales, pocas lecciones han de ser más elocuentes que las ofrecidas en nuestra tierra por el azúcar y el tabaco en sus notorias contraposiciones" (p. 18).

4 Nicolás Guillén between the son and the sonnet

1 This is the title of an essay on Guillén by René Depestre, reproduced in *Recopilación de textos sobre Nicolás Guillén*, pp. 121–125.

2 *Nación y mestizaje en Nicolás Guillén*, p. 65. Also pertinent is the following observation by Roberto Fernández Retamar: "[en la poesía de Guillén] se trata

de una aceptación de la tradición española. Junto al verso amplio y desigual, y al poema breve, casi siempre en forma de son, este empleo de las formas cultas de la poesía española (versos de arte mayor, combinaciones tradicionales como tercetos y sonetos) constituye una tercera línea de la obra de Guillén, que aparece aquí y va a continuar hasta nuestros días testimoniando la importancia otorgada por el poeta a su filiación hispánica" (*El son de vuelo popular*, p. 43).

3 All quotations from Guillén's poetry are taken from Nicolás Guillén, *Obra poética (1920–1972)* in 2 vols. Unless otherwise indicated, page references come from vol. 1.

4 In the original version, the third line of the second stanza read, "y no hay cuervo que manche la geografía de nieve."

5 On the angel-lady of courtly literature, see Maurice Valency, *In Praise of Love: An Introduction to the Love-Poetry of the Renaissance*, pp. 226–255; also useful are Irving Singer, *The Nature of Love: 2, Courtly and Romantic*, and Joan Ferrante, *Woman as Image in Medieval Literature*. The phrase *donna angelicata* goes back to Guido Guinizelli, the founder of the *dolce stil nuovo*.

6 On the motif of vassaldom, see Silvio Pellegrini, "Intorno al vassallaggio d'amore nei primi trovatori."

7 According to Nancy Morejón, this poem "aunque no aborda el tema de la trata y la esclavitud, sí asienta su filiación, su subrayada atención a la naturaleza racial – que no es otra cosa que la imagen del mestizaje – del abuelo negro (que sabremos esclavo, muchos años después, en 'El apellido')" (*Nación y mestizaje*, p. 250). In my view, the poem's filiation with the subject of the slave trade is somewhat more direct than one might suppose. For Morejón, "El abuelo" belongs to a textual constellation that also includes "Palabras en el trópico," "Balada de los dos abuelos" and "El apellido," poems in which the slave-trade is dealt with explicitly. The most thorough reading of "El abuelo" to date is by Keith Ellis in his *Cuba's Nicolás Guillén: Poetry and Ideology*, pp. 89–92. I should add that Guillén has a very different poem, written much later, that also needs to be inserted into this textual constellation; I refer to "La herencia" (from *La rueda dentada*, 1972; *Obra poética*, vol. 2, p. 287–289), which deals with the "remote descendants" of someone who left Cuba in the wake of the Castro revolution. Interestingly, here Guillén sees inheritance not as an enrichment but as an ignominious curse, a "kind of syphilis" that the exiled grandfather has passed on to his descendants.

8 According to Odilio Urfé, "De las manifestaciones más representativas de la identidad cultural cubana, y particularmente en lo que respecta al arte musical, el son cubano se destaca por ser, quizás, la expresión más característica y representativa de las surgidas de la entraña popular. Tal apreciación se reafirma si agregamos que el son cubano es la síntesis más decantada y original, realizada por nuestro pueblo y sus músicos más representativos con base en el caudaloso fondo integrado por las transculturaciones españolas y africanas" (as quoted in Nicolás Guillén, *El libro de los sones*, pp. 16–17). See also Ortiz, *La africanía de la música folklórica de Cuba* and Carpentier, *La música en Cuba*, esp. pp. 47–49.

9 The ambiguity extends into the prepositional phrase that follows, "junto a la fresca orilla." *Who* is next to the riverbank? Physically the grandfather, but since the granddaughter has been spiritually transported to Africa, she also might be said to be right there, by the riverbank, next to her grandfather.

10 The black slave, of course, is probably not the woman's literal grandfather, if we assume a modern setting for the poem, and if the woman is as white as she

appears to be. Just as Guillén telescopes the passage of time by brusquely flashing back to the time of the slave trade, he telescopes the woman's genealogy by transforming a distant ancestor into her grandfather.

11 We might also contrast the nightingale in "Tú" with the inexistent crow of "El abuelo" – "y no hay cuervo que manche la solitaria nieve . . ."

12 From an early review of *Cantos para soldados y sones para turistas* (1937), "Hazaña y triunfo americanos de Nicolás Guillén," p. 76.

5 Mulatto madrigals

1 Unless otherwise indicated, page numbers refer to the first volume of Guillén's *Obra poética (1920–1972)*. One curious thing about this poem about transubstantiation is that it ends with a literary transubstantiation, since the "white doves" of Nervo's "white rhymes" ("las palomas blancas de sus blancas rimas") recall the "dark swallows" of Bécquer's famous Rima LIII. Just as Nervo blanches the black roses of fate, Guillén blanches Bécquer's dark – but certainly not obscure – swallows. But Guillén's early poetry is shot through with undisguised echoes of Bécquer's *rimas* (see, for example, the sequence of poems entitled "Rima amarga," "Rima triste," and "Rima ingenua" [pp. 14–17]. Like many other poets before and since, Guillén found his voice by imitating others' voices, and his poems before *Motivos de son* are best seen as exercises in imitation of the fashionable poets of the day – Bécquer, Darío, Silva, and Casal, among others.

2 "Madrigal en el abanico de doña Fidelina de Castro" and "Madrigal exaltado" (*Poesías Completas*, pp. 1027 and 670, respectively).

3 The sonnet and the madrigal are closely connected in Guillén's work, as they are in Western poetic tradition. Symptomatic of this alliance is the fact that Guillén's first madrigal, entitled "Madrigal trirrimo," which appeared in *Camagüey Gráfico* in 1921, adopts the metrical form of the sonnet. If the sonnet is the genre in which Guillén wrote a majority of his early poetry, the madrigal is the label he affixes to poetry itself.

4 See also these lines from a poem similar to "Tú":

> Brazos que bien vinieran a la Venus de Milo;
> ojos con resplandores de estrella o de puñal . . .
> ¡Quién hubiera, señora, la gloria de ofrendaros
> el corazón y un madrigal! (p. 28)

Other references to the madrigal in the poetry of this period can be found in the following poems: "Jardín" (p. 7), "Manos, las de la Amada" (p. 54), "Laca" (p. 73), and "Ven al jardin" (pp. 75–78).

5 Jonathan Culler, *The Pursuit of Signs*, p. 140. On apostrophe see also Paul de Man, "Lyrical voice in contemporary theory: Riffaterre and Jauss" and Barbara Johnson, "Apostrophe, animation, and abortion."

6 As Lily Litvak has pointed out (*Erotismo fin de siglo*, pp. 30–41), the poetry of the *modernistas* and the European counterparts is full of lilies, lotuses, nelumbiums, and other flowers valued for their exotic names, shapes, or properties. I am grateful to María Salgado for bringing this reference to my attention.

7 "Más acerca de la poesía mulata. Escorzos para su estudio," p. 26.

8 In *Sóngoro cosongo* "Mujer nueva" precedes the two madrigals; although the former is not framed as an apostrophe, it deals with the same subject matter as the madrigals, and should therefore be considered along with them. One can look upon "Mujer nueva" as a record of the *results* achieved by the apostrophic form of the madrigals.

9 See G. R. Coulthard, *Race and Colour in Caribbean Literature*, pp. 87–96.

10 Ibid., p. 95. More recently, Lorna Williams has remarked that Guillén's madrigals draw a "machista portrayal" of black women (*Self and Society in the Poetry of Nicolás Guillén*, p. 20).

11 Significantly, in Emilio Ballagas's anthology, *Mapa de la poesía negra americana*, the poem appears under the title "Signo" (p. 119).

12 This relocation of the cognitive faculties may have something to do with Guillén's reading of Spengler in the late twenties and early thirties, since one of the well-known theses of *The Decline of the West* was that the enervation of Western civilization was reflected in – and caused by – an increasing cerebralization of culture. Compare the following passage from an essay by Luis Palés Matos written in 1927, also evidently under the influence of Spengler: "El sentido estético de la raza blanca ha penetrado en un estado de peligrosa cerebralización, anulando sus raíces cósmicas ... Yo no creo en ese arte ornamental de meras representaciones cerebrales; yo sólo creo en el arte que se identifica y confunde con la esencia misma de la cosa. Arte que sea lo menos arte posible, es decir, donde la aptitud de realización esté subordinada al golpe de la sangre y del instinto, que es siempre golpe certero, porque lleva detrás la experiencia milenaria de una especie" ("El arte y la raza blanca," p. 229). Guillén mentions his reading of Spengler in Nancy Morejón, "Conversación con Nicolás Guillén," p. 45.

13 It will be obvious that I am not convinced that Guillén's poetry bears out, as Cintio Vitier has claimed, "la tesis de la no-teluricidad esencial de lo cubano" (*Lo cubano en la poesía*, p. 431). As I have been arguing, the key to Guillén's poetry is rather the *mode of existence* of the telluric.

14 Dorothy Clotelle Clarke, "A chronological sketch of Castilian versification together with a list of its metric terms," p. 347.

15 Italian madrigals have a better defined identity, since they are often made up of two or three tercets followed by a couplet. On the madrigal generally see Alfred Einstein, *The Italian Madrigal*, and Edmund H. Fellowes, *The English Madrigal*. On the madrigal in Spanish literature see Rudolf Baehr, *Manual de versificación española*, pp. 402–407. Besides Cetina, other Spanish Golden Age poets who wrote madrigals were Quevedo, Jáuregui, Espinosa, and Soto de Rojas.

16 The fact that the madrigal does not possess generic indicia does not mean that there are not certain general attributes associated with madrigals. The point is that, without the title, these attributes are not sufficient to class a poem as a madrigal.

17 It may be worth remarking that, strictly speaking, there could be no caimans in the Zambezi, since this reptile is an American variety of crocodile. But this again illustrates the artificial nature of Guillén's primitivism; the *caimán* is there because it connotes nature-bound qualities that Guillén wants to highlight. The verisimilitude of putting this American reptile in the African river is as relevant as the lifelikeness of the woman herself.

18 The *silva* (or *sylva* or *selva*), which became current as a literary term in Spanish in the early seventeenth century, originally designated an amorphous, heterogeneous, or "wild" poetic composition. See Karl Vossler, *La poesía de la soledad en España*, pp. 98–104; and Eugenio Asensio, "Un Quevedo incógnito. Las *Silvas*," pp. 13–39. The semantic relation between *silva* and *selva* is well illustrated by the following excerpt from Pierre Bense-Depuis's *Apollon espagnol* (1644): "... les Espagnols en ont encore d'une autre sorte, aussi composée de vers Italiens,

qu'ils appellent d'un nom particulier *Siluas* comme qui diroit *Forest*, pour ce que dans vne Forest, le chesne, le hestre, le fousteau, & les autres sortes d'arbres s'y rencontrent pesle-mesme, sans aucun ordre déterminé, aussi dans les Silues Espagnoles, les vers Entiers & rompus y entrent confusément, sans qui'ils soient contraints à aucune suite de Rimes, qu'à celle qu'il plaist au Poète leur donner" (as quoted by Asensio, p. 27).

19 Nancy Morejón, "Conversación con Nicolás Guillén," p. 42.

6 The discourse of the tropics

1 I will be quoting *Trópico* from *Poema Mío* (1947), Florit's compilation of his poetry up to 1946. Page references will be given in the text. There are several book-length studies of Florit's poetry; two are worth mentioning: María Castell-anos Collins, *Tierra, mar y cielo en la poesía de Eugenio Florit*.

2 The *guajiro* is the Cuban farmer; the *diablito* is the dominant and most colorful figure in Afro-Cuban carnival celebrations. Constantino Suárez in his *Diccionario de voces cubanas* describes him as follows: "El negro que disfrazado con colorines y muy chocarreramente, va haciendo mil indecentes contorsiones, acompasadas por infernal gritería, que producen otros muchos individuos de su raza, quienes lo rodean y siguen a modo de procesión, la que toma el nombre de *comparsa de ñáñigos*" (p. 196). Ortiz discusses this figure extensively in *La fiesta afrocubana del Día de Reyes*. The *diablito* was a favorite subject of nineteenth-century illustrators like Landaluze and Mialhe. I should make clear that in contrasting these two figures I am drawing on the literary and artistic stereotypes rather than on the historical realities. On the *guajiro* as a character in Cuban vernacular theater, see Eduardo Robreño, *Como lo pienso, lo digo*, pp. 207–217.

3 Napolés Fajardo's pseudonym arises from the conflation of the English "cook," and the Amerindian word, "calambé," loincloth. "Cook-calambé," thus, equals "native or savage chef." The pseudonym was also supposedly an anagram of "Cuba clamé," and thus an anti-Spanish slogan. The poetic movement of which the Cucalambé is a part is known as "siboneísmo" because of its idealization of the Siboney indians, Cuba's noble savages; its best-known examples are José Fornaris's *Cantos del Siboney*, (1855) and Napolés Fajardo's *Rumores del Hórmigo*, (1856). On the *siboneístas* see Samuel Feijóo, "Sobre los movimientos por una poesía cubana hasta 1856," pp. 64–176; Cintio Vitier, *Lo cubano en la poesía*, pp. 133–178; and Julio Le Riverend, "El indigenismo en la historia de las ideas cubanas."

4 I allude specifically to Napolés Fajardo, for which see Samuel Feijóo, "Sobre los movimientos por una poesía cubana hasta 1856," pp. 151–170.

5 This is not to deny that the Afro-Antillean movement was also influenced by European literary currents; as is well-known, this movement began as a European fad, which was quickly assimilated by Antillean writers. Nonetheless, Cuba did have in Ortiz's research an important local precedent contemporaneous with the flowering of the European interest in the exotic *nègre*, and one which gave the Afro-Cuban writer a native archive from which to draw his documentation.

6 Juan Cristóbal Napolés Fajardo, *Poesías completas*, pp. 123–125. In this edition the lines read a little differently: "Ven, chinita, que ya empieza / a madurar la guayaba."

7 Florit records his debt to Góngora and the Generation of 1927 in "Una hora conmigo," pp. 162–164. In 1930 Florit also published some "Estrofas para un homenaje a Góngora" in *Social*.

8 The bipartite division may also have a native precedent in Regino Boti's *La montaña y el mar* (1921). I'm grateful to Jorge Olivares for bringing this book to my attention.

9 *Doble acento* (1937) is the title of the book of poems that Florit published after *Trópico*.

10 The antecedents to *Motivos de son* may be found in Ramón Guirao's anthology, *Orbita de la poesía afrocubana*.

11 It is not clear whether "de la tierra" refers to "canto" or to "envoltura." One possibility is that the prepositional phrase, much displaced, is part of a definition of the *décima*, the "clásica envoltura de la tierra." The reading would then be something like: "Since you, grateful song, have assumed the classic garb of this land [that is, the *décima*], then" etc. But the sense is not much changed if one assumes that the phrase modifies "canto." The reading then would be: "If you, grateful song of the earth, have assumed the classic garb, then" etc. The second construction is syntactically less violent (the hyperbaton is not so severe) but semantically less coherent.

12 This is part of Cucalambé's self-portrait:
    Rústico y pobre guajiro
    De estos terrenos feraces
    Canto mis bellos solaces
    Al templado son del güiro.   (*Poesías completas*, p. 59)

13 This positioning was already present in the opening stanza of "Inicial," where Florit conveys the dual subject matter of his poems by placing his song successively in a *nido* and a *manantial de altura* ("... detén el ala por mirar el nido / y luego bebe un manantial de altura").

14 José Lezama Lima, *Antología de la poesía cubana*, vol. 3, p. 89.

15 Not coincidentally, Balboa's poem was first published in the nineteenth century during the heyday of Romanticism in Cuba. For a discussion of the significance of this poem in Cuban romanticism, see Roberto González Echevarría, "Reflections on the *Espejo de paciencia*." On the catalogues of flora and fauna in romantic poetry, see Cintio Vitier, *Lo cubano en la poesía*, pp. 60–70, 134–142.

16 As quoted in Vitier, *Lo cubano en la poesía*, p. 139. Since the names of the fruits and plants mentioned here have no English equivalents, a translation is pointless.

17 I borrow the term "descriptive system" from Michael Riffaterre's *Semiotics of Poetry*, where it designates a network of associated descriptive commonplaces.

18 From José Fornaris, "La laguna de Ana Luisa," in *Poesías*, p. 169.

19 "Alusión y elusión en la poesía de Góngora," in *Estudios y ensayos gongorinos*, pp. 92–113. This essay was originally published in 1928 in the *Revista de Occidente*.

20 This poem, of which I only quote the initial and closing stanzas, forms part of *El son entero* (1947).

21 See Rorty, *Philosophy and the Mirror of Nature*, pp. 38–39 *et passim*.

22 "Claridad y belleza de las *Soledades*," in *Estudios y ensayos gongorinos*, p. 73. The essay was originally published in the *Revista de Occidente* in 1927.

23 Alfonso Reyes, "Compás poético," *Sur*, 1 (1931), 64–73.

24 "Poesía pura es todo lo que permanece en el poema, después de haber eliminado todo lo que no es poesía. *Pura* es igual a *simple*, químicamente" ("Carta a Fernando Vela").

25 *Poética: Ensayos en entusiasmo*, pp. 21–48. This important little book also includes essays on Nicolás Guillén, Manuel Navarro Luna, and Emilio Ballagas.

26 From "Palabras en el trópico" (*Obra poética*, vol. 1, p. 135). It is interesting that a few months after the appearance of *Trópico*, Guillén published a parody of Florit's book in the section "Ideales de una raza" of the *Diario de la Marina* (this section, where Guillén originally published *Motivos de son*, was a weekly supplement directed by Gustavo E. Urrutia and dedicated to the literary output of Cuba's "gente de color"). In his own *décimas* Guillén labels Florit an "anfibio músico," alluding to the land and sea sections of *Trópico*, but more pointedly perhaps to Florit's divided literary allegiances, halfway between the learned and the popular. Guillén's four *décimas*, which are still very funny, can be found in Samuel Feijóo's anthology, *La décima culta en Cuba*, pp. 311–312.

7 The creation of Juan Criollo

1 On *Juan Criollo*, see Juan Marinello, "*Juan Criollo*. Novela"; Manuel Pedro González, "La literatura de hoy: Carlos Loveira"; Marcelo Pogolotti, "El juancriollismo"; J. Riis Owre, "*Juan Criollo*, after forty years"; Sarah Marqués, *Arte y sociedad en las novelas de Carlos Loveira*, pp. 181–221; Luis Toledo Sande, "Balance de Carlos Loveira, novelista"; and Lourdes S. Herrera, *La novelística de Carlos Loveira*, pp. 115–134.

2 On the history of the term *criollo*, see José Juan Arrom, "Criollo: Definición y matices de un concepto."

3 References to *Juan Criollo* are taken from the first edition, 1927. The discursive equivalent of Loveira's novel might well be a work like Tom Mix's [José M. Muzaurieta] *Manual del perfecto sinvergüenza*, whose subtitle reads: "Prontuario de conocimientos útiles para los que aspiren a ser 'algo' en la vida pública." Muzaurieta's recommendations include such gems as: "Nunca diga lo que sienta ni sienta lo que diga"; "Cualquier procedimiento es bueno para triunfar"; "Diga que usted es un hombre honrado y verá que algo se le pega"; "Legal es todo aquello que le reporte a usted algún beneficio" (pp. 22–25). If one follows this advice, says the author, one will avoid "el doloroso papel de bobo" (p. 48) and triumph in public life, a goal within everyone's reach: "Eso le será fácil si usted es un poco vivo. ¿No lo hacen otros? Usted también puede hacerlo" (p. 30). Juan Criollo's career seems to bear out the soundness of Tom Mix's advice. From a generic standpoint, this forgotten but fascinating little book is interesting because of its "mix" of two very different genres: the *speculum principis* and the picaresque novel. The *Manual* is a *speculum* for *pícaros*, a textbook of political *picardía*. Mix's *Manual* has an important Cuban precedent in José Antonio Ramos's *Manual del perfecto fulanista* (1916).

4 According to Raimundo Lazo, for instance, "por su precipitación final, la novela se frustra" (*Historia de la literatura cubana*, p. 233).

5 The bibliography on the use of point of view in the picaresque novel is extensive; I have found the following studies particularly useful: Claudio Guillén, "Toward a definition of the picaresque," in *Literature as System*, pp. 71–134; Fernando Lázaro Carreter, "*Lazarillo de Tormes*" en la picaresca; and Francisco Rico, *The Spanish Picaresque Novel and the Point of View*.

6 See Philippe Lejeune, "L'Autobiographie à la troisième personne."

7 One may find an admittedly faint precedent for this grammatical split in *Guzmán de Alfarache*, where the narrator–protagonist sometimes addresses himself as a "you," thus underscoring the disjunction between his identities as

sinner and penitent. See Rico, *The Spanish Picaresque Novel and the Point of View*, pp. 42–43; also Francisco Ynduráin, "La novela desde la segunda persona. Análisis estructural."

8 I discuss the function of the packet of love letters in *Literature and Liminality*, pp. 77–81.

9 On the notions of *énoncé* and *énonciation* see Emile Benveniste, "L'Appareil formel de l'énonciation."

10 I take the term "focalization" from Gérard Genette, *Narrative Discourse*, pp. 189–194.

11 I am making here the same argument that others have made apropos of the apparent irregularities of *Lazarillo de Tormes*; see, for example, Claudio Guillén, "La disposición temporal del *Lazarillo de Tormes*."

12 In statements about his work, Loveira did not disguise their autobiographical character. At the time of his unexpected death in December of 1928, he was preparing a collection of stories under the title "Horas de vida." This title was appropriate, he said, "por tener [los cuentos] mucho de autobiográficos" (Carlos Loveira, "Para la nota biográfica," p. 38).

13 According to Toledo Sande, *Juan Criollo* is "el testimonio literario de la trayectoria vital del novelista" ("Balance de Carlos Loveira, novelista," p. 300).

14 I am alluding here to Juan Marinello's assessment of Guillén's poetry, quoted at the end of chapter 4.

15 For some general leads on the importance of the picaresque in modern Spanish-American fiction, see Jean Franco, *Spanish-American Literature Since Independence*, pp. 143–149. Frederick Monteser's discussion of the subject in *The Picaresque Element in Western Literature* (pp. 87–106) is too vague to be useful. On the other hand, the proceedings of the First International Congress on the Picaresque ("Primer Congreso Internacional sobre la Picaresca"), published under the title, *La picaresca: Orígenes, textos y estructuras*, contain several useful essays (see section XIII: "La picaresca en Hispanoamérica," pp. 1033–1158).

8 Shifting grounds

1 Rodríguez's words in the "Advertencia al lector," p. 7. Page references refer to the novel's definitive edition, *Ciénaga* (1937); the first version appeared under a somewhat different title, *La conjura de la ciénaga* (1923), which in the second version becomes the title of a framed narration included in the novel.

2 Of the few studies of Rodríguez's fiction, the most informative are Marinello's "Americanismo y cubanismo literarios" and Cira Romero's "Luis Felipe Rodríguez, testigo y narrador de una tierra oprimida."

3 Marinello, "Tres novelas ejemplares" (1937), pp. 83–99.

4 Some of the novel's commentators have also unknowingly fallen prey to the swamp's influence; according to Cira Romero, for instance, Rodríguez's fiction, which represents the author's attempt to "profundizar en sus propias experiencias y en el medio que lo rodeaba," reveals "una honda preocupación de signo telúrico" ("Luis Felipe Rodríguez, testigo y narrador de una tierra oprimida," pp. 277, 274).

5 Emir Rodríguez Monegal, "*Doña Bárbara*: texto y contextos," p. 212.

6 I might also point out that the Cuban marshlands were already a popular motif in the poetry of the *siboneístas*, as in Napolés Fajardo's "A Rufina desde una ciénaga."

9 *Land or language*

1 From Roberto González Echevarría's introduction to his edition of the novel (p. 15). González Echevarría continues: "En *Los pasos perdidos* se somete a prueba, no sólo la literatura hispanoamericana, sino la misma posibilidad de escribir desde Hispanoamérica. Son tan trascendentales las preguntas de las que surge esta novela de Carpentier, que debe ocupar un lugar de importancia, no sólo en la historia de la literatura, sino en la del pensamiento hispanoamericano" (*Los pasos perdidos*, pp. 15–16). Other page references in my text refer to this edition. My own discussion of Carpentier's novel does not attempt to do justice to these broad issues, on which González Echevarría's introduction provides a reliable guide; my aim is more limited: I will read *Los pasos perdidos* only in the context of Cuban criollism. Although Carpentier is deliberately vague in situating his novel, I am interested in the novel as a "Cuban" text, as a synthesis of that critical strain within Cuban criollist literature that has been the subject of this book.

2 Carpentier has expressed himself in similar terms. In his important essay, "Problemática de la actual novela latinoamericana," he remarks: "En cuanto a mí, creo que ciertas realidades americanas, por no haber sido explotadas literariamente, por no haber sido *nombradas*, exigen un largo, vasto, paciente, proceso de observación" (p. 12; emphasis in the original).

3 I take the terms "narrating self" and "experiencing self" from Shlomith Rimmon-Kenan, *Narrative Fiction: Contemporary Poetics*, p. 74.

4 In "Problemática de la actual novela latinoamericana" Carpentier analyzed the task of the Spanish-American writer by listing the "contexts" that must figure in his work; these contexts range all the way from the culinary to the political.

5 González Echevarría has discussed the contrasts in the handling of point of view between Carpentier's novel and the *Lazarillo* in "Ironía y estilo en *Los pasos perdidos*," pp. 38–39.

6 On the use of verbal tenses in the novel, see Klaus Müller-Bergh, "En torno al estilo de Alejo Carpentier en *Los pasos perdidos*" and Carlos Santander, "Lo maravilloso en la obra de Alejo Carpentier."

7 On the dating of the "diary" see Santander, ibid., pp. 112–114; Roberto González Echevarría, *Alejo Carpentier: The Pilgrim at Home*, pp. 183–184; Eduardo González, *Alejo Carpentier: El tiempo del hombre*, pp. 130–136; Emil Volek, *Cuatro claves para la modernidad. Análisis semiótico de textos hispánicos*, pp. 127–153; and, most recently, Eduardo González, "Framing Carpentier," 427–428.

8 See González Echevarría, "Ironía y estilo en *Los pasos perdidos*," p. 45.

9 As Eduardo González has indicated, "La narración mantendrá por todos los medios posibles la ilusión de que lo ocurrido está ocurriendo" (*Alejo Carpentier: El tiempo del hombre*, p. 125). For a somewhat different reading of the novel's opening, see Germán Gullón, "El narrador y la narración en *Los pasos perdidos*"; according to Gullón, the superposition of time-frames yields "una temporalidad 'intemporal', un ahora que sirve funciones espaciales tanto como temporales" (p. 506). See also González Echevarría, *Los pasos perdidos*, pp. 48–49.

10 I quote from the beginning of each tale and skip over the prologues and other preliminary matter, which have no parallel in *Los pasos perdidos*. The reason is worth noting: in *Lazarillo* as in *Pascual Duarte*, the preliminary documents serve to clarify the situation of writing. This is the clarification that the narrator of *Los pasos perdidos* studiously avoids.

11 In my view this is the reason for the prevalence of musical structures in the novel, for which see Karen Taylor, "La creación musical en *Los pasos perdidos.*" The author of *El acoso*, of course, was no stranger to the "musicalization" of fiction.

12 A suggestion advanced by González Echevarría, *Alejo Carpentier: The Pilgrim at Home*, p. 183.

Bibliography

Aguirre Beltrán, Gonzalo. *El proceso de aculturación*, Mexico City, Universidad Nacional Autónoma de México, 1957

Alonso, Carlos. "The *novela de la tierra*: the discourse of the autochthonous," unpublished Ph.D. dissertation, Yale University, 1983

Alonso, Dámaso. *Estudios y ensayos gongorinos*, Madrid, Gredos, 1955

Altamira, Rafael. *España en América*, Valencia, F. Sempere, 1908

Anderson Imbert, Enrique. *Historia de la literatura hispanoamericana*, 2nd edn, 2 vols., Mexico City, Fondo de Cultura Económica, 1970

Arrom, José Juan. *Historia de la literatura dramática cubana*, New Haven, Yale University Press, 1944

"Criollo: definición y matices de un concepto" in *Certidumbre de América*, 2nd edn, Madrid, Gredos, 1971, pp. 11–26

Asensio, Eugenio. "Un Quevedo incógnito. Las *Silvas*," *Edad de Oro*, 2 (1983), 13–39

Augier, Angel. "*Ciénaga*, novela cubana" (1937) in *De la sangre en la letra*, Havana, Unión de Escritores y Artistas de Cuba, 1977, pp. 215–218

Baehr, Rudolf. *Manual de versificación española*, trans. K. Wagner and F. López Estrada, Madrid, Gredos, 1970

Ballagas, Emilio (ed.), *Mapa de la poesía negra americana*, Buenos Aires, Editorial Pleamar, 1946

Barthes, Roland. *Writing Degree Zero and Elements of Semiology*, trans. Annette Lavers and Colin Smith, Boston, Beacon Press, 1970

S/Z, trans. Richard Howard, New York, Farrar, Straus and Giroux, 1974.

Beals, Ralph. "Acculturation" in A. L. Kroeber (ed.), *Anthropology Today*, University of Chicago Press, 1953, pp. 621–641

Benítez Rojo, Antonio. "Power / sugar / literature: toward a reinterpretation of Cubanness," *Cuban Studies*, 16 (1986), 9–31

Benveniste, Emile. "L'Appareil formel de l'énonciation," *Langages*, 5, no. 17 (1970), 12–18

Blanco Fombona, Rufino. "El criollismo," *Repertorio Americano*, 18 (1929), 263

Bloom, Harold. *The Anxiety of Influence*, Oxford University Press, 1973

Borges, Jorge Luis. *Ficciones*, Madrid, Alianza, 1979

Brathwaite, Edward. *History of the Voice*, London, New Beacon, 1984

Bueno, Salvador. "Don Fernando Ortiz: Al servicio de la ciencia y de Cuba" in *Temas y personajes de la literatura cubana*, Havana, Ediciones Unión, 1964, pp. 209–218

"Aproximaciones a la vida y la obra de Fernando Ortiz," *Casa de las Américas*, no. 113 (1979), 119–128

Campoamor, Fernando G. "Don Fernando Ortiz, el Maestro fuerte," *Repertorio Americano*, 47 (1952), 225–226

Carpentier, Alejo. *Los pasos perdidos* (1953), ed. Roberto González Echevarría, Madrid, Cátedra, 1985

"Problemática de la actual novela latinoamericana" in *Tientos y diferencias*, Montevideo, Arca, 1967, pp. 5–41

La música en Cuba, 2nd edn, Mexico City, Fondo de Cultura Económica, 1972

Cela, Camilo José. *La familia de Pascual Duarte*, New York, Las Américas, 1965

[Cicero], *Ad C. Herennium: De Ratione Dicendi (Rhetorica Ad Herennium)*, trans. Harry Caplan, Cambridge, Mass., Loeb Classical Library, 1954

Clarke, Dorothy Clotelle. "A chronological sketch of Castilian versification together with a list of its metric terms," *University of California Publications in Modern Philology*, 34 (1952), 279–382

Collins, María Castellanos. *Tierra, mar y cielo en la poesía de Eugenio Florit*, Miami, Florida, Universal, 1976

Corominas, Joan. *Breve diccionario etimológico de la lengua castellana*, 3rd edn, Madrid, Gredos, 1973

Correa, Gustavo. *Realidad, ficción y símbolo en las novelas de Pérez Galdós*, 2nd edn, Madrid, Gredos, 1977

Coulthard, G. R. *Race and Colour in Caribbean Literature*, Oxford University Press, 1962

Criado de Val, Manuel (ed.), *La picaresca: Orígenes, textos y estructuras*, Madrid, Fundación Universitaria Española, 1979

Culler, Jonathan. *The Pursuit of Signs*, Ithaca, Cornell University Press, 1981

Darío, Rubén. *Poesías completas*, 10th edn, ed. Alfonso Méndez Plancarte, Madrid, Aguilar, 1967

De Lope, Monique. *Traditions populaires et textualité dans le 'Libro de Buen Amor'*, Montpellier, Centre d'Etudes et de Recherches Sociocritiques, 1984

de Man, Paul. "Lyrical voice in contemporary theory: Riffaterre and Jauss" in Chaviva Hosek and Patricia Parker (eds.), *Lyric Poetry: Beyond New Criticism*, Ithaca, Cornell University Press, 1985, pp. 55–72

Depestre, René. "Orfeo negro" in Nancy Morejón (ed.), *Recopilación de textos sobre Nicolás Guillén*, Havana, Casa de las Américas, 1974, pp. 121–125.

Einstein, Alfred. *The Italian Madrigal*, trans. Alexander H. Krappe, Roger H. Sessions, and Oliver Strunk, 3 vols., Princeton University Press, 1949

Ellis, Keith. *Cuba's Nicolás Guillén: Poetry and Ideology*, University of Toronto Press, 1983

Feijóo, Samuel. "Sobre los movimientos por una poesía cubana hasta 1856," *Revista Cubana*, 25 (1949), 64–176
La décima culta en Cuba, Las Villas, Cuba, Dirección de Publicaciones de la Universidad Central de Las Villas, 1963

Fellowes, Edmund H. *The English Madrigal*, Oxford University Press, 1925

Fernández Retamar, Roberto. *El son de vuelo popular*, Havana, Letras Cubanas, 1979

Ferrante, Joan. *Woman as Image in Medieval Literature*, New York, Columbia University Press, 1975

Florit, Eugenio. "Estrofas para un homenaje a Góngora," *Social*, 15, no. 7 (July 1930), 37
"Una hora conmigo," *Revista Cubana*, 2 (1935), 159–167
Poema Mío, Mexico City, Letras de México, 1947

Fornaris, José. *Poesías*, prologue by R. M. Mendive, Havana, Imprenta del Tiempo, 1855

Franco, Jean. *Spanish-American Literature Since Independence*, New York, Barnes and Noble, 1973

García-Carranza, Araceli. *Bio-bibliografía de don Fernando Ortiz*, Havana, Biblioteca Nacional José Martí, 1970

Genette, Gérard. *Narrative Discourse*, trans. Jane E. Lewin, Ithaca, Cornell University Press, 1980

González, Eduardo. *Alejo Carpentier: El tiempo del hombre*, Caracas, Monte Avila, 1978
"Framing Carpentier," *MLN*, 101 (1986), 424–429

González, Manuel Pedro. "La literatura de hoy: Carlos Loveira," *Revista de Estudios Hispánicos*, 2 (1929), 188–189

González Echevarría, Roberto. "Ironía y estilo en *Los pasos perdidos*" in *Relecturas: Estudios de literatura cubana*, Caracas, Monte Avila, 1976, pp. 27–51
Alejo Carpentier: The Pilgrim at Home, Ithaca, Cornell University Press, 1977
"Lo cubano en *Paradiso*" in *Isla a su vuelo fugitiva: Ensayos críticos sobre literatura hispanoamericana*, Madrid, José Porrúa Turanzas, 1983, pp. 69–102
"The case of the speaking statue: *Ariel* and the magisterial rhetoric of the Latin American essay" in *The Voice of the Masters*, Austin, University of Texas Press, 1985, pp. 8–32
"Doña Bárbara writes the plain" in *The Voice of the Masters*, pp. 33–63
"Reflections on the *Espejo de paciencia*," *Cuban Studies*, 16 (1986), 101–121

Guillén, Claudio. "La disposición temporal del *Lazarillo de Tormes*," *Hispanic Review*, 25 (1957), 264–279
Literature as System, Princeton University Press, 1971

Guillén, Jorge. "Carta a Fernando Vela" in Joaquín González Muela and Juan Manuel Rozas (eds.), *La generación poética de 1927*, Madrid, Alcalá, 1966, pp. 239–240

Guillén, Nicolás. "Ortiz: Misión cumplida," *Casa de las Américas*, 10, no. 55 (1969), 5–6

Obra poética, 1920–1972, ed. Angel Augier, 2 vols., Havana, Editorial de Arte y Literatura, 1974

El libro de los sones, ed. Angel Augier, Havana, Letras Cubanas, 1982

Guirao, Ramón (ed.), *Orbita de la poesía afrocubana, 1928–37*, Havana, Ucar, García y Cía., 1938

Gullón, Germán. "El narrador y la narración en *Los pasos perdidos*," *Cuadernos Hispanoamericanos*, 263 (1972), 501–509

Gutiérrez de la Solana, Alberto. "En torno a Fernando Ortiz, lo afrocubano y otros ensayos" in Kurt Levy and Keith Ellis (eds.), *El ensayo y la crítica en Iberoamérica*, University of Toronto Press, 1970, pp. 81–87

Hartman, Geoffrey. *Criticism in the Wilderness*, New Haven, Yale University Press, 1980

Herrera, Lourdes S. *La novelística de Carlos Loveira*, New York, Las Américas, 1983

Hildebrand's Travel Guide: Cuba, Frankfurt, KARTO+GRAFIK, 1985

Jakobson, Roman. "On linguistic aspects of translation" in R. A. Brower (ed.), *On Translation*, Cambridge, Mass., Harvard University Press, 1959, pp. 232–239

Johnson, Barbara. "Apostrophe, animation, and abortion," *Diacritics*, 16, no. 1 (Spring 1986), 29–47

Juan, Adelaida de. *Caricatura de la República*, Havana, Letras Cubanas, 1982

Labra, Rafael M. de. *Orientación americana de España*, Madrid, A. Alonso, 1909

Latcham, Ricardo A. "La querella del criollismo," *Bolívar* (Bogotá), no. 34 (1954), 565–593

Laurence, Kemlin M. "The battle between Don Carnal and Doña Cuaresma in the light of medieval tradition" in G. B. Gybbon-Monypenny (ed.), *"Libro de Buen Amor" Studies*, London, Tamesis, 1970, pp. 159–176

Lazarillo de Tormes, eds. Everett W. Hesse and Harry F. Williams, Madison, University of Wisconsin Press, 1969

Lázaro Carreter, Fernando. *"Lazarillo de Tormes" en la picaresca*, Barcelona, Ariel, 1972

Lazo, Raimundo. *La literatura cubana*, Mexico City, Universidad Autónoma de México, 1965

Historia de la literatura cubana, 2nd edn, Mexico City, Universidad Autónoma de México, 1974

Leal, Rine. *Breve historia del teatro cubano*, Havana, Letras Cubanas, 1980

Lecoy, Félix. *Recherches sur le "Libro de Buen Amor"*, 2nd edn, ed. A. D. Deyermond, Farnborough, England, Gregg International, 1974

Lejeune, Philippe. "L'Autobiographie à la troisième personne" in *Je est une autre*, Paris, Editions du Seuil, 1980, pp. 32–59

Le Riverend, Julio. "El indigenismo en la historia de las ideas cubanas," *Islas*, 9 (May–August 1961), 53–68

Le Riverend, Julio (ed.), *Orbita de Fernando Ortiz*, Havana, Unión de Escritores y Artistas de Cuba, 1973

Lezama Lima, José. *Antología de la poesía cubana*, 3 vols., Havana, Consejo Nacional de Cultura, 1965

Litvak, Lily. *Erotismo fin de siglo*, Barcelona, Antoni Bosch, 1979

Lizaso, Félix. "Criollismo literario," *Cuadernos de la Universidad del Aire* (Havana), no. 35 (30 September 1933), 445–452

Loveira y Chirino, Carlos. *De los 26 a los 35: Lecciones de la experiencia en la lucha obrera*, Washington, D.C., The Law Reporter Printing Company, 1917

Los ciegos, Havana, Imprenta "El Siglo xx," 1922

Juan Criollo, Havana, Cultural, 1927

"Para la nota biográfica," *Social*, 14, no. 2 (1929), 38

McKendrick, Melveena. "The *mujer esquiva* – a measure of the feminist sympathies of seventeenth-century Spanish dramatists," *Hispanic Review*, 40 (1972), 162–197

Mañach, Jorge. *Historia y estilo*, Havana, Minerva, 1944

Marinello, Juan. "Un guacalito de cubanismos," *Archivos del Folklore Cubano*, 2 (1926), 228–236

"*Juan Criollo*. Novela," *Revista de Avance*, 15 May 1928, 130

"Americanismo y cubanismo literarios" (1932) in *Ensayos*, Havana, Editorial Arte y Literatura, 1977, pp. 47–60

"Margen apasionado" (1933) in *Ensayos*, pp. 63–71

Poética: Ensayos en entusiasmo, Madrid, Espasa-Calpe, 1933

"Hazaña y triunfo americanos de Nicolás Guillén" (1937) in *Ensayos*, pp. 75–82

"Tres novelas ejemplares" (1937) in *Ensayos*, pp. 83–99

"Don Fernando Ortiz. Notas sobre nuestro tercer descubridor," *Bohemia*, 18 April 1969, pp. 52–60

Marqués, Sarah. *Arte y sociedad en las novelas de Carlos Loveira*, Miami, Florida, Universal, 1977

Martínez Estrada, Ezequiel. *La poesía afrocubana de Nicolás Guillén*, Montevideo, Arca, 1977

Mayz Vallenilla, Ernesto. *El problema de América*, Caracas, Publicaciones de la Dirección de Cultura de la Universidad Central de Venezuela, 1959

Mix, Tom [José M. Muzaurieta]. *Manual del perfecto sinvergüenza*, Havana, Imprenta "El Siglo xx," 1922

Monteser, Frederick. *The Picaresque Element in Western Literature*, The University of Alabama Press, 1975

Morejón, Nancy, *et al.* "Conversación con Nicolás Guillén" in Nancy Morejón (ed.), *Recopilación de textos sobre Nicolás Guillén*, Havana, Casa de las Américas, 1974, pp. 31–61

Nación y mestizaje en Nicolás Guillén, Havana, Unión de Artistas y Escritores Cubanos, 1982

Müller-Bergh, Klaus. "En torno al estilo de Alejo Carpentier en *Los pasos perdidos*" in Helmy F. Giacoman (ed.), *Homenaje a Alejo Carpentier*, New York, Las Américas, 1970, pp. 179–207

Napolés Fajardo, Juan Cristóbal [El Cucalambé]. *Poesías completas*, ed. Jesús Orta Ruiz, Havana, Editorial de Arte y Literatura, 1974
Novás Calvo, Lino. "Mister Cuba," *Americas* (New York), 2, no. 6 (1950), 6–8, 46
"Cuba em pessoa," *Americas* (New York), 2, no. 7 (1950), 6–8
"Cubano de tres mundos" in *Miscelánea de estudios dedicados a Fernando Ortiz*, Havana, no pub., 1956, vol. 2, 1133–1141
Orbea, Ramón. *La reconquista de América*, Madrid, V. Suárez, 1905
Ortiz, Fernando. *Hampa afro-cubana. Los negros brujos*, Madrid, Librería de F. Fé, 1906
El caballero encantado y la moza esquiva, Havana, Imprenta "La Universal," 1910
La reconquista de América. Reflexiones sobre el panhispanismo, Paris, Paul Ollendorff, 1910
Entre cubanos, Paris, Paul Ollendorff, 1913
Un catauro de cubanismos, Havana, no pub., 1923
Glosario de afronegrismos, prologue by Juan M. Dihigo, Havana, Imprenta "El Siglo xx," 1924
La fiesta afrocubana del Día de Reyes, Havana, Imprenta "El Siglo xx," 1925
"Los negros curros," *Archivos del Folklore Cubano*, 2 (1926–1927), 209–222, 285–325; 3 (1928), 27–50, 160–175, 250–256; 3, no. 4 (1928), 51–53
"Más acerca de la poesía mulata. Escorzos para su estudio," *Revista Bimestre Cubana*, 37 (1936), 23–39, 218–227, 439–443
"Contraste económico del azúcar y el tabaco," *Revista Bimestre Cubana*, 38 (1936), 250–260
"La cubanidad y los negros," *Estudios Afrocubanos*, 3 (1939), 3–15
"América es un ajiaco," *La Nueva Democracia*, 21, no. 11 (1940), 20–24
Contrapunteo cubano del tabaco y el azúcar, prologue by Herminio Portell Vilá, introduction by Bronislaw Malinowski, Havana, J. Montero, 1940; rev. edn: Las Villas, Universidad Central de Las Villas, 1963; Caracas, Ayacucho, 1978, ed. Julio Le Riverend; English translation: *Cuban Counterpoint: Tobacco and Sugar*, trans. Harriet de Onís, New York, A. A. Knopf, 1947; edition used: Barcelona, Ariel, 1973
"Del fenómeno social de la transculturación y de su importancia en Cuba," *Revista Bimestre Cubana*, 46 (1940), 273–278
"Los factores humanos de la cubanidad," *Revista Bimestre Cubana*, 21 (1940), 161–186
"Por la integración cubana de blancos y negros," *Revista Bimestre Cubana*, 51 (1943), 256–272
El huracán. Su mitología y sus símbolos, Mexico City, Fondo de Cultura Económica, 1947
"La 'tragedia' de los ñáñigos," *Cuadernos Americanos*, 52, no. 4 (1950), 79–101
"Los negros y la transculturación," *La Nueva Democracia*, 31, no. 1 (1951), 34–38

La africanía de la música folklórica de Cuba, Havana, Publicaciones del Ministerio de Educación, 1950

"Cubanidad y cubanía," *Islas* (Santa Clara), 6, no. 2 (1964), 91–96

Owre, J. Riis. "*Juan Criollo*, after forty years," *Journal of Inter-American Studies*, 9 (1967), 396–412

Palés Matos, Luis. "El arte y la raza blanca" in *Obras: 1914–1959*, ed. Margot Arce de Vázquez, San Juan, Editorial de la Universidad de Puerto Rico, 1984, vol. 2, pp. 229–235

Pedreira, Antonio S. *Insularismo. Ensayos de interpretación puertorriqueña*, Madrid, Tipografía Artística, 1934

Pellegrini, Silvio. "Intorno al vassallaggio d'amore nei primi trovatori," *Cultura neolatina*, 4–5 (1944–45), 21–36

Pérez Firmat, Gustavo. "La palabra invisible: Manuel de Zequeira y Arango en la literatura cubana," *Crítica Hispánica*, 7 (1985), 65–73

Literature and Liminality. Festive Readings in the Hispanic Tradition, Durham, North Carolina, Duke University Press, 1986

Pérez Galdós, Benito. *El caballero encantado*, ed. Julio Rodríguez-Puértolas, Madrid, Cátedra, 1977

Pike, Frederick B. *Hispanismo, 1898–1936: Spanish Conservatives and Liberals and their Relations with Spanish America*, University of Notre Dame Press, 1971

Pogolotti, Marcelo. "El juancriollismo" in *La República de Cuba al través de sus escritores*, Havana, Lex, 1958, pp. 26–28

Prince, Gerald. "The diary novel: notes for the definition of a sub-genre," *Neophilologus*, 59 (1975), 477–481

Rama, Angel. *Transculturación narrativa en América Latina*, Mexico City, Siglo Veintiuno, 1982

Ramos, José Antonio. *Manual del perfecto fulanista*, Havana, Biblioteca "Studium," 1916

Reyes, Alfonso. "Compás poético," *Sur*, 1 (1931), 64–73

Rico, Francisco. *The Spanish Picaresque Novel and the Point of View*, trans. Charles Davis and Harry Sieber, Cambridge University Press, 1984

Riffaterre, Michael. *Semiotics of Poetry*, Bloomington, Indiana University Press, 1978

Rimmon-Kenan, Shlomith. *Narrative Fiction: Contemporary Poetics*, London, Methuen, 1983

Robreño, Eduardo. *Historia del teatro popular cubano*, Havana, Oficina del Historiador de la Ciudad de La Habana, 1961

Teatro Alhambra: Antología, Havana, Letras Cubanas, 1979

Como lo pienso, lo digo, Havana, Unión, 1985

Rodríguez, Luis Felipe. *La conjura de la ciénaga*, Madrid, V. H. Sanz Calleja, 1923

Ciénaga, Havana, Trópico, 1937

Rodríguez Monegal, Emir. "*Doña Bárbara*: texto y contextos" in Nelson Osorio *et al.* (eds.), *Relectura de Rómulo Gallegos*, Caracas, Ediciones del Centro de Estudios Latinoamericanos Rómulo Gallegos, 1980, vol. 1, pp. 211–220

Rodríguez-Puértolas, Julio. *Galdós: Burguesía y revolución*, Madrid, Turner, 1975

Romero, Cira. "Luis Felipe Rodríguez, testigo y narrador de una tierra oprimida" in *Nuevos críticos cubanos*, ed. José Prats Sariol, Havana, Editorial Letras Cubanas, 1983, pp. 274–286

Romero, Fernando. "Los *Estudios Afrocubanos* y el negro en la patria de Martí," *Revista Bimestre Cubana*, 47 (1941), 295–301

Rorty, Richard. *Philosophy and the Mirror of Nature*, Princeton University Press, 1979

Ruiz, Juan, Arcipreste de Hita. *Libro de Buen Amor*, ed. Julio Cejador y Frauca, Madrid, Espasa-Calpe, 1970

Santander, Carlos. "Lo maravilloso en la obra de Alejo Carpentier" in Helmy F. Giacoman (ed.), *Homenaje a Alejo Carpentier*, New York, Las Américas, 1970, pp. 99–104

Sarduy, Severo. *La simulación*, Caracas, Monte Avila, 1982

Servodidio, Mirella D'Ambrosio. *The Quest for Harmony: The Dialectics of Communication in the Poetry of Eugenio Florit*, Lincoln, Nebraska, Society of Spanish and Spanish-American Studies, 1979

Singer, Irving. *The Nature of Love: 2, Courtly and Romantic*, University of Chicago Press, 1984

Starobinski, Jean. *La Relation critique*, Paris, Gallimard, 1970

Steiner, George. *After Babel*, Oxford University Press, 1975

Suárez, Constantino. *Diccionario de voces cubanas*, Madrid, Imprenta Clarasó, 1921

Taylor, Karen. "La creación musical en *Los pasos perdidos*," *Nueva Revista de Filología Hispánica*, 26 (1977), 141–153

Toledo Sande, Luis. "Balance de Carlos Loveira, novelista" in *Nuevos críticos cubanos*, ed. José Prats Sariol, Havana, Editorial Letras Cubanas, 1983, pp. 287–303

Torres Rioseco, Arturo. *La novela en la América Hispana*, Berkeley, University of California Press, 1941

Valency, Maurice. *In Praise of Love: An Introduction to the Love-Poetry of the Renaissance*, New York, Macmillan, 1958

Vargas Llosa, Mario. "Primitives and creators," *Times Literary Supplement*, 14 November 1968, pp. 1287–1288

"The Latin American novel today," *Books Abroad*, 44 (1970), 7–16

Vitier, Cintio. *Lo cubano en la poesía*, 2nd edn, Havana, Instituto del Libro, 1970

Volek, Emil. *Cuatro claves para la modernidad. Análisis semiótico de textos hispánicos*, Madrid, Gredos, 1984

Vossler, Karl. *La poesía de la soledad en España*, trans. Ramón de la Serna y Espina, Buenos Aires, Losada, 1946

Williams, Lorna. *Self and Society in the Poetry of Nicolás Guillén*, Baltimore, Johns Hopkins University Press, 1982

Yndurái, Francisco. "La novela desde la segunda persona. Análisis estructural" in Germán and Agnes Gullón (eds.), *Teoría de la novela (Aproximaciones hispánicas)*, Madrid, Taurus, 1974, pp. 199–227

Index